Story Logic and the Craft of Fiction

Story Logic and the Craft of Fiction

Catherine Brady

Dear Kathy –
I hope you'll find something
here & there in these pages
to inspire your own writing.

Catherine Brady
6·16·12

palgrave
macmillan

First published 2010 by
PALGRAVE MACMILLAN

Palgrave Macmillan in the UK is an imprint of Macmillan Publishers Limited, registered in England, company number 785998, of Houndmills, Basingstoke, Hampshire RG21 6XS.

Palgrave Macmillan in the US is a division of St Martin's Press LLC, 175 Fifth Avenue, New York, NY 10010.

Palgrave Macmillan is the global academic imprint of the above companies and has companies and representatives throughout the world.

Palgrave® and Macmillan® are registered trademarks in the United States, the United Kingdom, Europe and other countries.

ISBN-13: 978–0–230–58055–8 paperback

This book is printed on paper suitable for recycling and made from fully managed and sustained forest sources. Logging, pulping and manufacturing processes are expected to conform to the environmental regulations of the country of origin.

A catalogue record for this book is available from the British Library.

A catalog record for this book is available from the Library of Congress.

10   9   8   7   6   5   4   3   2   1
19   18   17   16   15   14   13   12   11   10

Printed in China

for my students

Contents

List of Figures

Acknowledgments

I wish I could name all the students who inspired me to write this book. Whether we were tackling challenges in their manuscripts or admiring, debating, and dissecting the books we read together, their curiosity and inventiveness triggered mine. Because of them, I've had to keep learning how to talk about craft in a way that has immediate practical value and honors their high ambition for their work. Over and over, they have demonstrated that the best test of an idea is the response it fires in others. Teaching, like fiction writing, only really works if discovery is the end product.

This manuscript owes so much to Steven Kahn that I can never thank him enough. His insightful critical reading shaped the evolution of successive drafts, and his suggestions and support for this project kept me going. My editor, Kate Haines, encouraged me to write this book and offered excellent editorial advice as it developed. I also owe personal thanks to Ann Ryles, who commented on an earlier draft from the perspective of an ideal reader, alert, sympathetic, and generous. Thanks to the faculty development fund at the University of San Francisco, I could rely on the services of an efficient research assistant, Doris Hung, to help me track down resources and sources of inspiration. The illustrations for this book were provided by Alan Stonebraker, who was unfailingly professional and exacting in his work. Two of the chapters were previously published in very different form in *The Writer's Chronicle*, the journal of the Association of Writers and Writing Programs: "A Cage in Search of a Bird: The Elusiveness at the Heart of Story Structure" appeared in fall 2003; "Showing and Telling: The Necessary Partnership" appeared in May 1998.

1

Story Logic

Let's start with a story that has been told before, one that Edith Wharton lifted from the autobiography of Renaissance sculptor Benvenuto Cellini. One day when Cellini was very young, he and his father saw a salamander in the hearth, a rare sighting. The father boxed the boy's ears to make sure he'd never forget it. From this anecdote Wharton fashions a metaphor for writing fiction: "It is useless to box your reader's ear unless you have a salamander to show him. If the heart of your little blaze is not animated by a living, moving *something* no shouting and shaking will fix the anecdote in your reader's memory. The salamander stands for that fundamental significance that made the story worth telling."[1] To demonstrate that technique can accomplish little in the absence of animating substance, Wharton falls back on a story that offers the unapologetically fierce notion of boxing the reader's ears. At some risk to both parties. Smarting from the blow, the reader might bleat "What was that for?" when we hoped to evoke an ah! response of astonished recognition.

Like most writers, my students tend to be good at analyzing literature and gifted with an intuitive sense of storytelling. Verbal, well-organized, capable people, they discover that as soon as they master the skill to say exactly what they mean, their fiction dies at their own hand. Luckily, most of them are stubbornly persistent, and they're also curious, unafraid to question formulas. For the first graduate workshop I taught, I came armed with twenty pages of notes, no help at all when a student asked me, "Why *can't* we use cliché?" When I advised students to show, not tell, they had the wherewithal to say, "You don't complain when Chekhov does it." Called for some violation of the rules, they'd point out a published writer who "got away with it" and demand to know why the same rules didn't govern every situation.

The students' predicament is akin to that of medical students who dissect a corpse so they can label bones and muscles and tendons and identify where and how they connect, and yet this doesn't tell them very much about how to examine a living person and diagnose her symptoms correctly. This book evolved because, along with my students, I found it uninspiring simply to prescribe rules or conventions for writing fiction. Even worse, teaching formulaic skill sets—characterization in this box, setting in another—begs the question of dynamics, of how all the elements of a work of fiction are integrated to achieve particular effects. If we discuss point of view, we need to consider how this rhetorical device helps us to shape what's at stake in a story; if we analyze setting, we have to consider tropes (figures of speech) in order to understand the principles that govern selection of detail.

What matters most for apprentices is to cultivate the attitudinal stance of a creative artist. In a public lecture the painter Wayne Thiebaud once gave this answer to the question of how to train someone to draw: "I'd give him an egg, a pencil, and a piece of paper, and have him watch the way the light plays over the egg during the course of the day."[2] Thiebaud emphasizes a stance of heightened attentiveness, and condensed in the concrete terms of his answer is a viable principle, one that can accommodate a variety of strategies. Just because creative thinking is often intuitive, opportunistic, and spontaneous, it does not follow that its methods are irreducibly mysterious. But like Thiebaud, we can afford to be concrete in ways that embody principles and to be playful in the ways that art is. In a medium that works by metaphor, it makes sense to teach by metaphor and by paradigm. It also makes sense to learn on a case-by-case basis. Because we're interested in generating original work, we can't simply copy the methods of a specific story but have to seek principles that can account for why a craft choice works in a given context. We learn not exactly *what* to do but *how* to do it. This book emphasizes craft analysis of literary models because it is the best (and time-honored) way for writers to consider technique as "site-specific." For the same reason exercises at the back of this book emphasize practice that will broaden a writer's repertoire and processes that cultivate a particular stance toward the material.

I hit on the concept of story logic in an attempt to address the why and how of technique, which has to be fitted to the highly particular methods of persuasion that characterize art. How do you make your appeal to a reader? You strategize ways to make the experience of a story a reader's experience. You learn to be precise in generating meaning that is not stable and never entirely leaves the realm of uncertainty. To achieve both these ends, your primary methods must be literal and concrete.

Story logic rests on a basic trust in storytelling itself. Everyone has had the experience of reading a bad novel but being unable to put it down because he had to know how it turned out. The materials are so simple: a particular individual in a particular situation that poses some threat, enough that we are in suspense about the eventual outcome. Any credible story also offers us surprise, and this is true even of picture books for children. In Margaret Wise Brown's *Runaway Bunny* a little rabbit threatens to run away. He boasts that if his mother comes after him, he'll turn into a fish and swim away; she counters that she'll turn into a fisherman and fish for him. If he turns into a bird, she'll be a tree; if he becomes a sailboat, she'll be the wind that blows him home. Each event of a story triggers the next, and even a child can recognize an *implicit* causal chain: as the little rabbit's claims escalate, his mother matches him, but she doesn't simply block his fanciful wishes, she accommodates them. The pleasing surprise of this story is that it transforms a struggle into reassurance that a mother's love can meet any challenge, which speaks directly to the experience of a young child. Meaning resonates because the conflict between the desire for autonomy and the need for security also exposes the problem of negotiating between fantasy and reality.

Both the author of *The Runaway Bunny* and the author of *Ulysses* can proceed from this free gift of story itself, knowing that readers, including very young children, are already expert in the ways of story. Stories have a hold on our imaginations—as writers and as readers—because their particulars do not resolve in the form of unequivocal, exact statements. Their value lies in the richness of their implications, their capacity to shed meaning in many directions, not just one. Fiction is full of ideas, but they are the effluence thrown off by specific events, not a premise for which the story is a proof. Fiction offers at best tentative proofs, but it is not vague: it is *differently* precise than a rhetorical argument that makes its claims explicitly.

This is where story logic begins: how do I *enact* meaning? The stamp of art is all over the children's tale, because the writer has discovered the right plot for the idea. But "idea" is not exactly the right term. "Idea-welded-to-emotion" would be more accurate to the nature of storytelling and is central to its effects. Tolstoy didn't hesitate to make this his credo: "Art is the means of transferring feeling from one man's heart to another's."[3] Only when the reader steps in is the imaginative act of story complete; only when her feelings and her intelligence are called into play can fiction generate what Flannery O'Connor calls "experienced meaning."[4] To solicit the reader's imaginative engagement, fiction works primarily through the senses, a principle we can trace back to Aristotle, who said, "Nothing exists in the intellect that was not first in the senses."[5]

A paradox lies at the heart of story logic. If sensory detail grants immediacy to a story and coaxes emotional investment from the reader, it's also inexact. I might have a different take than you do on a man who holds doors open for women, and we both have to sift the many implications of sensory detail for those that provide clues to an author's intentions. But stories make a virtue of this necessity: they generate meaning that is intentionally unstable and "irresolute": on any given page, good fiction engages a reader in struggling to reconcile tension and inconsistencies. What's more, literal tension ultimately must stand for the symbolic; this kind of meaning is akin to that of dreams in so far as both draw on emotional logic—devious, associative, lateral, and inherently metaphoric—to substitute one thing for another.

Like a dream, a work of fiction can't be reduced to a single, fixed statement of meaning. As Flannery O'Connor has noted, a good story resists paraphrase: "any abstractly expressed compassion or piety or morality in a piece of fiction is only a statement added to it.... when you write fiction you are speaking *with* character and action, not *about* character and action. The writer's moral sense must coincide with his dramatic sense."[6] What does it mean to create a genuinely dramatic predicament? Not only is the outcome uncertain but the reader's feelings about it are unresolved until the very end. Charles Baxter observes that "it is not always enough simply to tell a truth in art, especially if the truth has no dramatic tension or has lost its emotional force."[7] Why does literal tension matter so much to story as art? Because it's the only springboard for generating figurative tension, and if fiction writers cannot declare meaning, they can exploit tension to pose it as a problem.

Framing a question

Plot is an attitude toward the subject as much or more than it is a technique—an instinct for selecting those moments in the story line at which events offer the greatest promise for provoking uncertainty in the reader. Meaning is only compellingly elusive when the reader must struggle to reconcile the tension that arises from plot. Chekhov once insisted that it is "not the business of the artist to solve narrowly specialized questions" and pointed out that this conception confused two distinct aims, "the solution of the problem and a correct presentation of the problem." The writer, like a judge instructing a jury, "is obliged to submit the case fairly, but let the jury do the deciding, each according to its own judgment."[8] Like a judge, the writer remains silent at critical junctures—but not silent on which information is relevant to judgment. No less an experimentalist than Milan Kundera affirms this as a universal principle of fiction: "A novel does not assert anything; a novel searches and poses questions.... The novelist teaches the reader to comprehend the world as a question."[9] To do so, the writer must first teach himself. In his brilliant polemic "Against Epiphanies," Charles Baxter notes that "a story, as Borges has shown, can be a series of clues but not a solution," because its true aim is "the enfolding of mystery."[10]

If you are to coax, prod, or detour the reader from a readiness to pass judgment, you must tackle what troubles your own understanding. In Katherine Mansfield's "Garden Party," the writer portrays her upper-class characters with a critical eye. When laborers arrive to prepare the grounds for a lavish party, Laura, the daughter of the house, treats them with romanticizing condescension, and the rest of her family, who manage the servants better, are preoccupied with enjoying the fruits of privilege. Only Laura hesitates when she hears that a laborer from a cottage nearby has been killed that day; she is laughed at for her naïve concern that the party will have to be called off, and her mother easily distracts her by having her try on a hat that will complement her dress.

Laura feels the intrusion of a harsher reality in ways that evoke sympathy yet also annoy a reader, and throughout the story it remains an open question whether this harshness can puncture the insularity of her milieu. After the party Laura does her bit for noblesse oblige, carting leftover food to the miserable home of the laborer's widow. When she is taken in to see the body of the dead man, already laid out, a humbled Laura murmurs to the corpse, "Forgive my hat."[11] This closing moment of the story constitutes a litmus test of the reader's own prejudices and predispositions: can Laura be forgiven her vanity because she responds with awe in the presence of death, or is her response just another transient romantic moment? Mansfield can remain silent on the answer because she has committed herself so fully to presenting the opposing arguments with equal conviction. She is neither dishonest about the failings of the upper class nor simplistic in subordinating the rich inner life of her main character to generalizations.

Generating a high ratio of subtext to text

A work of art doesn't just solicit imaginative engagement but intensifies it, particularly when it comes to feelings. Consider this example from the early pages of "Dimensions," a short story by Alice Munro. So far, the reader knows that Doree, the perspective character, leads a solitary life working as a hotel maid, but once had a husband and three children. As she's riding the bus to visit her husband (who's in prison, but the reader doesn't know this yet), Doree keeps herself "calm" by reading roadside signs: "both the advertising and the street signs. There was a certain trick she had picked up to keep her mind occupied. She took the letters of whatever words her eyes lit on, and she tried to see how many new words she could make out of them. 'Coffee,' for instance, would give you 'fee,' and then 'foe,' and 'off' and 'of,' and 'shop' would provide 'hop' and 'sop' and 'so' and—wait a minute—'posh.' "[12] Instead of telling us that Doree feels dread about the visit and explaining why, the writer poses a question by foregrounding Doree's need to rely on a trick to keep her mind occupied. Because it's an excruciatingly trivial trick, this extreme hints at its opposite, traumatic suffering. Munro helps the reader to intuit not just a terrible past loss but this awful emptiness as its consequence. We still don't know all the facts, but we *feel* them.

Not only does this paragraph count for its force on clues in earlier passages, it devotes a good deal of space to the word game in order to enact Doree's willed numbness and to suggest how she clings to randomness. Doree's predicament might be stated in fewer words, but strategic silence is not just a matter of the fewest words possible. It's a matter of how much implication a writer can generate for any given amount of words. A fiction writer strives to sustain an enhanced ratio of subtext to text, and any methods that achieve this justify themselves. How all the elements of fiction work interdependently to serve this end forms the subject for this entire book.

Story logic exploits silence. The conjectural process that is set going in a reader by strategic silence offers a beautiful mimesis for actual experience. When we watch two people negotiate a difficult task, we'll conjecture a whole history for their relationship. When the man who sits next to us on the airplane won't share the armrest, we'll draw conclusions about his character. In the same way we'll imagine a whole world from the distilled materials of a plot. Indirection in art is highly valued because it doesn't merely trigger such conjecture, it shapes it. On the one hand, a writer carefully selects for details that will impart a certain slant, helping to focus the reader's attention on some possibilities and not others. On the other hand, the writer leaves out in order to sustain the deliberate uncertainty of unresolved tension. In this risky negotiation—there's a hair's breadth between error and evocative openness of meaning—precision depends on *cumulative* clues.

As a living, *moving* something, a work of fiction depends on the ah! response of discovery and surprise: if all the clues are apparent from the start, the reader has no work and no such reward to anticipate. Because of this, the most powerful associations fiction can generate are buried associations. Plot is not merely more compact than the "whole story" it suggests, it's structured to direct our curiosity toward buried associations, as is suggested by E. M. Forster's often-cited distinction between story and plot: "In a story we say, 'and then?' . . . in a plot we ask 'why?' "[13] Rather than making causes and effects explicit, a plot functions more like a connect-the-dots diagram, with significant, puzzling gaps for the reader to fill in.

Let's start with a simple example. In an apocryphal anecdote that has circulated on the Internet for years, students are challenged by a teacher to compose the shortest story possible that incorporates religion, sex, mystery, and royalty. The winner? "My God," said the queen. "I'm pregnant. I wonder who did it."[14] Consider how much information is packed into this joke construction and how much dramatic event is packed into the white space between each sentence. Note also how even this truncated version of a plot refuses to stand still: the ejaculatory "My God" alerts us to anticipate some problem; since the announced pregnancy ought to be good news (queens are supposed to provide a royal heir) we don't know yet exactly how this poses a problem, and then the story culminates with a startling surprise. We have to discard our first assumption about the queen's pregnancy and instead consider the extent of her betrayal. Point of view and word choice also contribute to subtext and even accomplish subtle characterization. A queen who merely wonders "who did it" ascribes agency to others, not herself, and this casts her initial reference to God in a less than reverent light; point of view limits us to flippancy in a situation in which the consequences for carelessness loom large.

If these three sentences can generate such fullness of implication, artistic fiction produces exponentially more complex effects *and* entices us to want to pursue them. In analyzing the examples included in this book, I've often had to resist the temptation to unravel every last thread of implication, because if I did, this would be a two-volume set. But even a hasty reading of "The Garden Party" shows that a more complicated plot employs the same principles as the Internet anecdote. The story is plotted in just one day, the day of a party. The party is dispatched in just a few paragraphs; instead plot emphasizes the anticipation of it, including Laura's worry that the party will have to be cancelled, and the aftermath, in which some consideration for the dead man's family can be afforded. The plot structure pushes us to compare the scene in which Laura's distress is made to seem comically outsized and the final scene in which an act of charity is intended to suffice as an expression of concern. When Laura views the corpse, there is an oh-so-important gap between her vanity-tinged response ("Forgive my hat") and the circumstance of confronting death, one that puts the reader in the predicament of considering how genuine Laura's awe might be and *more*. How genuine is *our* awe? Can anyone break through ordinary vanity to either awe or compassion? This is not, as it turns out, merely a class issue.

Both these examples illustrate that you can't cleanly disentangle "plot effects" from point of view or imagery or tone or characterization. In some of the Internet versions of the queen's story, in place of "I wonder who did it," the queen says, "I wonder who the father is."[15] So much of the surprise and the subtext of the original is owed to word choice that strategically leaves out that it's hard not to see this as a plot choice too. "The Garden Party" offers a more complex example of how tightly interwoven all the elements of fiction really are. Because this story is written from the perspective of a girl whose manners aren't yet as smooth as those of her elders, we're able to sympathize with her awkwardness and her inability to find the right box for her feelings. The image of Laura's hat stands for a host of vanities, called up by the concise "forgive my hat," which is *also* an action that forcefully recalls the earlier scene in which the laborer's death was trivialized. The total effect of a work of fiction depends on dynamic interplay between all its moving parts and the way a writer orchestrates them to make silence speak.

Reading for story logic

One of the fundamental qualities of story logic is that it is playful. A good writer relishes the constraints of this game rather than regarding them as a burden. In *The Art of Fiction* John Gardner offers a metaphor for this in his description of a game called Essences. The player who is it thinks of a famous person and supplies some scant clue, such as "I am a dead European," and then the other players try to guess the name of the famous person, but they can't ask for facts, only for metaphor: "What kind of animal are you?" "What kind of weather are you?" The player who is it can only answer "tiger" or "cloudy." Gardner wants us to think of the writer as it and readers as the other players, who must rely on these answers to make the right guess: "Obviously the game cannot be played with the intellect; it depends on metaphoric intuition. Yet anyone who plays the game with good players will discover that the metaphors that describe the personage whose name is being sought have, at least cumulatively,

a remarkable precision."[16] In the game you play with your readers, your hands are tied: you can only give sneaky and partial
answers and are held to a fundamentally metaphoric mode of
thinking. But the game sure is fun. And note that the constraints force *both* the player who is it and the other players to
be inventive.

Which is exactly why reading matters so much to writers.
When we read great fiction, we're participating in the inventiveness of story logic, honing the same imaginative skills we need
as writers, and when we analyze how a literary work exploits this
logic, we enrich the pleasure of our reading experience and gain
models for our own writing. Writers read not only for meaning
but for appreciation of how a beautiful thing is made: "willya
lookit that!" is a valid part of our aesthetic ah! response. Any satisfying reading experience teaches us something else about story
logic: if every work of fiction can tap into these general principles, stories are only obligated to work out the unique logic
they establish for themselves. In a conditional, site-specific form
of learning, writers don't extract from their reading rules that
specify solutions but principles that allow for a highly varied
approach to problem solving. This is akin to Noam Chomsky's
notion of the deep structure of grammar: even very young children can apply generative principles as they construct a linguistic
expression unique to the immediate situation.

The principles of story logic can facilitate alert, receptive cri-
tiques of a manuscript in the workshop. To illustrate, I'll trace in
hypothetical form the specific discussion of a short story that is
a composite of the kind of first draft submitted in my workshop
many times. Here's a synopsis of the story:

> An old man who's recently lost his wife won't sell his house because
> the house holds memories of her. In the story's first scene a realtor
> approaches the widower, but he refuses to sell the house. In the next
> scene his adult son expresses concern for how he's managing on his
> own and warns the widower that he won't be able to keep up the
> house much longer. The realtor comes back and again offers to buy
> the house, but the man still refuses.

The sequence of events in a work of fiction reveals a great deal
about its logic. We can read the son's warning as a form of escalating pressure; in the face of this, the man's refusal to sell remains a

constant. But this sequence comes awfully close to reiterating the refusal, not advancing it; nothing shakes up the static equation between attachment to house and attachment to wife. The story remains at a standstill, and it's in danger of being sentimental. An artistic plot progresses by exposing *hidden* tension, unveiling by degrees the cost of choice. If we trust the power of virtually any story to throw off something elusive, we can investigate what the writer has given us in an effort to help her uncover tension implicit in the material. How can the present action trouble the widower's understanding of his attachment to his wife and to mourning?

One of the consequences of trusting in the story logic of a given manuscript is generosity, a willingness to see the potential of the work. Because stories have an unruly and inherent tendency to shed meaning in *so* many directions, in this first draft the writer might not have registered all the possibilities or figured out which of them might be relevant to tension. Since money is involved, the notion of value might be in play. Does the profit promised in the realtor's offer threaten to cheapen the widower's attachment? How might the son's concern call into question the man's capacity to sustain intense mourning indefinitely? Are there any clues that the man's determination masks something other than love, perhaps an effort to make reparation for failures in his marriage—or to deny them? Because reader's interests and tastes vary, the writer has to listen for some inward flicker in response to any of these possibilities; she can effectively act only on those that reignite her own engagement with the material. But the more possibilities the writer can tackle, the better, with the limitation that they must ultimately make sense in relation to each other.

By paying attention to the possible multiple meanings of value (material and emotional) in the story, the workshop readers gave the writer something to go on in revision. In responding to a first draft, readers often say they want more information. Frustrated guessers in the game of Essences may demand that the player who is it shout out the name of the famous person rather than ask him to refine his metaphoric responses. In this instance some readers asked for more information on the history of the marriage, and others for facts that would clarify the man's relationship with his son. If the hard-pressed writer responds to these requests by filling in all the blanks, the revised draft usually doesn't satisfy readers any more than the first one did. Typically, the story feels thinner.

The real "missing information" in this plot was that it wasn't exploiting some visible cost to suggest the hidden cost for the widower's intensity of feeling. In the revised draft the writer submitted to the workshop, she added a new scene just before the final scene in which the realtor repeated his offer. There's a storm, and the roof starts leaking, and the widower sets out pots all over the house to catch water dripping from the ceiling. Now when the realtor makes his second appearance and takes in all the pots, he makes a lower offer for the house. In the second draft the story's logic changed. Because it now began with the offer of a high price and ended with a lower offer, we could ask about diminishing value in relation to the association between wife and house; because the house sprang leaks in the rain storm, the evidence of its failure further reinforced the notion of the widower's diminishing power to sustain mourning. So *this* is where the story was headed.

Once the writer got this implicit causal chain underway, the workshop readers could ask different questions of the evolving draft. Readers were still unsure about how each scene triggered some escalation of the stakes in the next, and (surprise!) they weren't satisfied with the writer's effort to give them more factual answers on the length of the marriage, the alienation of the son, and so on. At this stage in the game of Essences, the right questions from readers and the right answers from the writer both depend on interrogating the sensory reality of the story; ideas have no other way to enter the work. Is there a nick on the banister that the widower never got around to repairing when his wife was alive? Does he always run his hand over it as he goes downstairs, and does he ever forget to do this? Does the roof leak because the widower forgot some routine maintenance? What about those pots he set out to catch leaks? Is there a circle of dampness on the carpet around each of the overflowing pots? Or is dripping water pinging in the pots as he refuses the realtor one more time? How can the material qualities of the rain storm scene flow over onto the final scene, helping readers to see the widower's second refusal to sell the house as different from the first?

The writer will have to go off alone again to write the next draft. But she is now working in the realm of the concrete and has acquired the patience to compose a plot, which requires that we resist the temptation to make meaning clear in one fell swoop. In lieu of further explanation the writer is more likely to attempt something like a bank shot in billiards, aiming at a certain point on the table rim because she calculates the ball will come off at an angle that will get it into the pocket. Story logic is crooked logic.

2

The Elusiveness at the Heart of Story Structure

In graduate school I balked at formulas for plot. They were boring. I didn't want to winnow the stories that fanned out from the one I'd meant to write or concede that the still moments gummed up the works, couldn't make what seemed to be the required sacrifice. My instructors were very nice about these formless musings. They'd say, "Isn't that a pretty sentence!" Later, editors were not so nice. They'd complain that a story had too many characters, or it got bogged down in the past, or it was too dense, too quiet, too girly. I tried to quit writing and even enrolled in a graduate program in counseling. But guess what? In San Francisco, the city where I live, there is roughly one licensed therapist for every eight people. Those were even worse odds for success. So I went back to stories.

I had to make some unholy compromises between what compelled me to write and the basic box of story structure. But I began to trust that I might have the principle right even if I'd been getting the execution wrong. When you write a story, you have to create a coherent character and imagine a plot that feels complete, but as demanding a task as this is, it really serves as camouflage for *what else* is going on. There's always a story beneath the surface story, suggested by what gets left out or goes unexplained, by images that disturb us or make us uncertain, by actions that convince us but also astonish us. We're ultimately more fascinated by the story that won't fall completely into place, that resists being explained away. I'm still trying to pull off stories that don't fit neatly into the box. But everything wild and astonishing and heartrending in a story depends on that box being there.

The standard diagram for story structure looks more like an inverted checkmark than a box. Freytag's pyramid was originally designed to depict the dramatic structure of a play. Plenty has been said about the rules for this paradigm. A story should begin with an initial situation about to be destabilized; its bulk should be devoted to rising action in which pressure steadily escalates;[1] increments of tension in the rising action should peak in a crisis, or climax;[2] the crisis must fall off to some resolution.[3] Presented with Freytag's pyramid, you might, like me, protest its reductionism rather than bending to the yoke. The basic formula for plot structure provides a template for devising a narrative, not its raison d'etre. Though suspense is essential, a story satisfies not because it pursues a literal chain of events but because it manages to make those events stand for something else. When the reader, not the writer, supplies the connection between the two, meaning is experiential.

In his essay "What's a Story?" Leonard Michaels cites Kafka's one-sentence parable, "A cage went in search of a bird," in which both literal and figurative tension are swiftly accomplished by the paradox of caging a creature meant for flight. As Michaels observes, the parable "plays with a notion of.... containing the uncontainable" and can be read as an allegory for story, which is "an artifice of form...in deadly pursuit of a spirit."[4] Every good story seeks to impose form on what cannot finally be grasped by form—to prove the elusiveness of meaning through the exacting effort to capture it. Great stories are fundamentally about their silences, "the story that got away." Story logic exploits gaps and ellipses in a plot—the interstices between the bars of the cage— to suggest what is not on the page, the elusive bird for which the cage was built. The pressure for economy in a short story makes it a perfect vehicle for considering how writers make choices about such gaps, but the principle holds true for a plot of any length.

Because conflict in a story exists in order to generate conflict within the reader, it paradoxically works against resolution at the level of meaning at the same time as it works toward crisis and resolution at the literal level. This is why Freytag's pyramid and other notions of story that depict plot as a single unbroken line prove inadequate: they don't account for how a series of events can suggest a figurative central tension that remains unstated and unresolved—the elusive hidden story. A good plot doesn't dodge the confining paradigm of rising action, climax, and resolution but makes it serve this dual aim.

If you think of a story's momentum as deriving from complicating the literal stakes, not just raising them, you'll be freed of a strictly linear notion of how rising action escalates pressure. In the rising action you have to manage what the reader knows in the moment against what she doesn't know yet in two ways: the literal tension remains unresolved on any given page, and the buried associations that connect it to figurative tension are merely hinted at, not declared. When you effectively plot a literal gap in a story, you provide a logical gap for the reader to fill in with an invisible *because* clause. If your story proceeds from a scene in which two lovers quarrel to a scene in which one of them is looking for an apartment, you're offering a hint: *because* of the quarrel, one person has reconsidered the relationship. A still more ambitious plot exploits story logic to suggest hidden tension. Say instead that in your story's first scene the lovers plan a vacation together and then one of them searches for a separate apartment. Suddenly, it's more problematic to supply the invisible *because* clause, and the reader, who must read on in order to keep puzzling this out, can only provisionally fill in the gap. Rising action does not build a tightly linked chain of cause-and-effect but troubles a strictly literal reading by highlighting gaps in logic that the reader can't yet resolve.

When the potent charges laid in the rising action fire simultaneously at the climax, a story offers a convincing surprise. In terms that do not require realization in the form of an epiphany, the climax can be defined as a decisive action that convincingly reconfigures what has come before; at this moment, the visible story comes closest to the hidden, untold story. The tension between order and elusiveness at the heart of every good story culminates in the resolution, which propels the reader in opposite directions at once, intimating the specific literal consequence of the crisis action (the future of a character, as if his or her life will continue past the final page) while ultimately reasserting the instability of meaning. But on changed terms. Particularly in a short story, the climax rearranges the elements in play much like a slight twist of the kaleidoscope radically transforms randomly aligned crystals into a beautifully coherent pattern, and resolution lasts only as long as is necessary for the reader to recognize this new symmetry.

Plot as objective correlative

Every element of fiction can be employed to generate experienced meaning, but the first breakthrough you must make in learning to think like an artist is to understand that story structure depends not on baldly advancing a literal conflict but on constructing a plot that articulates the exact parameters of the secret at the story's heart. The clues to figurative tension—imagery, detail, recurrence, sequencing, and diction—will remain inert, incapable of supporting a coherent subtext, unless the right literal central tension aligns them, like a magnet drawn over iron filings.

Plot functions as "the chain of events" T. S. Eliot referenced when he defined the objective correlative: "The only way of expressing emotion in the form of art is by finding an 'objective correlative'; in other words, a set of objects, a situation, a chain of events which shall be the formula of that emotion, such that when the external facts, which must terminate in sensory experience, are given, the emotion is immediately evoked."[5] That's a mouthful, but it expresses an artistic principle of long standing: meaning must be embodied in the literal. An objective correlative works much like a metaphor; the writer suppresses one partner to a comparison (the idea or emotion) but so arranges the other partner (literal element) that the reader will intuit and supply the "silent" partner. Instead of announcing that a walk in the rain is like a baptism, the writer depicts a character turning up her face to feel rain drops thumbed on her forehead, and so on. Eliot's reference to a *chain* of events should alert us that the whole action of the plot works as a correlative: strung on the scaffold of plot structure, literal events enact the implicit tension of the hidden story.

Perhaps the raw material for your story is a dramatic situation in which a woman decides to leave her husband. What triggers the wife's decision to act? What costs will she incur if she leaves? What secret harmony in this relationship might belie her dissatisfaction? The aim of your final draft is to sustain tension around these questions—to recreate this conjectural process of discovery, not share your conclusions about it. If you plot only the surface story, you'll tend to fill in every necessary logical step, to focus on justifying the literal action. Such stories feel deterministic to a reader, and they tend to culminate in a predictable climax. Knowing this, you successively discard plotting a year's worth of arguments or plotting the wife's discovery that her husband has pruned to a stub her favorite rose bush. No hidden tension possible in either scenario, although the second is a bit closer to the notion of a literal act suggesting its figurative partner. Instead you decide to plot an evening when husband and wife pick up a hitchhiker—a young and charming female hitchhiker, who prompts the husband to regale her with stories that amuse his wife too. When they drop off the hitchhiker, she asks for money for food, and the fate of the marriage hinges on the husband's response. Now you are plotting two stories, with the precisely suggestive literal tension calling up the unstated and *unresolved* question of his capacity for generosity in the marriage. The literal action possesses open possibilities: his wife could decide to leave because he gives the hitchhiker his last twenty dollars or grudgingly hands over a few coins. You still have work to do to avoid an obvious match-up, but you're on the way.

As you compose a first draft, try this strategy of telling one story in order to tell another. Approached in the most literal-minded way, this will deflect your attention from making a point and force metaphoric thinking along an axis of tension. Instead of steering your character straight at realization (an epiphany too much on *your* mind), struggle with the mechanics of making one story yank another to the surface. This will lead you to discovery. I can vouch for it.

Plotting "two stories," the literal and the figurative

Plot choices can transform what might otherwise be only an anecdote. Consider this predictable dramatic situation: A woman bumps into her ex-husband while she's running errands. She's affectionate, but he still bears a grudge. Before they part, he gets in one last dig, a chain of events culminating in little more than petty retaliation. Since this is the action of Grace Paley's story "Wants" (just three pages long), we can learn from her how the transformation from anecdote to story is accomplished. On her way to return long overdue books, the narrator meets her ex-husband on the library steps. She hails him as "my life," earning an immediate rebuff: "What life? No life of mine."[6] Following her to the check-out desk, he makes the wild claim that they divorced because she never invited the Bertrams to dinner. She blithely grants his point but makes hilariously irrelevant excuses for her behavior—she was distracted by her children, her sick father, the start of the Vietnam War. As she pays her fine and decides to renew the books (read so long ago she's forgotten them), her ex-husband admits to one good memory of sitting over coffee in the morning, but this provokes a disagreement over whether they were really so poor back then. Countering the narrator's rosy view one last time, he declares she'll never want anything. The action circles back to the opening moment: she sits on the library steps to ponder his accusation before she resolves that this time she'll return the books before they are overdue.

The decision to return the library books is all that this story requires, all that any story requires if its writer understands how to structure literal tension so it supports a figurative payoff. Paley can generate vast effects because she has chosen exactly the right action to locate tension in her material: this chance encounter, long after the fact of mutual hurt, focuses our attention not on blame but on the mysterious survival of attachment, in the form of two seemingly irreconcilable alternatives, the narrator's casual affection and her ex-husband's bitterness. Literal tension coaxes the reader to attend to this discrepancy: as soon as the husband rebuffs his ex-wife, he follows her to the check-out desk to revive an old grudge. He is *not* finished with her. For him the past is a source of grievance, while for her it's a source of nostalgia. These two accurately rendered and opposed attitudes articulate the story's silence about the other possibility open to both of them: regret.

The literal tension superbly aligns other narrative elements to suggest the parameters of this hidden story. From the first exchange ("my life" and "no life of mine"), the characters enact the problem of proportion. Time enters the story immediately and in hyperbolic terms—the library books have been overdue for eighteen years; the characters were married for twenty-seven years; as the narrator notes, one of the books, *House of Mirth*, also spans twenty-seven years. Disproportion is mirrored in the action; the trivial looms large in his complaint about her failure to make a dinner invitation, and her list of excuses equates large reasons with small. Plot doesn't require any further fleshing out of their history and would even be undermined by it; what

matters are their mutually exclusive views, more telling than
the missing "accurate" account of their failed marriage. The
trivial again looms large as the literal action of returning overdue books alerts us to another gap: completion of this task easily
erases regret and obligation. Paley has sly fun with the connotations of *renewal:* the narrator is satisfied that the librarian has
now "wiped the record clean"—unlike her ex-husband, who does
not want her to forget her more substantial failure with him.[7]
Cumulatively, plot enacts the hidden tension.

In the climactic action the ex-husband boasts that since their
divorce, he has done well and is looking forward to being able to
purchase a dreamed-of sailboat. "But as for you," he says, "you'll
always want nothing." The narrator finally feels her ex-husband's
fury, like a humble "plumber's snake working its way through the
ear down the throat, halfway to my heart."[8] An insult that hits
its mark constitutes the slight shift by which the climax radically
reconfigures the tension arising from their opposed attitudes.
The ex-husband links time to material accomplishment before he
defines the narrator's inclination to be interested in everything as
wanting nothing. Stung, the narrator sits on the steps to compose
a mental list of her wants, a comparatively long resolution for so
short a story. She wishes to have been married her whole life to
her first husband or her second; it would take that long to "get
under the rock" of a man's reasons, and "a whole life...is really
not such a long time." Underscoring this disconnect between the
brief span of human life and the vast arc of natural time, the narrator observes that the sycamore trees on her street, planted when
her children were young, are now in "the prime of their lives."[9]
Her desires too now bear some new correspondence to the passage of time: her wish for more time to get to know her men is
the closest she can come to regret and to satisfying her husband's
demand for a tangible accounting. (Thus, plot aligns the toting
up of numbers that has occurred throughout the story.) Isn't she
as accurate as her husband in recognizing how little time we are
given to achieve the things that matter to us?

Because the literal tension contains built-in allusions to impermanence, the hidden story can pursue questions about how
ephemeral all desires might be. This long resolution nails the
literal consequences of the insult while simultaneously refram-
ing the tension implicit in the disproportion between good
intentions and their realization. When the narrator resolves
to return the library books on time, "which proves...I *can*

take some appropriate action, though I am better known for my hospitable remarks," her predicament is embodied in an evocatively trivial final action, one that is merely planned, not accomplished.[10]

It's harder to conceive of plot as engineering a relationship between a visible story and a hidden one, but it's a lot more fun. While an obvious match won't make for a good-enough game, provocative matches between literal and figurative tension can be achieved in many ways. The plot of Junot Díaz's "Fiesta, 1980" splices past and present action to exploit disjointed parallels between them. The story is literally about silence, since the ten-year-old narrator and his older brother, Rafa, both know of their father's mistress but have never told their mother of her existence. The present action begins as Yunior's immigrant family gets ready to go to a relative's party and ends as they drive home. The immediate dilemma is that the boy vomits every time he rides in his father's new VW van, and so that he won't throw up on the way home, his father has forbidden him to eat at the party. The story would offer such a neat (and disappointing) correspondence if the reader could equate throwing up with a traumatic response to the affair, but Díaz immediately throws a wrench in the gears: Yunior began throwing up in the van before he ever met the mistress.

The visible story, the literal suspense, has to do with whether Yunior might evade his father's prohibition and partake of the feast at the party. Redirecting the reader's anticipation of discovering trauma to this substituted dilemma, Díaz orchestrates the present action so that it alludes to what's missing from the story, any blame the narrator might attach to Papi for his affair. At the outset Papi berates Mami for letting Yunior eat before they set out for the party and predicts that Yunior will throw up as a result; this readiness to lay blame spotlights his son's reluctance to do the same. The mistress is shoehorned into the story not because of any expressed distress but because she once played a practical role when Papi stopped at her house after Yunior vomited in the van. When Mami blesses her sons with a traditional Dominican blessing before they leave for the party, her touch mirrors its inverse in the past action, the mistress roughly toweling the narrator when she cleaned him up, "like I was a bumper she was waxing."[11]

Papi sent for his family only after years of living alone in the United States. A stranger to his sons, he relentlessly finds fault with Yunior, who accepts this as his fate. ("It was like my God-given duty to piss him off.")[12] Rafa inches away from Yunior as soon as their father starts to yell, ready to sacrifice Yunior or his mother whenever loyalty might bring Papi's wrath down on him as well. "When I was in trouble," Yunior confides, "he didn't know me."[13] Throughout the story Rafa reenacts the father's abandonment of the family and manages to get everything forbidden to the narrator, food at the party, his father's tolerance, the sexual interest of girls. To reap similar rewards, Yunior must emulate Rafa and his father, and the only fly in the ointment is that the new-car smell of his father's van bothers him. On the way to the party, he throws up, and his mother gets out of the van with him, as she does whenever he's ejected for this offense. A reader has to be alert to guess at an invisible *because* clause: the fly in the ointment is now linked to Yunior's feelings about his mother, not the mistress.

Once the family arrives at the party, the present action again evokes the signal action of the past, the sons' complicity in their father's secret. Among the guests is a boy who is improbably mute—not deaf, but unable to speak. During the evening Yunior's aunt invents an excuse to be alone with Yunior, ostensibly to sneak him food; in this supremely right action, when satisfaction of desire is greedily accepted by Yunior, the aunt, suspicious of Papi, tries to pump the boy for information. Yunior remembers his mother doing the same thing a short while before and meeting with the same response from him: silence. And yet the whole night Yunior has been imagining his father's public exposure, has been "waiting for a blowup."[14] The longed-for literal satisfaction supplied by the plot—Yunior devouring the pastries his aunt gives him—evokes its figurative opposite, unsatisfied hunger for justice.

The story's ending offers a wonderful payoff for the spliced plot, forging one last off-kilter connection that realigns past and present *and* future. In a flashback section Yunior recalls his mother grilling him, and in retrospect he questions his silence: "Later I would think, maybe if I had told her, she would have confronted him, would have done something, but who can know these things?" In the next section the family heads home from the party. As soon as the van gets underway, Yunior feels ill: "I started feeling it again." The deliberate choice of the indefinite pronoun reconfigures the crucial link between the memory and the present moment in which Yunior can only call his mother's name, substitute for the warning he has never issued. When both his literal and spiritual nausea are superimposed by the figuratively open pronoun, the literal action finally veers closest to the underlying story. The crisis translates swiftly to a resolution that's accomplished in just a sentence: "Finally, I said, Mami, and they both looked back, already knowing what was happening."[15] For a reader who remembers that Papi has twice proved accurate in predicting his son would throw up, meaning is crystallized. Yunior's cynicism and his fatalism about the future, about how everything "turned to shit," protects him against his father's brutality, yet it also makes him like his father, silent and complicit in betrayal. The *real* story—of his instinctive protest against realpolitik—has never happened on the page, and yet the structure of the story enables the writer to articulate what is never directly stated.

Taking risks in plotting

Every good story has to risk being obscure, aimless, about nothing, if it is to sustain that "something wild," not within reach, not enclosed in the story because it cannot be named or identified in any single passage. Federico García Lorca spoke of this quality as "duende," the aesthetic equivalent of the unruly, often diabolical sprites of Spanish folklore. In writing a first draft, we're often tempted to discard plot developments that are inconsistent with a single, clear trajectory, treating them as error or digression instead of entertaining the possibility that a story's impulse to unravel itself is productive and necessary. Because they must refuse to reveal their secret too soon, good stories teeter on the narrow boundary line between Poe's "unity of effect" and digression.

In his magical realist fiction Gabriel García Márquez exuberantly courts this danger. In "Light is Like Water," a family has moved from an unnamed Latin American country to a landlocked city in Spain. The two boys, seven and nine, yearn for a rowboat, a wish granted by their parents as a reward for good work at school. When their parents aren't home, Toto and Joel discover that they can create a sea of light on which to row their boat. The narrator impudently interrupts the story to take credit for this: "This fabulous adventure was the result of a frivolous remark I made while taking part in a seminar on the poetry of household objects. Toto asked me why the light went on with just the touch of a switch, and I did not have the courage to think about it twice. 'Light is like water,' I answered. 'You turn the tap and out it comes.'" One might be distracted forever by the evocativeness of that reference to "the poetry of household objects." A *digression* sets off the chain of events that constitutes the story's plot; the narrator's statement makes possible the boys' adventure. They break a light bulb, and when light pours like water from the broken bulb, they let it run to a (manageable) depth of three feet. But temptation entices them, and next time they invite their classmates on their adventure and let the light/water flow and flow: "It spilled over the balconies, poured in torrents down the façade, and rushed along the great avenue in a golden flood."[16]

García Márquez indulges himself again in a list of the beautiful absurdities that follow when the family's apartment is "brimming with light"; the furniture floats about the room, household objects "in the fullness of their poetry flew with their own wings," musical instruments drift among "bright-colored fish."[17] Because of this, the story's climax comes as a nasty shock. The boys have turned on so many lights that they drown in the flood, along with all their classmates, "eternalized in the moment of peeing into the pot of geraniums, singing the school song with the words changed to make fun of the headmaster, sneaking a glass of brandy from Papa's bottle." All the children die in the disaster in a city whose population "had never mastered the science of navigating on light."[18]

This story might be neatly translated as allegory. The rowboat is given in return for the boys' obedience, a perfect fit with the moralistic conventions of fable, which reward virtue and punish misdeeds. Or we might view the plot as a predictable conflict between the superego (the parents) and the id (the children). In either case the flood can be read as punishment for rebellion. Only when we register that the real plot is buried in ornamentation—in the story's digressive elements—can we progress from a fixed reading of its meaning.

What aspects of the story escape containment? First of all, the parents, those representatives of stern morality, are neither paragons nor tame conformists. The father buys the boat because he has bet the purchase against his sons' improvement in school, without first consulting his wife, "who was more reluctant than he to pay gambling debts," and thus we can assume that he has other gambling debts as well.[19] The boys can embark on their adventures because their parents are at the movies, enjoying *Last Tango in Paris* (which depicts acts of sodomy), and in the flood the television floats along with the other furniture, still tuned to the "final episode of the midnight movie for adults only."[20] These details undermine the parents' authority more by nibbling at its edges than by condemning it. Second, the boys *do* achieve their hearts' desire by capitulating to the demand that they perform well in school; the carrot-on-a-stick morality doesn't defeat their wishes or seem to harm them in any way. Finally, on their "fabulous adventure," the boys and their classmates pee on geraniums and steal sips of brandy, petty acts of rebellion that recall the parents' "naughty" rather than truly transgressive interest in sexuality.

The brutal surprise of this story's climax might meet with argument in a workshop: the writer should prepare the reader. But García Márquez fully honors the principle that a climax reconfigures what has come before. By this story's logic, structure heightens dissonance in order to unravel a moralistic interpretation. A disaster of unanticipated proportions feels *more* like a betrayal to the reader when it follows on the heels of a languid list of the impossibly beautiful effects of the flood. This is the predicament García Márquez wants to dramatize. He has to slap the reader hard in order to dislodge any notion of the imagination as charming diversion; it not only proves itself destructive but also refuses to distinguish between the comic and the tragic, as the story itself refuses to distinguish between light and water. By fiercely disrupting the expected causation (the neat allegory) and remaining silent on the impediments to fluid interpretation, García Márquez can pressure the reader to conjecture a hidden story. Anyone who thinks of magical realism as "whimsical" should be really uncomfortable, but all of us belong to the population that has yet to master the strenuous demands of navigating on light.

García Márquez achieves his aims in this story by anticipating at every moment the reader's efforts to register the action as having fixed symbolic import—in essence, the reader's desire to discover the bird in the cage. The truth is that readers bring to each story the most basic expectations of plot, but the best writers are more interested in messing around with those expectations than in fulfilling them in tidy fashion. As fiction writer William Gass once acknowledged, "The thing one wants to do with stories is screw them up."[21] A close look at each of the stories discussed so far reveals that the template for structure is bent and hammered to serve a unique dramatic situation, though you could profitably imitate the way each writer sets up (screws up) the climax and learn a great deal about how to gamble with the reader's expectations rather than simply satisfy them.

Because of their conventionally realistic surface, the experimental nature of Alice Munro's short stories is often underestimated, yet her work consistently demonstrates that stories are always and finally about the story that didn't get told. In "Fathers" Munro rather pointedly makes this case by offering us two separate plot lines to complicate our pursuit of a third, elusive story. The retrospective narrator tells us the story of two girls she barely knew in childhood. Each girl's story is told in turn, emphasizing the bifurcation of the plot line. First, the narrator tells of her acquaintance with Dahlia Newcombe, a year older, a popular girl whom the narrator admires. Because both live in the country, they walk home together from the high school in town. After her father, Bunt, attacks her with a shovel, Dahlia runs away from her family's farm and goes to live with her older sister in town, so she and the narrator walk together only one more time. Dahlia takes the narrator along to spy on Bunt, confessing how much she'd like to kill him, and the narrator feigns ignorance of the family's brutal life—the subject of much gossip—and manages not to betray any shock at the violence of Dahlia's feelings. She concludes that Dahlia brought her along because "she just wanted somebody to see her hating him."[22]

After a space break the narrator relates her acquaintance with Frances Wainwright, a younger child whom she knew four or five years before she met Dahlia. (Munro wickedly frustrates even the reasonable expectation that she will tell her story chronologically.) Frances's parents have asked the narrator to walk her to school and befriend her, and the narrator satisfies the outward form of the request by walking with Frances every day but then hiding from her at lunch time and joining in when the other girls tease her. Retrospectively, the narrator declares she isn't sure whether she led the teasing or merely went along with it. When Frances's parents are forced by poverty to leave town, they invite the narrator over for a farewell dinner. The narrator accepts only because she knows she won't have to see Frances again, and she spends most of her visit devouring movie magazines, the only interest she shares with Frances. Playing out a fantasy of serving a meal in a fancy restaurant, Frances's parents prepare exotic food, dote on the girls in ways that the narrator views as obsequious, and display a helplessness about practical matters and an indulgent, sexual affection for one another that, in combination, make the narrator queasy. Feeling "off balance," the narrator does not "tell about any of this at home."[23] This section of the story provides a mighty interesting epilogue for the Wainwright episode, and it's a terrific plot decision to include it. After the Wainwrights have moved away, the house they lived in falls apart, and although "no trespassing" signs are posted, the narrator, along with other kids, pokes around in the ruins. The section's last paragraph consists of one sentence: "No movie magazines came to light."[24] Nothing of the mirage of tenderness remains, only the disquiet it provoked in the narrator.

The story makes one more leap, to a section that reads like a coda for the other two and begins, "I did tell about Dahlia."[25] Now the narrator claims the story as her own, offering us clues by which we can re-read Dahlia's and Frances's stories as hers. She relates how she parlayed Dahlia's confession of her desire to kill her father into edifying gossip for her parents and reflects that "we could conduct this conversation so easily, without its seeming ever to enter our heads that my father had beaten me."[26] Plot structure aligns literal with figurative meaning: the period when her father beat her was "in between" her acquaintanceship with Frances and her acquaintanceship with Dahlia, just as her hidden story lies "in between" the other two. In laying side by side the bullying Bunt Newcombe and the solicitous Mr. Wainwright, Munro collapses the distance between tenderness and brutishness, compressing and contaminating what lies between them, the blinkered decency of the narrator's parents. This is the story that got away, the story of that unstable continuum. At the climax the narrator admits "the shame of being beaten, and the shame of cringing from the beating" and connects it with the "queasiness" Mr. Wainwright made her feel: "There were demands that seemed indecent, there were horrid invasions."[27]

The plot structure forces us to attend to gaps in the logic here: for the obvious connection with Dahlia the narrator now substitutes a link to Mr. Wainwright, whom she's carefully omitted from the tales she packages for her parents. Munro has seeded disruptive information throughout the story to help us interpret this gap. For example, Munro makes recurring references to the fixity of small town judgments, unclouded by pop psychology theories or any "thought of intervention": brutal Bunt Newcombe is accepted simply as "mean," "born that way"; Dahlia's athletic prowess gives her a chance to "slip free" of the stigma of "the business of her family," known to everyone; the narrator refines her skill at mimicry and retails town gossip in just such a way that her parents will read her as neither too vulgar nor "too smart." In contrast to "horrid invasions," small-town mores find a place for cruelty to lie undisturbed, accommodate people who are "born that way" rather than pursue motive. The story's climax culminates when the narrator nostalgically recalls the flat certainty of her elders at that time, "mysterious, uncomforting, unaccusing."[28]

In an earlier version of this story, published in *The New Yorker,* Munro ends the story on this note.[29] But in the revision that appears in her collection *The View from Castle Rock,* she shifts from the very beginning to the very end of the story a block of text that includes the narrator's response to a newspaper account of Bunt Newcombe's death, which occurred not long after the spying episode. The newspaper account, identifying Bunt as "beloved husband" and ending with a soothing Bible quotation, enacts the euphemisms by which conventional morality dodges close scrutiny. (Allow me to elbow you here: remember the stress on movie magazines, which also offer up a doctored version of reality, in the Wainwright section?) The story then concludes with this paragraph: "Dahlia Newcombe could not possibly have had anything to do with her father's accident. It happened when he reached up to turn on a light in a hanging metal socket, while standing on a wet floor in a neighbor's stable. He had taken one of his cows there to visit the bull, and he was arguing at that moment about the fee. For some reason that nobody could understand, he was not wearing his rubber boots, which everybody said might have saved his life."[30] Just as the newspaper sanitizes the grotesque death and brutal father, the narrator attempts to write herself out of Dahlia's story. But careful word choice in this paragraph perversely identifies the narrator with *both* Dahlia and Bunt. There's no need to reiterate the obvious (Dahlia couldn't have killed her father), except to cover for her own link to Dahlia, and we've just caught her donning rubber boots to preserve herself from the potency of fierce hatred. For some reason.

This clue may have been revealed too soon in the earlier version of the story. In this slot the newspaper account rings against the last line of the Wainwright story ("no movie magazines came to light"), and the narrator's comments on it invoke the last line of the Dahlia story ("she just wanted somebody to see her hating him"). Thus this placement helps us to recognize the unity of a story in which the narrator struggles to disown her ugly impulses and disavow the possibility of tenderness—at crippling cost. As a preface this paragraph did not have the force of revelatory surprise, but as a resolution, inflected by the adjectives *mysterious, uncomforting,* and *unaccusing,* it hints more forcefully at what has been left out of the plot, ensuring that the reader will recognize how closely the subterranean story is entwined with the bifurcated surface story. Placed here, the passage ensures that we'll read backward to see a beautifully distinct pattern in crystals that were only hazily in focus before, a swift realignment of literal and figurative that constitutes one of the key satisfactions a short story can offer.

Munro's story practically shouts its faith in the pursuit of what's not stated, what isn't there on the page, through its tour de force orchestration of two separate stories, neither of which is whole, both of which are required to suggest the hidden story that lies in their interstices. All great stories evoke the story that *isn't* contained within the literal elements of the plot by funneling toward a crisis and resolution while simultaneously unraveling themselves. Sustaining the tension between these two poles makes a story capable of generating "felt experience"—emphasizing the search over its conclusion, approaching more closely to meaning without ever capturing it, a cage in search of the elusive bird.

3

Chapter Structure and Shapeliness in the Novel

In the well-known biblical story, Delilah seduces Samson in order to discover the secret of his strength and then plots to cut a lock of his hair, leeching him of his power so she can turn him over to the soldiers who will chain him. In 1628, when Rembrandt took this betrayal as his subject, he was faced with finding a new way to portray an already familiar drama weighted with iconographic gestures and details—Delilah poised with scissors in hand, a bare-chested Samson displaying rippling muscles. As historian Simon Schama has noted, Rembrandt solved this dilemma by finding a masterful way "to suggest an entire story encapsulated in a single moment."[1] (See Figure 3.1.) Delilah occupies the center of Rembrandt's painting, while Samson, his back to the viewer, rests his head in her lap, his face obscured by locks of hair, though the brightest light falls on his supine form. In the background a soldier charges forward from the shadows, and behind him another helmeted soldier, dimly outlined, peers past the curtain that hides his body from our view. The army of men required to subdue even a weakened Samson is merely suggested, and its charge strongly contrasted with the limp, fully clothed form of Samson. If Delilah has been in on the plot, she looks up at the advancing soldier with an expression of startled surprise, and her hands betray conflict, one buried in Samson's golden locks, the other sifting a swatch of hair.

No scissors in sight, just as none of the weapons in this picture lies in plain view. Samson's sword is sheathed in its scabbard; the advancing soldier's sword is cut off by the edge of the picture frame, though light glints on its handle; and the second

Figure 3.1   Rembrandt van Rijn, *Samson and Delilah* (1628)
Bildarchiv Preussischer Kulturbesitz/Art Resource, NY.
Gemaeldegalerie, Staatliche Museen, Berlin, Germany.

soldier's drawn sword is merely a slice of darker shadow against
the dim background. Instead of the expected symbol of the scissors, Delilah's caressing hand evokes her past sexual intimacy
with Samson. Instead of the muscled torso of conventional representations, we see the vulnerable soles of Samson's feet, and

his terrifying power is only implicitly suggested by that second soldier who hangs back, afraid to enter a moment too soon. The viewer is denied any glimpse of Samson's reaction or Delilah's deed of cutting his hair, unfulfilled expectations that heighten our awareness of what is *about* to happen.

This painting has much to teach us about how to plot a narrative. If Delilah were looking up with a cunning smile, we'd recognize the outlines of the story of betrayal but there would be no plot. Arrangement in the painting encompasses more than the inclusion of the central actors. It involves timing, the play of light, and choices about where detail is heavily worked, where roughly sketched or even left out—in essence, the overlay of complex plot patterns on the template of story. Spatially arranged to emphasize tension, the painting is also temporally situated at the periphery of the grand dramatic action: suspense reaches its highest pitch at the off-balance moment when both past and future impinge on the present. In other words, the painting exhibits the key qualities of a well-made chapter by structuring action so that it flows over the boundaries of the frame.

When you embark on a novel, you might begin with the notion that it's simply a story on a grander scale. That scale quickly becomes a terrifying abyss, and solving the problem of finding an idea "big enough" to carry a novel can get diverted into an attempt to pack in one plot crisis after another, jam the gaping pit as full as possible. Such a novel proceeds at a relentless pitch until the reader, if not the writer, suffers from adrenaline exhaustion, and when you substitute mere event for plot complication, you'll be beset by problems with continuity. Conversely, you might happily assume that now you have room to tell "the whole story" at a leisurely pace, when actually knowing which events to leave out is as crucial to the plot of a novel as it is to the plot of a short story. In this conception, elements of backstory and subplots tend to exert drag on forward momentum; you might develop a character's relationship with his parents as a sidebar that gives a fuller sense of who he is without regard for how it advances the literal tension. (Because you're writing a novel about character, and you shouldn't have to stoop to cheap tricks.) In both approaches subplot is typically conceived of as a way to vary the main action (or simply to produce more of it)—as embellishment rather than necessity dictated by the trajectory of the central plot. Neither choice puts emphasis on moments at which something is *about* to happen. As a result, you're likely to err on either side of the correctly "off balance" structure, writing shapeless chapters that fail to advance a central dramatic conflict or chapters that fully resolve conflict, with no dramatic carry-over. If a story's plot moves like an avalanche, a novel's plot moves like a glacier, and all the rocks and boulders picked up along the way determine its amassed power to alter the landscape.

In composing a novel you must whittle a story to the fewest possible plot events, integrate subplots, structure chapters to heighten anticipation and postpone resolution, and figure out how to sustain coherence without sacrificing suspense. Taken together, these strategies elongate or interrupt the simple chronological march of time for the purpose of deepening the reader's curiosity about causes or consequences or both. Considering how plot will segment story matters greatly even if you're writing a novel that does without chapter divisions.

Plot as arrangement

Plot constitutes an extreme abbreviation of story, leaving out so much, yet a novel's plot must do so in ways that generate a proliferation of consequences and implications. In other words, you want to find the simplest central plot line possible to support as much complication of motive as possible. William Faulkner's novel *Intruder in the Dust* exemplifies the kind of simplicity that generates figurative complexity. This novel takes as its story template the form of a mystery novel, and its plot can be paraphrased accordingly: an old man, arrested for murder, must rely on the aid of two adolescent boys and an old woman to exonerate him when no one else presumes him innocent. But what does Faulkner leave out that we might have expected from a mystery? There is no roster of suspects to be winnowed. Instead of depicting a detective's effort to piece together clues from various sources, Faulkner delivers key evidence in one dramatic moment fairly early in the novel. The detective in this story is the suspect, Lucas, whose fate hangs in the balance and who is locked in a jail cell for most of the action. Rather than tying up plot strands with finality, the key evidence provokes further difficulty and delay.

Faulkner also leaves out two events that would have central importance in a genre novel. About halfway through the novel, in order to buy time for the main characters to supply evidence without provoking violence, Lucas must be spirited out of his jail cell. While this action matters to story, its logistics do not, so the fact that Lucas has been moved out of harm's way is withheld until the last paragraphs of the chapter and reported in just a single sentence. Faulkner also leaves out the dramatic action that would constitute the culminating event in a genre novel: the sheriff captures the murderer off-stage while the reader instead spends time with Chick, his uncle, and an old white woman, Miss Habersham, as they anxiously await news of the outcome. The accomplishment of tasks implied by a crisis is superfluous to plot unless it has the potential to complicate conflict.

In a procedural mystery, plot progresses by the revelation of fact. In a literary novel, plot progresses as revelation triggers some new uncertainty or tension. In the first case the reader adds up the facts in order to arrive at a satisfactory answer. In the second, the reader is provoked by gaps in the story, forced to continually revise whatever understanding has been established by the facts, to keep compounding the initial literal question with qualifications. In *Intruder in the Dust* the logistics of identifying the perpetrator, which form the heart of a procedural, matter only as they touch on the novel's themes. Ultimately, this is a novel about the dangerous duality of the Southerner's code of honor and about the psychic scar of racism, both for the old black man, Lucas, and the white boy, Chick, who feels conflicted about helping him and is the novel's main character. Though the story belongs to Lucas, the plot belongs to Chick, a decision analogous to Rembrandt's choice of Delilah, whose conflict is the central one, as the focal point of his painting.

The economy demanded by plot is served by carefully arranging the main characters in relation to one another in ways that focus attention on a central conflict. In Faulkner's novel Chick is initially compelled not by a sense of justice but by the need to square his account with Lucas, whom he insulted several years ago, an insult Lucas will not let him forget. Because the murder victim, Vincent Gowrie, is a white man from Beat Four, a corner of the county known for its racial hostility and violence, background information about the significant threat of racial violence arises in the wake of the action. Because the code of his society dictates that Lucas cannot accuse a white man of a crime, he can't report the truth to his lawyer, who conveniently happens to be Chick's uncle Gavin, and must rely instead on Chick, triggering the plot.

Subplot as necessity

Subplots help a writer to continue entailing complications for the central conflict by taking advantage of careful arrangement of the main players. The structure of *Intruder in the Dust* is so simple that it's fairly easy to see how the pressure of time—the necessity of finding evidence in time to prevent a lynching—links plot and subplot. As the novel opens, Chick is part of the crowd awaiting Lucas's arrival at the jail, and when he fetches his lawyer uncle to represent Lucas, Gavin can't make any headway with his client. Alone with Chick for just a moment, Lucas demands that the boy dig up Vincent Gowrie's body to prove the bullet in the body didn't come from Lucas's gun. Implicit in this outlandish demand is Lucas's expectation that Chick still owes him; their shared *past* triggers the main action of the novel. On his return home Chick discovers his uncle consulting with Miss Habersham, whose interest in Lucas's fate stems from the fact that his dead wife once worked for her. Chick sneaks out of the house and enlists the help of his friend Aleck, who is black, and just as they're heading off to the graveyard, Miss Habersham surprises them and argues that they'll need her truck to succeed. When these three go to dig up the grave under cover of night, they make the novel's key discovery.

Because a man's life is on the line, Chick is torn between loyalty to his community and his sense of justice, forced to question his culture's mores. His subplot relationships with his uncle, Aleck, Miss Habersham, and the sheriff and his fear of the mob enable Faulkner to give dimension to the murder mystery plot. Chick relies on his uncle Gavin as moral compass and mentor, yet like everyone else, his uncle assumes that Lucas killed a man, and he can't acknowledge Lucas's dignity. His cynicism constitutes a defense against moral uneasiness, making him an image of the man Chick might well become. Because of gender, race, and/or age, Miss Habersham and Aleck and Chick are outsiders to the power structure, which makes them the only people Lucas might persuade to act on his behalf. Aleck, as Chick's boyhood friend, provides a potent reminder that the caste lines drawn according to race are countered by the daily reality of close contact, and so does Miss Habersham, who adheres to a Southern code of honor that obligates her to care for Lucas even as its etiquette sustains discrimination. In order to clear Lucas, even the sheriff must dance around dangerous social rules: to exhume the body officially, he must negotiate with the dead man's volatile family.

Subplot delivers the social manners of this community in terms of how they impinge on the actions the main characters can take at any given moment. Background figures do not need to be etched in bright light in order to have dynamic force in a plot. The periphery of this plot is alive with suggestive reminders of the will to violence, in the form of the crowd gathering at the jail and on the town's streets, the armed deputies recruited to guard Lucas, and so on. Like the minor character of the sheriff, the people of the county are largely in the shadows in the background, analogous to the onrushing soldiers emerging from shadow in Rembrandt's painting, yet the pressure of their presence matters to the whole effect.

Chapter structure and strategic postponement

Effective chapter divisions tend to splice plot at moments when literal discovery generates new pressure on characters—pressure that is only felt in the next chapter or chapters, that has *yet* to be acted upon, so that the action overflows the "frame" of the chapter. Chapters, unlike stories, must incorporate the literal consequences of what has come before and set up literal obligations ahead, and yet each must also present a complete action (though this can be broadly defined).

In *Intruder in the Dust* the crisis is named in the very first sentence: "the whole town (the whole county too for that matter) had known since the night before that Lucas had killed a white man."[2] If a fact (in this case, a presumed fact) starkly sums up the literal stakes, the writer does not have to embellish it in order for the reader to remember it, and the reminders incorporated as the narrative unfolds can be equally simple and compressed. With this teaser in place, as Chick waits for Lucas to arrive at the jail, Faulkner turns to a flashback set four years earlier. Chick, hunting with Aleck, has fallen into an icy river. Lucas offers the hospitality of his house, but provoked by his imperiousness, Chick offers coins in payment. When Lucas refuses the money, Chick tosses the coins on the floor, and chapter 1 closes as Lucas orders Aleck to pick them up. Lucas's victorious rebuke imparts a sense of a completed action, yet the scene carries over into the next chapter, which begins as the two boys depart from Lucas's house and Chick feels the first pangs of shame. The obvious way to segment the past and present action would have been to complete the scene at the jail with Lucas's arrival and then turn to a flashback chapter. Faulkner's strategy refuses to segregate the past from the present moment, and it cuts across the grain by splicing both the past and present scenes across chapter boundaries.

We're propelled across the white space of the chapter division by our eagerness to witness Lucas's arrival, only to discovery that the past-action scene is also not finished. How does the writer buy the reader's patience for this foray into the past and pay other kinds of dividends on curiosity? Faulkner's second chapter directs us *backwards* as well as *forward* by revising the reader's understanding of the initial encounter between Lucas and Chick: their contest is not about one-upmanship but about which of them behaved like a true gentleman. The chapter begins as Chick walks to the creek, takes the coins from his pocket, and throws them into the water. What's so perfect about this action is its doubleness: we don't know yet whether Chick is rejecting the fact that Lucas bested him or the realization that he behaved badly in offering the coins in the first place, and Chick doesn't know yet either. In his interior monologue fury constitutes his primary emotion—"*We got to make him be a nigger first. He's got to admit he's a nigger*"[3]—and yet the fact that Lucas shamed him counters this insistence on caste superiority.

Faulkner nests within this flashback another episode in which Lucas refused to allow a white person to treat him with contempt, inciting a physical attack. This is germane to character development—impossible not to admire Lucas's sense of his own dignity and to understand that the impulse to admire may be bound up in Chick's rage—but it also matters to plot development, because we're reminded of the novel's first sentence and faced with the possibility that Lucas might easily get into a situation in which he had to defend himself against a white man. We don't know yet if he did. Strategic postponement whets the reader's appetite to know more at a complicated psychological level but it never fails to anchor that curiosity in the literal tension of the novel. It's OK—in fact, it's a *really* good idea—if the reader burns for answers to these literal questions.

Holding off on returning to the present, Faulkner reports Chick's subsequent efforts to bestow gifts on Lucas (to make him take the money), which Lucas cleverly frustrates, and then draws out Chick's actions on the day that Lucas is brought to jail, elongating narrative time at the moment when Chick, like the reader, anxiously anticipates Lucas's arrival. Plot "swells" time in order to heighten tension and intensify our anticipation of conflict, not just the next event. The stakes are raised by the time Lucas walks on stage: Chick has a troubled conscience and wants to blame Lucas for it, and he's struggling to believe Lucas has just freed him of further obligation. When Lucas spots Chick in the crowd waiting at the jail, he tells him to fetch his uncle. Now Faulkner gets maximum dramatic force from brevity: Lucas's simple statement (an order) demolishes Chick's prolonged, conflicted rationalization in an instant. Chick obeys him. The chapter is and is not a self-contained universe: Chick's shame and rage prove useless against his nagging sense of debt, but consequence flows over to the next chapter and pulls the reader with it, welding literal and figurative curiosity. How much will Lucas ask of Chick, and will he be able to give it? Will this gesture clear his conscience?

Good plotting jumps the gap between chapters; the potboiler withholds a fact for the future while in a work of art, meaning, not just the discovery of fact or consequence, is suspended across that gap. Because Faulkner shamelessly takes advantage of cliffhanger chapter endings, he shows how the revelation of a crucial fact at chapter's end can be exploited for dramatic momentum. Chapter 3 ends with Lucas's outrageous demand that Chick dig up a grave in the middle of the night; chapter 4 ends when Aleck, Chick, and Miss Habersham discover that the body in the grave is not that of the murder victim; chapter 7 ends with a return trip to the graveyard to discover the grave empty, and so on.

To consider how Faulkner exploits revelation of fact, we can look closely at chapter 4, which ends as Alec, Miss Habersham, and Chick stare into the opened grave. We recognize a completed action (mission accomplished) and an incomplete one (this bodes well for Lucas but it's not the incontrovertible evidence they came for) that raises unanswered literal questions. Who put the body of another man in the grave? Why? An amateur would have dwelled on the characters' reactions at the gravesite, most likely having them address the questions in the reader's mind and worry about the next step in their thwarted effort, draining off dramatic momentum rather than banking on it. What we don't know yet keeps us hooked, so Faulkner skips over their reactions and in chapter 5 jumps to the moment when Aleck, Chick, and Miss Habersham return to town, the white space emphasizing that their discovery compels further action and it's already underway. The three then go with Uncle Gavin to Sheriff Hampton's home to seek his help, and Hampton insists on making breakfast before they proceed. The exhausted Miss Habersham refuses to be dismissed from duty until the men prevail on her to sit at the jail, since the presence of a "white lady" will protect Lucas from a mob. Though she gives in, she also demands to be driven home first, and the chapter ends with Uncle Gavin answering, "yessum."[4]

Faulkner doesn't need a cliff-hanger ending here because he's still "riding" the energy released by the revelation of a fact that complicates the literal problem *and* his main character's conflict. In this subplot chapter social customs are observed to a T: Aleck eats alone in the kitchen while the others eat in the dining room, and the men dominate Miss Habersham but are also bested by her ability to capitalize on her protected status. Why is Sheriff Hampton in this story at all? Because he cares about justice too, even if he wouldn't risk what Aleck, Miss Habersham, and Chick have risked for it. Because this community does have values that can redeem it and support its idealists, the reader shares Chick's conflict, and shares it intensely, since Aleck's solitary meal, at a moment when his courage ought to be acknowledged, forcefully reminds us of the ingrained habits of racism. Literal suspense is in abeyance in this chapter so that emotional tension can peak. The consequences of discovering the wrong body ripple outward to encompass family and cultural loyalty, not just the next step to be taken.

Since the discovery threatens the taboos of Chick's social order, it could fuel racial violence rather than prevent it, so Chick's conflict continues to be heightened by the pressure of time. In the next chapter he goes home to his anxious mother, a chafing reminder of his youth in stark contrast to his growing realization of the enormity of his actions, further consequence for the cliff-hanger ending of chapter 4. Only now does Chick recall what happened at the graveyard and realize he and his cohorts nearly surprised the murderer in the act of switching bodies. (He caught and killed someone else digging up the grave to look for evidence.) This plot fact has been withheld until the reader can fully appreciate the danger in light of Miss Habersham's frailty, Chick's vulnerability, Aleck's relegation to the periphery, and the profound cognitive dissonance engendered by the customs they observe.

Faulkner demonstrates that the really developed action of a novel occurs before or after decisive action, in the lead time *or* the lag time between literal revelation and its emotional cause or consequence. (In a bad plot the big external and internal crises tend to be simultaneous rather than "out of sync.") By taking advantage of postponement, an opportunity denied to a short story writer, you can complicate conflict and establish continuity.

Of course, this is also a license to let plot tension flag. You can counter this with a terrific tactical weapon: the exploitation of the "looming event." Once a literal pressure or unresolved conflict has been established, a novelist can take advantage of this to explore character in more quiet ways. *Intruder in the Dust* offers many fine examples of this. In the opening chapter, because we recognize the implicit threat in the crowd gathering at the jail, we're more than willing to turn with Chick to flashback because we want to know what stake he has in Lucas's fate. The quiet early morning breakfast in chapter 5 is infused with tension not only because we want to know what happened after Aleck, Miss Habersham, and Chick discovered the wrong body in the grave but also because consequence is so clearly complicated when they revert to the caste rules of their society. At the novel's conclusion the arrest of the guilty man must wait until after a subplot chapter in which plot developments threaten Chick's relationship with his uncle. After a second visit to the graveyard, this time with the sheriff, Chick and his uncle return home through a deserted town, the crowd having vanished as soon as word of Lucas's innocence got out. When Chick voices contempt for the mob, his uncle abandons his habitual stance to counsel idealism: "Some things you must never stop refusing to bear."[5] The plot may have been largely resolved, and there are only two more chapters, one an epilogue, but the reader has been given compelling reasons to keep moving forward: will

Chick's sense of honor be corroded to passive disillusionment and alienation?

When the central conflict of a chapter is completely self-contained, suspense suffers, since you've answered the literal questions that might keep a reader going, and so does figurative tension, which is felt most strongly at those moment when things are *about* to happen. As you struggle with your own novel, imagine that you must "buy" time to explore quiet byways with the coin of literal tension. To take advantage of a reader's anticipation of an upcoming event, try moving a lifeless passage so that it falls between a crisis and the reaction it provokes. Placement alone will boost its power, and you can exploit the unstable "between-ness," in which previous tension flows over and future action is foreshadowed. One of the by-products of such a move is the breadth of characterization possible only in a novel.

Tangential developments and coherence

Because a novel's plot can take advantage of postponement and tangential developments, it can digress from a strictly linear story line far more than does this particular example of Faulkner's work. For contrast, we don't have to look any farther than Faulkner's more experimental *As I Lay Dying*. In this multiple-perspective novel the Bundrens cart the reeking corpse of the family matriarch to a cemetery far from home. One chapter, in the perspective of her adult son Cash, offers a numbered list of reasons why a beveled edge is useful in carpentering a coffin, and the next, in the perspective of Cash's little brother, consists of the single sentence "My mother is a fish."[6] Because of what's been left out of the plot, Faulkner generates tension from this sequence in which Cash's effort to reduce the experience of death to a utilitarian task is countered by the child's starkly simple reference to the stench of decay. Shapeliness in this novel, as in *Intruder in the Dust*, derives from the writer's understanding of how plot diverges from story, how its gaps both suggest and distort the story template, the simple synopsis of the action.

In J. M. Coetzee's postmodern novel *Diary of a Bad Year*, chapters radically fragment the story line in ways that ultimately deliver a coherent plot. The novel is divided into two parts, Strong Opinions and Second Diary, and its chapters are

divided into three strands, an essay in its entirety and two narrative strands. The essays, most of which decry the brutal politics
of contemporary life, are being composed by C., a renowned
seventy-two-year-old novelist whose resemblance to the author
is provocative but deliberately unsteady. C.'s diary entries constitute the second strand. The third, which does not begin until
chapter 6, is the first-person narrative of Anya, C.'s beautiful
young neighbor. By titling each chapter after the essay it contains ("On the origins of the state," "On anarchism"), Coetzee
stresses the seemingly arbitrary division of chapters by topic,
the contradictory pull between the self-contained unit and the
interdependent part of a whole. He also lets the reader in on
his intention to bend a nonfictional mode to the laws—and
revelations—of plot and to make these three strands cohere
as *one*.

The three strands of the novel unfold "simultaneously" on
the page, each separated by a bar that visually stresses the tension between continuity and fragmentation. (Figure 3.2 provides
a representation of two successive pages.) Gaps and tangents in
the plot are lent emphasis by this layout, even more so because
in each short chapter the diary and Anya's narration are often

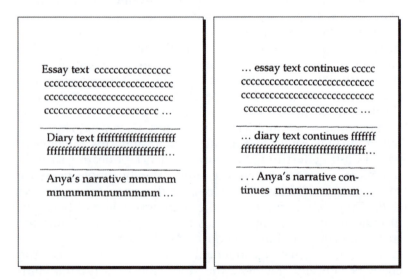

Figure 3.2   Page layout in *Diary of a Bad Year*
Illustrator: Alan Stonebraker

delivered in snippets of just a few lines per page. The plot advances only by the tiniest increments in any chapter; a single scene in either narrative strand might carry across ten or more chapters. Do you read this novel page by page or skip ahead to complete one strand at a time? In metafictional terms this structure highlights the process of reading a literary work: it exerts a powerful horizontal (forward) pull as we attempt to "complete" from segments of plot the coherent story, interrupted by the bars on the page but flowing right over the boundary line of the chapter break, and a powerful vertical pull as we read back and forth between the three strands, seeking parallels and hidden connections.

As with Faulkner's novel, subplot and plot (such as they are in the two narrative strands) are tightly entwined by necessity. There are just three main characters, whose biographies emphasize the lines of tension: C. is a white South African transplant to Australia who has wearied of writing novels. As an immigrant from the Philippines, Anya brings a different set of historical referents for colonialism, which colors her confidence in her sexual power. Alan, the boyfriend who supports her, is an "investment consultant" who cheerfully abides by the dog-eat-dog capitalist ethos that C. condemns in his essays. Perhaps echoing C.'s exhaustion (as he tells Anya, "To write a novel you have to be like Atlas, holding up a whole world on your shoulders"[7]), the plot is stripped to bare bones, with few sense details, scant reference to setting, and plot advances accomplished largely through dialogue. Coetzee also honors the principle of simplicity by boiling down the plot to just a handful of scenes that emphasize the core conflict: the predatory potential in each of the main characters. C. contrives to get close to Anya by offering her an exorbitant salary to serve as his secretary, typing up the essays he dictates and returning the file on disk. Anya shares the essays with Alan, who derides their out-of-date morality and astutely suspects that C. hired Anya for reasons other than her typing skills. After Anya figures out that C. is dying, probably of Parkinson's disease, Alan tries to enlist her in a scheme to embezzle the considerable fortune C. intends to leave to an animal-rights organization. The scenes in these two narrative strands take up less than two-thirds of each page, and Coetzee performs the magic trick of generating an increasingly complicated causal array from this literal progression.

Both the "digression" of the essays and the three-part structure of each chapter contribute to this achievement. From the outset the reader is struck by the distance between C. as essayist and C. as diarist. In chapter 1 the diary records his first glimpse of Anya in the laundry room of their apartment complex. Though he objectifies Anya as a bimbo with a booty, C. claims a "metaphysical ache" at the sight of her in "red shift and thongs." When he adds a correction—"Thongs of the kind that go on the feet"—he betrays what he's going to some lengths not to call by name.[8] Above the bar on the page, he's a disembodied mind; below, a crass old lecher. Structure enhances literal tension, forcing us to move back and forth between the two strands: "metaphysical ache" links the moralistic essays to a lust that mocks high-mindedness. By the end of this chapter C. is interrogating the building manager in an effort to identify his neighbor. The potent symbolic curiosity Coetzee has aroused in the reader is anchored in our literal curiosity about whether C. will initiate contact with Anya and how that relationship might unfold.

Despite all the trappings of metafictional experiment, Coetzee, like Faulkner, obeys the fundamental plotting law of suspending consequence across the chapter break even as he pays out the first installment on plot expectation. The second chapter shifts to a new essay topic, yet the title, "On anarchism," deftly recasts the previous action (intellect cannot govern unruly impulse), while the next diary entry propels the plot as C. reports thanking the manager for revealing Anya's name. Chapter 1's essay argues that identity is the property of the state, which asserts control over helpless individuals via bureaucratic requirements for identity papers, and now this tangent colors our reading of C.'s effort to discover Anya's identity.

Subtle echoes between the essays and narrative strands may constitute a departure from standard tactics but nevertheless underscore the chapter's true function of structuring information in ways that amplify the figurative meaning of literal tension. (Even the delayed introduction of Anya's narrative strand complicates the initial duality of mind/body by granting the object of C.'s lust status as a subject.) On page 15 an essay that declares "democracy is totalitarianism" concludes: "Then ask yourself: Who serves whom? Who is the servant, who the master?" In the diary strand just below the bar on this page, Anya is answering C.'s nosy questions by identifying Alan as "my partner."[9]

This playful juxtaposition invites us to doubt the truth of her statement and teaches us how to read the novel. The "consequences" for an essay also flow over chapter boundaries, even if the essays don't. The payoff for the chapter 1 essay on identity slowly accrues as questions of identity and integrity filter into the characters' personal relationships.

The essays constitute not interruptions but a form of strategic delay that allows the sparse literal tension available in any chapter to be read on figurative terms. For example, in chapter 13, "On the body," C. notes in his essay that humans, in contrast to animals, think of their bodies "in the relation of possessor to the possessed." In his diary he records a "bad dream" about dying. On the same page, in Anya's narrative strand, Alan continues a conversation with Anya, begun in the previous chapter, in which he urges her to be wary of C. "plagiarizing" her life for his writing, insisting, "You have an identity, which belongs to you alone. It is your most valuable possession."[10] On the very next page C. wonders if his dream suggests that "this young woman who declines to call me by my name, instead calling me *Señor*" (refusing to grant *his* identity) may be "the one who has been assigned to conduct me to my death," while just below the bar Anya and Alan debate whether C. is writing pornographic fantasies about her.[11] *That's* dramatic tension.

Thanks to reverberations in the white space, chapter 13 delivers a completed action *very* broadly defined, draws on its predecessors for effect, and introduces as-yet unresolved complications. Just when we might be ready to write off C., Anya shrugs at Alan's effort to persuade her that he's a predator, and C. reveals a very different kind of longing for her, a completed action. When Alan views the situation as rife with possibilities for a lawsuit, he commodifies identity in a way that corresponds to the chapter 1 essay but has not been predicted by it, and he comically subverts C.'s philosophical musings on possession. The mystical dream recorded in the diary eludes C.'s deterministic definitions of identity and Alan's reductionist views, introducing instability by complicating C.'s motives and undermining the authority of the essays. Each strand of the narrative is now revising our reading of the others, re-enacting on multiple dimensions the dilemma of identity—physical, cultural, political, intellectual, and spiritual. By page 60 Coetzee has brilliantly suborned the essay form to the functional principles of fiction.

Where a traditional novel might rely entirely on past event to continue fueling tension, these chapters recruit the terms and ideas of the essays and recombine them in relation to the dramatic action. Many of the essays in the early chapters focus on the collective shame and responsibility of human beings for the evils committed by the state. C. reports in his diary that Anya, bored with his outrage, has begun to challenge him on this notion of a shared burden of dishonor. How does she counter his argument? She tells him a story. At a much younger age she was gang-raped by three men but had the courage to press charges, despite the warning of a police captain that this dishonor would stain her, and thus she can declare that C. has made himself "miserable over nothing."[12] When C. sardonically probes at her logic—"And I would be very surprised if in your inmost depths they did not continue to dishonor you"[13]—Anya flies into a rage. Because C. makes his claim about Anya's "inmost depths" in a chapter titled "On asylum in Australia," the reader can supply a reason for Anya's fury: C. can look at her ass all he likes, but he can't presume to know the private asylum of her soul.

The plotting of the story is exquisite at this stage. In chapter 23, C. gets a note from Anya declaring that she won't work for him anymore, and the diary ends as he begins his reply, *"Dear Anya,* I wrote," a cliff-hanger chapter ending if ever there was one. The diary strand resumes in the next chapter by immediately impressing on the reader C's desperation: *"You have become indispensable to me."*[14] In counterpoint to this plot development, in the third strand Alan inadvertently betrays to Anya his plan for swindling C. and parries her objections, with his successive revelations engineered so that the plot literally jumps across the white space at chapter's end.

Over chapters 24–29 Coetzee interrupts C.'s effort to compose a reply to Anya and suspends its consequence (her response). Coetzee banks on this looming event as C. muses on the nature of his essays before adding to his letter a postscript in which he offers to write "a second, gentler set of opinions" to please her.[15] This allows time for the very literal conflict in the third strand to reach its peak. In chapter 30, the penultimate chapter of part 1, C. records in his diary Anya's arrival at his door just as in the third strand Alan is urging her to give his scheme more thought. By timing as simultaneous on the page Anya's appearance at the door and Alan's urgings, which actually preceded it,

Coetzee jams up the chronology of his plot so that *structure* can make visible the moment when subplot (Anya's relationship with Alan) intersects with plot (Anya's relationship with C.) to become one story—Anya's story. It's breathtaking to see plot enact meaning so fiercely. The timing generates literal suspense—does Anya agree to resume typing for C. in order to further Alan's plans?—and generates figurative tension by forcing the reader to compare two very different assaults on Anya's integrity. On moral principle C. insists that dishonor has invaded her inmost depths, while out of opportunistic greed Alan attempts to recruit her to share in *his* dishonor.

As the much shorter part 2 (Second Diary) begins, the plot promises of part 1, permuted but nonetheless literal, propel the reader forward: Will C. revise the essays, and if so, will this merely be a ploy motivated by lust? Will Anya reconsider Alan's swindling scheme? Are these men fundamentally alike in exploiting her? In these concluding chapters Coetzee takes full advantage of his novel's structure to dramatize consequence. Anya's influence is demonstrated in C.'s essays as scathing judgment gives way to anguish, while his diary entries are literally taken over by Anya's voice as he records a long, long letter from her, written after she has left Alan and moved away to start over on her own. Anya's sense of her own integrity (and C.'s) is felt as the novel's structure enacts its content, with the bars between the three strands no longer isolating mind from body or one self from another. At the close of the novel, in the third strand Anya relates her efforts to keep track of C.'s health from a distance, so that when he dies she can return to "hold his hand"—to serve as the mystical companion of his dreams.[16] Alongside the paeans to great artists in C.'s second set of essays, Anya's colloquial voice, dominating both narrative strands now, articulates an equally impressive imaginative achievement.

Coetzee's experimental form posits an elegant variation on a universally applicable principle: both continuity and suspense in a novel's plot depend on reworking what has come before. Tension is sustained over the long haul not just because new problems arise but because old ones re-emerge, and in different permutations. Mere story consists of one event leading to the next, which leads to the next, like this:

$$A \to B \to C \to D \to E \to \ldots$$

But in a novel's plot each subsequent event totters on under the accumulated weight of the past:

$$A \to B_{(A)} \to C_{(A)} \to D_{(B)} \to E_{(A, C)} \to F_{(A, B, C)} \to G_{(A, B, E)} \to H_{(A, C, F, G)} \to \cdots$$

The further along you are in a novel, the more you bank on reconfiguration of the past for meaning. (No matter how tenuously "the past" might be defined.) The ending of a novel coasts gloriously on all that has come before. To see how this holds true for a more conventional novel, you only have to think back to *Intruder in the Dust*. In the closing scene of the novel, Chick is with his uncle at his law office when Lucas comes to pay for his legal services. Gavin, who assumed along with the mob that Lucas had killed a man, charges two dollars, a charity that invokes all the other moments of caste privilege in the novel and reminds us that his society compromises efforts to be honorable. Lucas counts out nickels and pennies in payment, which would be only comic if it did not call up the coins Chick threw at him long ago as well as Chick's ensuing effort to free himself from obligation. This memory is reconfigured one last time when Lucas demands a receipt. A moral debt has yet to be paid.

As you consider the story material for your own novel, you can take many lessons from these two very different writers, neither of whom shies from basic storytelling strategies. First, you don't have to make any apologies for shamelessly engineering literal suspense via chapter structure. Second, when you consider which elements of story to plot, you must work both forward and backward, considering which actions can generate sustained consequences and which can call the past back into play. It matters less to plot a "big" event than to plot one that can heft the weight of the past. Third, conceive of plot as a deliberately off-balance arrangement of story material. Your plot energy should be disproportionately expended on moments when you can prolong the reader's anticipation of a coming crisis or when you can draw on the energy discharged by a literal discovery to fuel quiet moments in which consequence can resonate.

Finally, at those key nodes in the plot when some literal tension is resolved, you must also generate some new instability, one that the reader can't yet see in clear outline. If your main character suddenly quits his acting career in Los Angeles and takes off for his rural home town, the reader shouldn't yet know all the reasons he's done so and should be able to piece this together only as the past impinges on the next action and the next. If he settles down comfortably to watch TV with his boyhood friend as soon as he arrives in town, your plot has come to a grinding halt; if his friend first offers him a cornucopia of drugs reminiscent of the Hollywood parties he's just fled, you have the kind of instability that is essential, a motion shot in which the outlines of what is about to happen are blurred by reverberations from the past.

4

Three Key Strategies of Story Logic

When he was two years old, my son woke up one morning and reported, "Dream two gorillas chasing you." My son referred to himself as "you," his version of the royal *we,* but he also understood that the same pronoun would do to address his father and me, his devoted courtiers. He had just moved from his crib to a bed, and we worried about him waking before we did and wandering alone through the house. So we had no trouble deciphering his dream. We must have scared him more than we thought, rushing every morning to scold him about staying in bed instead of fawning over him, as custom demanded. The gorillas probably owed something to a recent visit to the zoo, where the howling monkeys had terrified him. A mellow baby, our son had just entered the era of tantrums—the era of his own howling. So the dream hid a complicated set of associations with his recent past, the contentment of babyhood, and even his own anger, provoked by our inexplicable transformation. Its one-sentence plot might be diagrammed as shown in Figure 4.1. Fiction that is any good has much in common with the dream mechanisms illustrated in this diagram. A linear plot can carry all this weight too, compressing a host of associations that unlock its multi-layered meaning. Both arrow and array.

A well-made fiction differs greatly from a dream. It offers a complete narrative arc, not a fragment, and its sequence of events makes literal sense. Yet just as in a dream, meaning depends as much on form as on content. Story logic exploits sequence to cue us to submerged connections, and it employs compression (a single image linking many associations) and displacement

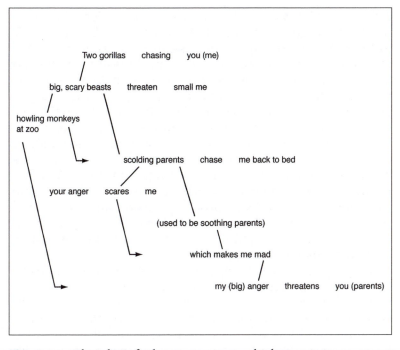

Figure 4.1 The "plot" of a dream generates multiple associations
Illustrator: Alan Stonebraker

(a skewed emphasis on a seemingly peripheral element) to sustain an enhanced ratio of subtext to text. Any given element does not yield its full meaning by itself; only when the reader traces associative connections and attends to sequence can she confirm the meaning diffused throughout the whole. Dreams and fiction are open to multiple interpretations, generating not an either/or statement but an either/and statement. Once we trace possible associations, the action of my son's dream can be read as "scolding parents scare me" *and* as "my anger threatens my parents." Because there *is* a relationship between these alternates (anger makes a monster of you), neither cancels out the other, as it might in a logical argument, and together they enrich meaning.

Usually only the dreamer can guess at the fragmentary meaning of a dream, but a fiction writer tries to define a range of interpretation for many different readers. As a deliberate construction, a narrative is like a joke, which also draws on the logical displacement that operates in dreams. In her essay "Mom's on the Roof," Antonya Nelson highlights this resemblance: "Humor is rooted in what is called 'appropriate incongruity,' the understanding of an appropriate intermingling of elements from domains that are generally regarded as incongruous."[1] Like jokes, stories deploy appropriate incongruity even in their structure: "A punch line, like an epiphany, serves to realign our understanding of characters, relations, situations, or events. It insists on an absent logical step in the process of cognition."[2] Consider this familiar joke: *Knock knock.* Who's there? *Orange.* Orange who? *Orange you going to invite me in?* The punch line offers an appropriate incongruity that satisfies because its surprise depends on an absent logical step, the comparison the listener must make (orange you? aren't you?) in order to recognize the auditory substitute as a *viable* alternative for a derailed content expectation.

Story logic helps you to suggest the absent logical step in plot—to hint at it by arrangement, not explicit statement. When you write fiction, you are in the peculiar position of striving to discover and exploit multiple connections among the elements of a narrative and simultaneously working to submerge all surface traces of this coherent "argument." Hemingway's famous iceberg theory indirectly alludes to this dilemma: "If a writer of prose knows enough about what he is writing about he may omit things that he knows and the reader, if the writer is writing truly enough, will have a feeling of those things as strongly as though the writer had stated them. The dignity of movement of an ice-berg is due to only one-eighth of it being above water."[3] "A feeling of those things" seems so imprecise, yet that is just the point.

Although the Russian formalist critic Victor Shklovsky makes a strange bedfellow for Hemingway, he analyzes how literature makes meaning in ways that correspond entirely with Hemingway's "feeling of those things." Shklovsky coined the term *defamiliarization* for any methods by which a writer engenders this kind of knowing, distinct from the narrowly focused knowing that operates when language provides only pragmatic cues. Defamiliarization is a matter of gestalt: it denotes an adverbial quality, *how* the writer's selection of detail, image, and diction imparts something more than the merely functional. Conventional representations of experience trigger an automatic response to information; drivers do not attend to the color of a traffic light except to register a signal to stop or go. Defamiliarization bypasses reflexive knowing much as dreams bypass the mechanisms of repression. Contrasting "poetic" language with "practical" language, Shklovsky defines defamiliarization as an effort to counter "habitualization": "And art exists that one may recover the sensation of life; it exists to make one feel things, to make the stone *stony*. The purpose of art is to impart *the sensation of things* [italics added] as they are perceived and not as they are known. The technique of art is to make objects 'unfamiliar,' ... to increase the difficulty and length of perception because the process of perception is an aesthetic end in itself and must be prolonged."[4]

At first it may seem that Shklovsky's vehemence about prolonging perception runs counter to Hemingway's insistence on leaving out, but the two are intimately related strategies. In writing fiction, you can afford to leave out certain material, such as explanation, provided that you successfully substitute a displaced emphasis on "sensation" that forces the reader to conjecture the absent logical step. What is off kilter or unexpected often makes the best candidate for this job: something on the periphery is suddenly lit by a spotlight. Mario Vargas Llosa once declared that the writer must be a "fetishist," citing as an example the novels of the obscure eighteenth-century French writer Restif de la Bretonne. Although Bretonne accurately reported many of the social customs of his day, in his novels "men fall in love with women not for the beauty of their faces, the slenderness of their waists, their good breeding, or spiritual charms but ultimately for the beauty of their feet or the elegance of their boots."[5] Because of Bretonne's helplessness in relation to his obsession, he could not generate meaning from this oddity, but as Vargas Llosa points out, "all creators of fiction are embroiled in the same process, though less thoroughly and blatantly."[6] For the writer as for the fetishist, the peripheral detail looms large, but with any luck, the difference is that a reader ultimately recognizes the accuracy of this displaced emphasis rather than resisting it.

Integrating story logic strategies

To engage a reader in experiential knowing and in conjecturing what has been left out, you can draw on three related craft strategies: the peripheral detail, recurrence, and sequencing. Rather than portray a character weeping to signal grief, you instead find a peripheral detail or gesture to embody grief in a fresh way, prolonging a reader's perception of it. You can, for example, focus the reader's attention on a character's inconsequential gesture, such as pouring tea into a cup without spilling it, and employ diction that will transfer the emotion onto the action. In other words, you find an objective correlative that is just strange enough: the teacup filled to overflowing, the liquid trembling with surface tension, can make the reader *feel* a barely suppressed grief in a way that no statement could. Where the fetishist points so insistently at the fetish object that no surprise—no discovery—can come of the effort, the writer must rely on understatement. A detail or a gesture ceases to be peripheral if you overstate its importance, just as in telling a joke, you can give away the punch line before it's delivered by overemphasizing some necessary linguistic setup or conveying information in the wrong sequence.

Recurrence, the second strategy, helps you to diffuse meaning in a way that is cumulative. Because of recurrence (of actions, phrases, objects, or images), any one moment in the text can be traced to multiple others, a network that reinforces and complicates the linear sequence of plot. Chekhov makes brilliant use of recurrence in "Anna on the Neck," and just one of many instances will illustrate its exponential power. A harmonium appears twice in this story, in which an impoverished widower marries off his daughter to a wealthy older man who hopes a beautiful wife can advance his career; in exchange, he might be tapped for a loan. At first so terrified of her moralistic husband that she can't eat in his presence, Anna sneaks home for a meal with her father and two little brothers. After dinner her father plays the harmonium, trying "to wrest from it pure and harmonious sounds," but capable only of making it wheeze and growl. Petulantly, he blames his sons: "You have spoiled the instrument!"[7] Eventually Anna serves her husband's ambition by winning male admirers, thus gaining power over him. In the story's last paragraph there's a glancing reference to the harmonium, which has been sold for debt, confirmation that Anna has cut ties to her family. Recurrence works best at the periphery, and here it overlays triumph with loss: like the harmonium, Anna was sold for debt; she too is a beautiful instrument, spoiled by the uses to which her husband and father have put her. Because of the time elapsed between one instance and the next, the reader's imagination fires connections, and meaning resides in those connections, not the single instance. Studying brain chemistry, neuroscientists have discovered that memories are not stored intact in particular brain cells but are reconstituted as electrical impulses travel the branching pathways between one cell and another. Memories reside in the synapses, a particular network of connections triggered in response to some stimulus. Similarly, recurrence works because it exists "in the synapses."

The third strategy, sequencing, draws on one of our basic assumptions about story, which is that an event that follows on another is caused by it. Because a writer can exploit this expectation, chronology can suggest causality. In the realm of reasoning we're cautioned not to mistake correlation for causation; crime rates may be higher in cities that have colder winters, yet this doesn't mean cold weather causes crime. But fiction, which appeals to emotional logic, is bent on making this mistake all the time and can deviously insinuate cause and effect via sequencing. If a man kicks the dog and in the next scene his lover feeds the man's dinner to the dog, we intuit the second action as a consequence of the first, especially if a space break entices us to fill in the blank. Reverse the order of the man-kicking-dog sequence, and a new causal chain is implied: because his lover fed the man's dinner to the dog, the man takes out his anger on the animal. In either case the lovers' anger at *each other* can be understood from sequence alone. Moreover, special figurative emphasis is lent to what occurs just before or after a space break. Think back to Chapter 2 and recall how the ending of Alice Munro's "Fathers" cashes in on the strategic placement of key sentences at the end of previous sections. Sequencing helps us to generate subtext in the white space of a chapter or section break, to hint at the hidden story via an invisible *because* clause, or to suggest submerged symbolic connections.

Tapping into dream logic

Like many surreal stories, Naguib Mahfouz's "The Conjurer Ran Off with the Dish" operates so thoroughly from dream logic that it's easy to trace its relation to story logic and to see how these three craft strategies work in concert. Mahfouz's fable corresponds utterly to an archetypal dream structure in which repeated attempts to complete a task are thwarted because one or another necessary component goes missing. On his mother's instructions a hungry boy makes several trips to purchase beans for their breakfast, but each attempt is foiled by some unanticipated condition: the beanseller asks whether he wants the beans with oil or butter; then he wants to know which kind of oil; then he asks for payment and the boy discovers he has lost the piaster his mother gave him to pay for the beans; then the boy forgets to bring a dish to carry the beans home. When the mother first sent her son on this errand, she announced, "It is time for you to be of use," and each time he returns home for further instruction, she berates him.[8] Like the beanseller who harangues the boy on each trip, she speaks for utilitarian reality.

How does Mahfouz weight this archetypal plot with rich, utterly unique associations? The carefully orchestrated sequence of the boy's repeated attempts helps a reader to register change: at first the obstacles to achieving adult competence are, to the boy, random and external, but on his third trip he spots a conjurer performing tricks for a crowd of children and gets sidetracked by his own desires: "My feet dragged as my heart was pulled toward them. At least let me have a fleeting glance."[9] Defeat changes him, and on his next trip he's distracted by a "peep show" offering imaginative tales of "chivalry, love, and deeds of daring," and this time he "gazed in fascination, completely forgetting the conjurer and the dish."[10] Countering any simple dichotomy between ego and id, the "picture stories" of the peep show proffer ennobling qualities, and when the captivated boy retells these romantic tales to himself, a young girl overhears him and triggers the next event in the story by responding. When the boy and girl find a secluded spot where they can kiss, Mahfouz emphasizes peripheral details: they sit together on a "stairway that went nowhere," and the narrator finds the kisses still sweeter because of the candy the girl has been eating, "red-and-white sweets called 'lady's fleas.' "[11] *Willya lookit that* awesome example of fetishism! If the candy evokes comparison with the beans as satisfaction for hunger, it also evokes the body in gross terms, tainting the sequence in which tales of chivalry lead to chaste kisses. Either/and. And then the girl runs off because she too must complete an errand for her mother—finding a midwife, another realistic dimension of sexuality still veiled from the boy.

Because he has dallied with the girl, by the time the boy returns to the beanseller, no more beans are left, but instead of again passively enduring the seller's wrath, the boy fights back, throwing the dish at the man. Sequence tells us that the interlude with the girl has sprung the boy free of the cycle of failed attempts, and rebellion in turn engenders a new kind of foresight. His head still filled with "dreams of heroism and valor," the boy resolves to spend the piaster on "some sort of enjoyment" "before being punished."[12] He knows now that reality demands he pay for his pleasure, but one more disturbing lesson remains. Recalling the delight of kissing the girl, he returns to the stairway, where he spies a man and a woman having sex, which arouses "curiosity, surprise, pleasure, and a certain amount of disquiet." When the man slaps the woman and she retaliates, the boy flees: he cannot reconcile himself to the discovery that pleasure offers no real escape from struggle and may be as labyrinthine in its demands as the reality principle. The boy immediately registers that he is "lost," with "no idea of where I was"; reinforced by recurrence (remember the stairway that went nowhere), sequence establishes the literal and figurative consequence of what he has witnessed.[13] The story's ending offers this appropriate incongruity in place of uncomplicated wish fulfillment.

Sequencing to generate subtext

In "The Gambler, the Nun, and the Radio," Ernest Hemingway so successfully keeps seven-eighths of the iceberg under water that the literal plot strikes a casual reader as random; it doesn't yield meaning unless we attend to the story logic that cues us to its submerged story. Hemingway beautifully illustrates how important sequencing is to meaning in a realistic story, and his strategies also suggest that plot construction itself might be predicated on looking to the periphery. The main character, Frazer, has been hospitalized for weeks with a badly broken leg, and the story opens when he encounters Cayetano, a man brought into the hospital with a gunshot wound that may paralyze him. Tangential contacts among Frazer, Cayetano, and a nursing nun, Sister Cecilia, suffice for a plot. Entering the story without preamble, Hemingway deliberately imposes on the reader a confusion about facts that mirrors the many misunderstandings among the characters: Cayetano is mistaken for a poor farm worker because he's Latino and doesn't speak English; a second, unintended victim was shot as well; and so on.

The story's nine sections maximize the effect of space breaks and underscore that they function as more than mere indicators of the passage of time. The first scene is actually broken in two by a space break: in section I Cayetano, interviewed in his hospital room, refuses to identify his assailant for a police sergeant and is abetted by Frazer, and in the very short section II Frazer talks to the sergeant in the corridor afterward. Why insert a space break at all? In the first section the reader can't quite keep up with the action: there's no apparent reason for Cayetano to lie, declaring he was shot by accident, or for Frazer to support him. When the official interpreter embellishes Cayetano's story, the police sergeant gets Frazer to translate in his place, but with no better results. Like the official interpreter, Frazer does not relate precisely what Cayetano says, but unlike the other interpreter, Frazer investigates Cayetano's motives, telling him that he can "with honor" denounce his assailant.[14] Cayetano is curious too, because he asks about Frazer's broken leg. To add to the comedy, the police officer blurts, "I don't give a damn who shot you, but I've got to clear this thing up."[15] Subtly, the reader is asked to trust Cayetano and Frazer, who are interested in more than facts. In section II, as Frazer chats with the sergeant, we learn that he's confined to a wheelchair and has endured a series of surgeries after his leg failed to heal. Frazer reassures the irritable sergeant that despite his own efforts to subvert the man's aims, he's "not sore." Because of the space break, Hemingway can underscore tension between Frazer's affinity for Cayetano in the first section and his detachment in the second section.

In section III Sister Cecilia visits Frazer's hospital room to report on Cayetano's progress. Where Frazer cultivates detachment, Sister Cecilia is extravagantly effusive; to her, Cayetano is "beautiful," "a fine patient" who suffers in silence, in contrast to the other victim in the same shooting, whose screaming belies the comparatively minor nature of his own wound. She declares Cayetano must be "a thoroughly bad one, he's so fine and delicately made," adding (unnecessarily), "I always like the bad ones." This section, only two paragraphs long, concludes as Sister Cecilia announces her intentions:

"I know he's not a beet worker. His hands are as smooth and not a callous on them. I know he's a bad one of some sort. I'm going down and pray for him now. Poor Cayetano, he's having a dreadful time and he doesn't make a sound. What did they have to shoot him for? Oh, that poor Cayetano! I'm going right down and pray for him."

She went right down and prayed for him.[16]

Both recurrence and sequencing are at work in this hilariously mimetic close to the section: Sister Cecilia's absolute statements are translated immediately into action, a consistency between her internal code and her behavior that contrasts sharply with the apparent inconsistency in Frazer's approach to his role as translator. The scene has been distilled to its essence: it's so simple for Sister Cecilia to act.

Hemingway begins section IV with the sentence "In that hospital a radio did not work very well until it was dusk."[17] Especially after a space break, we tend to read the next plot development as consequence, and Hemingway exploits this to suggest Frazer is reacting to Sister Cecilia's unqualified feelings for Cayetano. Juxtaposition strongly hints that the radio should be considered in relation to prayer, on the surface a distortion of perspective, especially since the stations Frazer listens to for most of the night offer mindless escape. Presumably he lies awake because he's in pain, but the writer refuses to confirm this. In leaping to the peripheral detail of the radio, Hemingway defamiliarizes the experience of pain and also complicates Frazer's dilemma by "precise imprecision." Because the reader has to assume the fact of pain, its nature may be as much psychological as physical. In this section, most of which occurs in Frazer's thoughts, even the revelation of the next plot fact is defamiliarized. Since the wheelchair "had proved to be premature," Frazer, once again confined to bed, resolves that "it is really best to be in bed if you are in a hospital. . . . If you stay long enough in a room the view, whatever it is, acquires a great value and becomes very important and you would not change it, not even by a different angle."[18] These physical circumstances acquire symbolic value because of the writer's careful attention to the periphery and to sequencing, which contrasts Frazer's prolonged thoughts with Sister Cecilia's immediate action.

Section V begins as Sister Cecilia visits Frazer a second time. Frazer is listening to a Notre Dame football game on the radio, but Sister Cecilia is so anxious she can't bear to listen and instead drops by for intermittent reports on the score. Between visits she prays for Notre Dame to win. Recurrence (she even announces, "I'm going right down to the chapel to pray"[19]) underscores the dilemma of perspective: her prayers for Cayetano, equated with the radio by the space break between sections III and IV, are wedged into another distorting equivalence, compounded by the fact that Sister Cecilia readily ascribes sacred connotation to Notre Dame (Our Lady). In her indiscriminate investment she embodies what Frazer believes he desires: for her the view is always the same.

In this, the longest section in the story, Hemingway strings together scenes separated by gaps in times, a strategy directly opposed to his strategy at the story's opening. Only by attending to sequence could a reader hope to decipher a plot as fragmented and elliptical as this one. Section V incorporates four scenes: Sister Cecilia's evening visit; Frazer's report to her the next morning on the victory of Notre Dame; a visit to Frazer from "some Mexicans," three men whom Sister Cecilia has recruited to visit Cayetano because "it's wicked the way no one has come to see him"; and Frazer listening to the radio after these men have left.[20] Strategic use of the space break also involves knowing when not to insert it. By grouping together these varied scenes at about the halfway point in the story, Hemingway pushes his reader to perceive tension in seeming equivalences. In each of these contiguous scenes, the relation between form and content is called into question: Sister Cecilia responds to dilemmas large and small by observing the form of prayer; she insists on satisfying the form of correct community behavior toward Cayetano without regard for the essence, since she has had the police force the three visitors to comply; Frazer satisfies good form by offering excellent liquor to these men when they stop by his room; and finally, after his visitors leave, Frazer again listens to the radio, "turned to be as quiet as possible and still be heard," merely observing the form of listening to news of the world beyond his room.[21]

In these last two scenes, sequence reinforces the notion that Frazer retreats from insight as well as connection to others. Frazer manages to honor form but betrays uncertainty about its efficacy, particularly when, after he declares to his visitors his respect for Sister Cecilia, he informs them that "it is necessary to be very strong against something"—a negative stance that contradicts Sister Cecilia's fervent efforts to be *for* something but holds in common with her the hunger for some unshakeable principle.[22] Frazer is usefully vague (precisely imprecise) with respect to the values that underlie any *form* of investment.

Section VI is a brief paragraph long, and by now the reader has been trained how to read this story. When the three visitors, musicians, make another trip to the hospital, they bring beer "but it was not good beer," a lovely peripheral detail that matters greatly to the attentive reader who understands that violations of form may matter more in a world in which the values it's meant to serve are uncertain. This time, Frazer "did not feel like talking" because "his nerves had become tricky." There's also an allusion to a hidden fact, Frazer's past experience recovering from a wound: "he resented being forced to make the same experiment when he already knew the answer. Mr. Frazer had been through this all before. The only thing which was new to him was the radio. He played it all night long, turned so low he could barely hear it, and he was learning to listen to it without thinking."[23] This is such a fine example of carefully understated recurrence, which locates meaning in the synapses. The phrase constitutes only a small variation on the reference to the radio's volume at the close of the previous section, but changing *context* continues to advance the reader's cumulative reading of its diffused symbolic import. The reader must now redefine Frazer's pain in psychological *and* existential terms and consider further the threat that the intrusion of others poses to detachment, Frazer's chosen stance toward what he must endure. The strategic sequencing of references to the radio at the beginning or end of sections also contributes to the reader's ability to decipher the importance of the radio in relation to the symbolic system of the story as a whole, posed in the equivalent series of terms in its title (standing for hedonism, dogmatism, and stoicism).

Section VII opens as Sister Cecilia talks to Frazer about her ambition to be a saint, unnervingly at odds with detachment, but as he did in the first scene, Frazer observes form by lying, politely affirming her desire just as she observes form by lying to him about how much better he looks. She orchestrates a visit between Frazer and Cayetano, which takes place in section VIII. Stoic Cayetano reveals that he makes a living as a small-time gambler, and because he fleeced the impoverished farm worker who shot him, he regards it as a matter of honor not to name his assailant. Cayetano believes in luck, even though he seems condemned to bad luck. It's no accident that this debased reliance on mere luck follows on the heels of Sister Cecilia's outlandish ambition to be a saint, the one investment too paltry and the other too grandiose for Frazer to embrace as principle. In their dialogue Cayetano and Frazer dance around the problem of adopting a detached attitude toward fate.

As the scene closes, the best either can do is to wish the other luck, but the troubling nature of connection is demonstrated almost immediately when the next and last section opens: the three Mexican musicians have returned to play "cheerful" music for the patients, and Frazer, listening from his room, for the first time imagines the other residents of the ward, cataloguing in detail the injuries other patients have sustained.[24] Sequencing underscores this empathy as consequence of his visit with Cayetano. All by itself, a space break can supply an invisible *because* clause, drawing our attention to chronology as causality.

The musicians again stop by Frazer's room and take up a debate begun in section V, when one of them argued vigorously that religion was the opium of the people. In another first, Frazer attempts a hierarchy of forms, but if dogma (religious or Marxist), hedonism, and even stoicism constitute no more than efforts to escape circumstances that must be endured, can one make distinctions among better and worse forms? He can arrive at only one absolute, the necessity of withstanding misery, which frightens him enough that he retreats (again). He has been "thinking well, a little too well," and as soon as his visitors depart, he will "play the radio so that you could hardly hear it."[25] He still clings fiercely to a view that "remains the same," yet the arc of change for the reader is something fierce, underscored by recurring references to the radio: neither studied detachment nor fellow feeling can diminish the threat that the good form Frazer honors may be nothing more than meaningless static.

Re-sequencing as a revision strategy

In a literary masterpiece sequencing can seem preordained: the writer's choices seem so perfect for his aims that it's difficult to work backward to imagine the strategic decisions made along the way. My graduate students benefit from studying sequence in published stories and novels, but they fully grasp the idea only when we apply the same approach to drafts of their own work and they can see how re-sequencing might solve the problems their peers have identified in the manuscript. Two former students have graciously given me permission to analyze how sequencing improved successive drafts of their work. "Thoughts and Prayers," by Ann Ryles, is a story about a young girl, Jenna, set during the last summer before she leaves for college to study music.[26] Jenna and her boyfriend, Tom, decide to attend the funeral of his cousin, Randy, largely because this trip offers a last chance for them to be alone together. Jenna understands herself as pragmatic, even when it comes to assertiveness about her sexual needs, and she has never seen any reason to tell Tom about her baby sister, Frances, who died in a freak accident when Jenna was only seven. The funeral for Tom's cousin is a shabby affair, and afterwards, Randy's younger brother, Kyle, insists that Tom and Jenna join him and his girlfriend, Angie, for a boat ride— Randy would have wanted them to party in his honor. At the lake, when Angie proposes to Jenna that they swap partners for the afternoon or engage in a threesome, Jenna balks, but after the boat ride (skipped over in the plot) she has sex with Kyle, presumably because she guesses that Tom was tempted by the same proposal.

In the first draft it's unclear what's at stake for Jenna or how events change her. Is the problem merely survivor guilt? Is the central conflict her choice between "good behavior" and "bad" as a response to loss? Or does Jenna have sex with Kyle just to get even with Tom? Is a *guess* enough to trigger this action? And how is her pragmatism about sexuality related to her feelings about her sister's death?

Sequencing matters to a reader's understanding of how a central conflict unfolds, and in the first draft significant background material was included but in an order that didn't help to reinforce escalating pressure. Scenes in the present action were spliced with scenes of Jenna speaking to her therapist about her sister's death and about her relationship with Tom. Immediately following the scene in which Angie propositions Jenna, Ryles placed a therapy session in which Jenna confides to her therapist that she was drawn to Tom because he was an "average" guy. Essentially, the author's hand was showing in this "explanatory" sequence, which sequestered information that ought to have been in play in the previous scene. Furthermore, this therapy session occupied a "hinge location": as the second-to-last scene, it must forcefully suggest the absent logical step (what triggers Jenna's decision to sleep with Kyle), but it wasn't offering the reader enough to go on in conjecturing motive. Fairly late in this first draft, at the lake, Jenna thinks about composing a piece in memory of Frances but finds that the notes running through her head are from the theme song to *Love Story*. This is also a form of sequestering information. The message, delivered at one go, is only too clear: Jenna's desire for some ennobling memorial is blocked.

If the arc of change has to do with Jenna relinquishing her hold on sanitized notions of memorial and grief, then the order of her memories and of key images and actions matters very much as far as enabling the reader to see her give ground in the wake of pressure. In the second draft Ryles chose to restructure the story, cutting the therapy sessions and substituting a few memories integrated with the present action. Before they join Kyle and Tom on the boat, Jenna and Angie rub sun tan lotion on each other, an eroticized prelude for Angie's proposition. This time, in the present action, Angie freely admits that Kyle is far too small town for her but "good at getting me off," and then asks Jenna, "How about Tom?" Jenna answers, "Fine," and adds, in her thoughts, "And normal.... But *normal* would sound worse to Angie than *fine*." Jenna's motives for being with Tom can now be exposed in a flashback triggered by the present action: "Tom had sought her out at a keg party, out of the blue, and come on to her. She'd never expected someone like him, so regular and average, to have any interest in her." There's also beautiful patterning in Jenna's refusal to admit the "whole story" to Angie, just as she has never admitted to Tom that she had a sister, and she keeps other secrets connected to her fear of impermanence, so strategic placement now puts the past dynamically in play.

In the revised draft Jenna think of the song she'd like to compose for Frances, and only of this song, during the funeral service at which no music is played and no one stands up to memorialize Randy. Now the information is in tension with the scene, and we're able to read Jenna as striving for a euphemistic normalcy, destabilized but not yet overturned by events. The writer has also created an opportunity to exploit recurrence. For the crucial hinge location, Ryles incorporated a new present-action scene showing Angie, Kyle, Jenna, and Tom on the boat, "celebrating" Randy—ultimately, a better way to *insist* on the absent logical step. On the boat Tom privately admits to Jenna that Angie also propositioned him—now a fact, not a guess—and then Angie, disappointed that Jenna won't indulge her fantasy, lets slip that Tom told her Jenna was "kinky." This term is linked, via recurrence, to a chain of related words for deviance in the story, and once the problem of not being like others has been defamiliarized as sexual kinkiness, the writer can link this with Jenna's experience of death. Jenna's normal guy thinks she's kinky, and only after this blow does the *Love Story* theme come into Jenna's head, interfering with her thoughts of her song for Frances. To establish a clear arc of change, all Ryles had to do was move information to the right spot and capitalize on recurrence. Now we *see* Jenna begin to lose her sense of herself as safely normal in the wake of pressure that exposes her secret, the profound fear that her sister's death has marked her as a freak. The action provokes a conclusion not on the page, informing Jenna's subsequent decision to have sex with Kyle: it may not be possible to salvage some untroubled stance toward death and loss.

Sequencing operates at the macro-level in terms of the order of scenes (including the placement of flashback) and on a micro-level, where the order of sentences in a given passage can suggest what's been left out. To illustrate how this contributes to dramatic dialogue, let's consider how re-sequencing sentences strengthens the ending of a scene from J. Q. Stuckley's manuscript, a comic novel.[27] The narrator, Jim, works for a Silicon Valley Internet company that is making profits hand-over-fist; like his co-workers, Jim makes extreme concessions to the demands of work in exchange for the glittering (but elusive) promise of stock options.

Early in the novel Jim goes on a blind date with Maria. (He works so many hours a week he doesn't have time to meet women.) Over dinner Maria, the founder of a start-up company, drops hints that she's about to close a fantastic deal, perhaps to persuade him she's a good catch and perhaps to tempt him to engage her company's services. She even takes business calls during the meal. Jim feels put off by her inability to pay attention to him yet suckered by his high-tech culture's infatuation with quick riches. As Jim walks her home, Maria invites him to come up to her apartment so she can show him a marketing brochure for her new company. Is this an excuse for a sexual seduction, or is the business deal the real seduction? What the writer needs to show at the conclusion of this scene is Jim's inability to distinguish the difference and his consequent uneasiness about what he really values. In the first draft, here's how the scene ends:

> I told her that the wine and my bike ride had knocked me out, which was true. And I had to get up early Sunday to work, which was also true.
> **"Could I take a rain check on the brochure?" I said.**
> She said, "As soon as you told me you worked for an Internet company, I knew we'd hit it off."
> Even if I was a troll or had a huge fever blister on the tip of my nose?
> She pecked me on the cheek and we held the embrace for a long moment. I wondered if maybe this had all been a defense mechanism on her part. Maybe she started companies and took them public to avoid getting hurt by guys. Maybe she was really a scared little girl, trying to find genuine connection in this cold world.
> **"I would like to see that brochure some time,"** I said.
> She smiled. "I'll call you."
> I walked off into the night, examining one thought as I climbed the hill toward my apartment building a few blocks away. If I didn't feel connection with Maria—the most alpha of dot-com alpha females—then who was my ideal woman?

The boldfaced sentences in this passage reiterate Jim's key response, equivocation, in essentially the same terms before *and* after Maria's overture, so that we can't read him as reacting to pressure. (Recurrence does not equal redundancy.) Furthermore, this text is too careful to explain itself as it goes, with Jim articulating in thought the uncertainty that should arise from the action itself. Sequence also blunts Maria's enigmatic "I'll call you" by making it an unambiguous trigger for Jim's shift from his perception of her as "scared little girl" to the notion of her as "alpha female," shutting down interpretation rather than fueling it.

The writer has yet to discover that sequencing can coax the reader to supply explanation and can help him to structure a scene that dramatizes the pressure on Jim and culminates in surprise, as in this possible revision of his response to Maria's invitation:

"I have to get up early Sunday to work," I said. Which was true.

She said, "As soon as you told me you worked for an Internet company, I knew we'd hit it off."

Even if I was a troll or had a huge fever blister on the tip of my nose?

She gave me a peck on the cheek.

Maybe she started companies and took them public to avoid getting hurt by guys. If I couldn't find connection with Maria—scared little girl? dot-com alpha female?—then who was my ideal woman?

"I would like to see that brochure some time," I said.

She smiled. "I'll call you."

In their first exchange in this revised passage, Jim's evasion is now implicit, which leaves an opening for Maria to react to subtext. When she overlooks the ambivalence of his comment, she affirms what they do have in common: it's a point of pride to work on Sunday. A stronger causal sequence is also established. If in his thoughts Jim challenges Maria's affirmation, her kiss provokes him to consider an unspoken implication of her statement: like him, she is looking for a partner. Because reordering now juxtaposes "scared little girl" with "dot-com alpha female," Jim's *uncertainty* about Maria's motives provokes him to hedge his bets at the close of this scene. The placement of Maria's response in the prime final slot means that the writer doesn't have to spoil ambiguity by declaring her to be one or the other.

Fundamentally, the related strategies of looking to the periphery, recurrence, and sequencing rest on cultivating receptivity to the open-ended nature of story logic. You *can* learn this particular way of seeing. It's a time-honored tradition for any apprenticeship in art. In the visual arts the term *negative space* refers to the space around an object or between its parts. By paying attention to the contours of this space, an artist can render the shape of an object without having to outline it in sharp relief. Art students are routinely asked to practice this way of looking, and the typical advice lines up with Shklovsky's and Hemingway's mutual emphasis on "the feeling of things": "Instead of painting what is in front of us, we paint what we know and remember about the subject...when painting a mug, we start thinking 'I know what a mug looks like' and don't observe the precise angles of this particular mug. By changing your focus away from the mug and to the negative spaces—such as the space between the handle and the mug...you have to concentrate on what's in front of you and can't work on 'autopilot.' "[28]

Only the precise shading of negative space will suggest what you haven't made explicit. Sequencing can feel transparently obvious if you are not careful to look to the periphery—to emphasize the detail or action that won't be recognized by the reader as decisive until cumulative clues bring its importance into view. Technically, it can be very difficult to discern the right degree of insistence on an absent logical step. If a writer compiles important information in a single location instead of diffusing meaning through sequencing and recurrence, the result is tantamount to finger pointing. You've got to put a little more faith in your reader. Skilled writers also devote time in revision to strengthening the torque at the space break, contemplating the best candidate for the marquee slot just before or after that break. And they consider how any recurring elements might be strategically placed in relation to plot action so that meaning will be sparked in the synapses.

Revision is not engine repair; it's not possible to lift out the carburetor, repair it, and simply return it in order to make the whole engine run properly. A work of fiction functions more like an ecosystem, in which the interaction between living organisms means that the effects of a small specific change might be amplified throughout the whole network. Sometimes you can fix a flawed ending by making changes to a much earlier page; sometimes a passage that doesn't work simply needs to be relocated to an appropriate niche; always you should anticipate that a change to one passage might reveal unanticipated possibilities or problems elsewhere in the manuscript. In composing and revising, you must question the draft, fully aware that the meaning embedded in the material may or may not reveal itself but trusting in the natural gift that makes every dreamer a genius at symbolic structure. And you must learn to ask *different* questions: What accidents of proximity reveal provocative associations? What *don't* I know yet? What if this came first, and that came second? What's that *thing* floating on the periphery of my vision? Where have I seen it before? Why has it come back now? When all else fails, you can move things around without knowing why the draft doesn't work, reshuffling sentences, taking this one out and putting that one back in just to see what might emerge from random changes. In the kinesthetic play of ordering and reordering events and scenes and sentences, the trick lies in keeping a loose hold on intention while staying alert for any opportunities that arise. By lucky accident and persistence, playfulness can arrive at the right arrangement to make silence speak.

5

Captured in Motion: Dynamic Characterization

With the air of an Old World pater familias, my husband's father fully inhabited his own authority until his death at age ninety-two. When other people were perplexingly irrational, Ernest wasn't alarmed but wryly, scathingly amused. If he raised an eyebrow, you would of course correct the error of your ways. He was a creature of habit because habit was orderly, and keeping a steady course had enabled him to rebuild his life in the United States after he and his wife, Ilse, fled Nazi Germany in 1938. He smoked exactly five cigarettes a day and had just one scotch before dinner, and dinner always began with a soup course because he liked soup and Ilse doted on him. When we were newlyweds, my husband and I took a trip with Ernest and Ilse. Since Ernest never hurried for any reason, we didn't head to the airport until very late, and by the time we got there, we had only about twenty minutes before our flight was scheduled to depart. If we ran to the gate, we might make it, but Ernest stopped to survey the long line at the ticket counter and said, casually, "I have to buy the tickets."

I'm telling you this story so that we can start simple as we consider what may be the most challenging aspect of fiction writing. Characterization depends not just on craft but on complexities of human psychology that a reader may understand differently than the writer, yet its fundamental components can be stated in simple terms. The first principle of characterization is singularity—the details that enable a reader to feel she knows an individual, which novelist Marilynne Robinson calls "the best privilege fiction can afford, the illusion of ghostly proximity to other human souls."[1] Mutual pleasure is at issue here too: I want you to enjoy Ernest as much as I did. And it's worth noting that we'll relish the idiosyncrasies of villains as readily as we delight in the traits of heroes.The second key principle is potent contradiction, because when a reader has to try to reconcile inconsistencies that *matter*, character is revealed, not just described. Fiction halts at the doorway to explanation, deliberately granting only a partial glimpse. If I've arranged the particulars of this family anecdote just right, the partial glimpse should evoke a richer experience because of what it doesn't resolve: How could someone so rational not grasp that he'd run out of time? Given his life experience, how could Ernest blithely trust that luck would go his way? Why *wouldn't* a man whose wife ironed his boxer shorts every week expect that the plane would wait for him? (And yes, we did make that plane.)

Fictional characters are convincing not because they are "lifelike" but because the reader's engagement with them is. Compelling characters both confirm our understanding of experience, invoked as we measure their motives and behavior against our own, and refine it by confronting us with what we can't or don't dare articulate, by claiming our sympathy despite our reluctance, by posing possibilities we didn't imagine but will believe. Characters are "real" when they can involve readers in this mimetic play. Whether a writer's frame of reference is realistic or surreal matters less than the power to persuade readers of a privileged glimpse into the inner life of character that tantalizes us with what remains uncertain and cloaked. We know the character, and yet we don't—not completely.

Literary scholar Robert Alter calls this "the purposefully troubling representation of character."[2] Looked at from the writer's perspective, the project is more speculative: we attempt to confront what most puzzles us in human nature rather than conceive of story as a proof for our convictions. Echoing Chekhov's insistence that the writer formulate a question, Grace Paley cheerily proposes this as first principle: "If, before you sit down with paper and pencil...it all comes suddenly clear and you find yourself mumbling, Of course, he's a sadist and she's a masochist, and you think you have the answer—*drop the subject*."[3] A writer works best from his "ununderstanding" of human relationships: "he simply never gets over it...like an idealist who marries the same woman over and over again."[4] Your aim is not to get an absolutely certain take on your character's motives but to be transfixed by complexities that exhaust the explanations at hand in your cultural moment, whether they are psychological or sociological or religious. Critics have spent centuries analyzing Hamlet because he richly rewards psychoanalytic, Marxist, and structuralist interpretations (and could probably accommodate any new -isms handily) but also possesses some residual mystery that compels another attempt and another. His motives will always be ambiguous, his character never entirely "of a piece."

When you struggle to create completely consistent characters, you risk being enslaved by a deterministic, reductionist psychology, and you're likely to produce flat characters who neither convince nor trouble a reader. Because it's so hard to tell the difference between raising too many questions and raising the right questions about character, the workshop can foster a consensual notion of plausibility that demands an answer for every question. As a consequence, you may settle for a character who "makes sense"—accommodates the prejudices of your peer group—rather than risk creating a character whose nature simply seems inconsistent and muddied. Sometimes only a fine line separates a workshop debate mired in confusion about a character's nature and motives and one in which even opposing arguments are grounded in the same precise evidence and a shared recognition of the stakes, with the latter being proof of success, not grounds for revision.

The technical challenges of writing a compelling character are rooted in the dilemma of knowing *how* not to know. What makes a character elusive rather than vague, intimately understood but not entirely predictable? Whether the writer gives us in detail the character's thoughts and style of dress, as George Eliot does, or asks us to know a character through his manner of speech rather than his appearance, as Grace Paley does, characters compel because their nature is made up of qualities that strike us as coherent but possess the charged instability of the atoms that make up matter. The traits of dynamic characters are unstable in relation to each other, "reliable" only so long as competing forces (internal as well as external) remain in balance. The tension of instability engenders plot: we may anticipate a character's choices and actions but cannot predict them.

A literal plot engineers a submerged story (hidden tension) because of how it arranges what's visible. The same principle holds true for characterization: readers are able to conjecture the hidden motives (and potential) of character from what's visible— what's literally clear. The relationship between character and plot is something like a Mobius strip that reverses on itself endlessly: you need a plot to reveal character, and you need a character capable of setting a plot in motion. What strategies shape a dynamic character? You root the character's central desire in a core instability, a potent contradiction that is key to the capacity for change and for surprise. You reveal character through the right action, the visible granting a partial glimpse of the hidden. You exploit the power of one character to expose what lies beneath the surface of another, with dialogue as a prime vehicle for achieving this.

These strategies rest on a writer's allegiance to the particular. The pleasure a reader takes in vivid characterization is grounded in language itself. In *Madame Bovary,* after Emma and her husband, Charles, return from a ball at a château, she chafes at her dull life, firing the maid and training a raw new replacement to put on airs. And then Flaubert gives us an image that confirms Emma's dissatisfaction while enabling us to see it new: "She devoutly put away in her drawers her beautiful dress, down to the satin shoes whose soles were yellowed with the slippery wax of the dancing floor. Her heart was like these. In its friction against wealth something had come over it that could not be effaced."[5] This image compels as much by its beauty as by its accuracy. Yet those yellowed soles would not lodge like a fish hook in the reader's heart except for keen sensory precision, which transforms Emma's petulance, witnessed in all its dreary pettiness, by engendering a sympathy that counters moral disapproval. Sensual particularity not only fosters identification but also grants readers a degree of literal certainty that is essential if they are to engage in reconciling contradictions of character.

The core instability of a dynamic character

Apprentice writers are typically advised to create a central character whose desire is strong enough to drive a plot. Taken at face value, this good advice yields a static character. As a work of fiction progresses, the issue is not whether desire remains the same or changes. It's that desire is revealed as dimensional, not unitary but a dynamic compound of wishes and motives. "I want to break up with my boyfriend" might carry within it fear of intimacy, thwarted desire for a father's love (past history), boredom, hankering for risk, and some inchoate dissatisfaction with a settled but secure relationship. A central character convinces and surprises us because her desire entangles motives that sometimes converge and sometimes conflict, a core instability. Consistently inconsistent character emerges from this interplay rather than from cleanly isolated traits. Story logic resides in the synapses.

While inner conflict conceivably might cleave along clear lines, as in "I want to drink a glass of red wine, but it gives me a headache," a simple polarity doesn't present a rich enough dilemma for fiction, which is always aimed at the ambiguity of choice and its hidden costs. In the drafts of stories that I see in workshop, one of the common problems is that the writer fails to pursue motive in dynamic terms, as something unstable and not fully dimensionalized until the climactic action. If at the outset we understand that a mother allows her teenage son to get away with murder because she feels guilty for divorcing the father he loves, the plot can only reiterate the point. But let's say she also resents her husband because he tolerated *her* bad behavior when the marriage was breaking up. Here's a core instability that will be susceptible to pressure, an inconsistency that promises complex motives that aren't yet visible to us. Rather than reduce motive to a single explanation, the real problem you face is to compound motive rather than declare it—to know how not to know.

Ambiguity is launched from literal clarity, and so nailing the consistent traits of characters can help us to generate open questions about their nature. At the beginning of James Joyce's story "The Dead," the main character, Gabriel, arrives at a party given by his ancient aunts; snow is falling in Dublin, and he enters the house wearing galoshes. In front of their hosts his wife needles him because he insists that she too wear "goloshes" for fear she'll catch "a dreadful cold"; his provincial aunts have to ask what these new-fangled galoshes are. Gabriel's insistence clearly conveys cautiousness, but this is bound up with his striving for refinement, ambiguously tinted, since, as his wife notes, "Gabriel says everyone wears them on the continent."[6] When he chafes at Gretta's teasing, Gabriel betrays insecurity he does not consciously own. His entwined traits of caution and pretension make for an unstable mix because they might reinforce *or* run counter to each other. If the galoshes merely stood for a fixed trait of cautiousness, the characterization would feel thin, but Joyce focuses our attention on dynamics. The writer's job is not to show that a character is cautious but *how* he is cautious.

One could say that in "The Dead" Gabriel has a simple central desire: for others to think well of him. But from the start this desire is entangled with fear of ridicule (caution) as well as condescension, a core instability. As the story progresses, Gabriel meets with many kinds of opposition: the maid takes offense at a patronizing remark; his wife teases him; his aunts' reverence toward him is undercut by their provincialism; another character turns his scorn for Irish nationalism against him; when he toasts his aunts' hospitality, he offers polite encomiums that belie his snobbery. The scales wobble because pressure complicates our reading of his motives: if Gabriel harbors pretension, we come to recognize refinement as well as defensiveness in his responses to his claustrophobic social world. If he betrays timidity in how he conceives of his superiority, this becomes tinged with concern for others and sensitivity to their perception of him. So should we wish for his escape or his comeuppance?

Just before they leave the party, Gabriel sees his wife standing at the top of the stairs listening to a song, and he is aroused, eager to be alone with her. The galoshes return to the story in the form of two subtle echoes. As they walk to their hotel, Gretta has "her shoes in a brown parcel tucked under one arm," an indirect allusion to the galoshes on her feet.[7] When they are finally alone in their hotel room, she shocks Gabriel by tearfully revealing that the song reminded her of Michael Fury, a boy who courted her long ago. Waiting outside her grandmother's house on the last night of Gretta's visit, this frail boy withstood cold rain for a chance to see her and died a week later. "I think he died for me," Greta says simply; she had run out to him that night, afraid he would "get his death in the rain," a delicate echo of Gabriel's concern for her.[8] Recurrence helps us to measure Gabriel's fall.

Joyce purposefully troubles his reader's inclination to judge: the sight of Gretta on the stairs, when the reader might identify most strongly with Gabriel's romantic vision of himself, triggers his fall in an unexpected direction. At first solicitous when Gretta cries, Gabriel betrays himself by retreating to condescension. If Joyce had not earlier nailed down this fixed quality, the reader wouldn't realize fully the stakes in these changed circumstances, which depend on what remains an open question—whether condescension is a necessary, if crippling, defense of a sensitive soul. This question allows for many cross-sections of the moment: Gabriel's habitual weapon is ineffectual against his wife's stark assertions, which are *more* impervious for being naïve. She counts on his sympathy (remember the shoes tucked under her arm), while she has in secret preferred the mere memory of this boy to her husband's refinement. The crudeness of his social world, against which Gabriel has struggled, may also be a property of passion, incompatible with gentility. Dynamic characterization makes possible multiple readings of character, none of which contradicts the others. (In contrast, contradiction between possible readings usually signals muddied characterization, not mystery.)

At this moment Gabriel faces a choice that has a high price tag: humiliated, he can continue defending his ego or sacrifice it to the refinement of insight, forfeit one kind of superiority for another. Now he sees his public self as "ludicrous."[9] He and the reader have moved on from the dilemma of social embarrassment to the dilemma of bitter self-knowledge, not because his desire has been altered but because it has been more fully revealed. Frustrated in his wish for esteem, Gabriel makes one more shift: he surprises us by summoning genuinely finer feeling, pity for the thwarted passion of his wife and her lover. But is this still condescension? Because this is a great story and not merely a good one, pressure breaks through the crust of character in ways that not only satisfy us with psychological acuity but also make the character's dilemma our own.

Character revealed through action

Only Gretta's intimate confession of her passion for another man could have pierced the armor of Gabriel's social persona. Like Joyce, in composing fiction you have to ask what external force will be strong enough to destabilize internal contradictions in ways that compel a decisive response. Readers will never feel they know a character if they're limited to learning only what she'll admit, which is why fiction constructed so that a main character is largely alone, lost in thought, usually fails. In the absence of literal pressure readers cannot measure what a character is willing to reveal against what she betrays inadvertently, cannot get a partial glimpse of some hidden potential. When it concentrates the core instability of character, the right action cloaks even as it reveals. Consider the difference between a woman who cries because her lover jilted her and a woman who cuts his letters into tiny pieces before returning them in the mail. The latter response is both more particular than the first and more enigmatic, since the seeming absolute severance cloaks a furious need to communicate. If Joyce had ended "The Dead" with Gabriel feeling merely embarrassed (desire thwarted) or determined to defend his superiority (desire on steady course), the character would strike us as entirely exposed, and his desire would be flattened to mere conceit. Instead, he is moved to tears, and the reader is forced to further conjecture by a fellow feeling that both evinces sympathy and contrasts sharply with unequivocal passion. What we already know of the character is reconfigured to lead to a new unknown.

At pains to be believed, you may settle for a character whose responses to his circumstances are utterly reasonable and appropriate, but such a character will behave predictably, and thus you will have nothing surprising to reveal about human nature. To create a character whose actions remain well within the scope of "realistic" expectations misses the point, since it can't yield discovery, a distinction Milan Kundera emphasizes in *The Art of the Novel*: "A novel examines not reality but existence. And existence is not what has occurred; existence is the realm of human possibilities, everything that man can become, everything he's capable of."[10] Flannery O'Connor poses the problem more concretely: "I lent some stories to a country lady who lives down the road from me, and when she returned them, she said, 'Well, them stories just gone and shown you how some folks *would* do,' and I thought to myself that that was right; when you write stories, you have to be content to start exactly there—showing how some specific folks *will* do, *will* do in spite of everything."[11] A compelling character dwells in a liminal terrain just at the outer reaches of plausibility, and it's better to risk a reader's resistance than to constrain character to a more temperate zone of possibility.

Action that concentrates a core instability helps a writer to tackle the inherently risky proposition of *making* us believe what some folks *will* do, so it's instructive to look at two writers who might inspire you to push your characters to extremes. In Haruki Murakami's surreal story "Sleep," the narrator, a dentist's wife, suddenly finds that she no longer needs to sleep. By day she adheres to routine, and by night she takes advantage of her freedom to read and eat chocolate. Like many Murakami characters, she strives to rationalize what is happening as if it were only a slight variation on the normal. The potential privilege results only in minor, secretive changes in her behavior; reading comes across as a placid version of voyeurism. This "under-reaction" also exists at an extreme reach of plausibility, so the writer is helping us to see the arc of the pendulum's swing.

The narrator's core instability—desire for some reprieve from monotony and an inability to shed habit—can be concentrated in a single culminating action only because of the increasing tension between her presumed freedom and the few uses she can make of it. Soon she begins to drive around at night to while away these extra hours, a dreary match for her daytime routine, until one night she parks her car in a remote area where violent assaults have been reported. She still understands change as arbitrarily imposed: "All the memories I have from the time before I stopped sleeping seem to be moving away with accelerating speed. It feels so strange, as if the me who used to go to sleep every night is not the real me.... This is how people change."[12] And then two assailants approach the car, trying to break in and rocking it from side to side; if insomnia has not freed her from living as if she's never really awake, she has finally sought something perilous enough to pierce the dullness. The story ends as she sits "locked inside this little box," waiting for the men to tip over the car.[13] In this purposefully shocking right action, rebellion is still tinged by passivity, even at the cost of her life.

A novel often requires more elaborate preparation if a writer is to redraw the boundary lines of plausibility. Theresa, the sixteen-year-old narrator of Alice McDermott's *Child of My Heart,* spends her summers babysitting and caring for the neighbors' dogs, and she feels superior to the adults in her world, who neglect their children or purvey blithe platitudes. One of her charges for the summer is her adored eight-year-old cousin, Daisy, and when Theresa begins to suspect Daisy might be seriously ill, she hides this so that Daisy won't be sent home to her parents, who practice benign neglect. This action smacks of childlike wishful thinking but is *also* shaped by a shrewd lack of faith in adults, a core instability that drives the novel. Desperate for some magic to dispel this curse, Theresa begins paying serious attention to the artist whose toddler she cares for, a dissolute old man whom she has previously regarded as merely peripheral. In the culminating action of the novel, she succeeds in seducing him. Her action closely holds a mystery *and* reveals its essence: she chooses the one adult who is unfailingly, if brutally, honest with her and is also waging his own war against mortality.

This action is so surprisingly out of bounds for the character that it takes McDermott the length of a novel to foreshadow it and to *deflect* a reader's realistic revulsion at the idea of sex between an old man and an underage girl. If we are to register this as an effort to trade youth and beauty for the artist's power to remake the world—to ameliorate harsh reality—McDermott must carefully set up this action by focusing attention on the problem she wants to foreground. A key scene precedes the sexual encounter between Theresa and the old man, and it occurs not long after his wife has abandoned him and their child, Flora. Theresa entertains Flora and Daisy by decorating a tree with lollipops, tying each one to the branches with kite string; she describes this as "working" (with the word in quotes), an ironic echo for the artist's efforts. When he comes out of his studio to watch them, Theresa is reminded of the "disappointed slouch to his stance as he looked at his handiwork, the canvases filled with black and gray and white paint, slashed and smeared."[14] While Theresa and the children work on the tree, he goes back to his canvas: now she and he compete in their efforts to transform. His acknowledgment of her aims is confirmed when he joins Theresa and the two girls on the grass, and they share aloud what they see when they look up at the clouds—a boat, a city skyline, a castle. During this game, the old man surreptitiously touches Theresa. If the consummately right action in this scene isn't purely innocent, because of it the act of seduction isn't purely predatory either.

The implicit equality that is established between the artist and Teresa will also flow over onto the seduction. Just as his honesty contrasts with the euphemisms of other adults, now his willingness to engage in imaginative play makes him the only adult who treats this as serious endeavor, valid even if it cannot stifle Flora's cries for her mother or heal Daisy. In risking futility Theresa and the artist are also matched; as he rises from the grass, she notes *this* effort: "blades of grass falling from his fingers, as if he had been torn away from the lawn where we'd been lying, had tried to hold on, as if he had struggled not to raise himself but to stay."[15] Not only has her magical thinking been granted credence by his attention, his failing vitality grants power to this teenage girl, thus combating the reader's reservations about their sexual encounter.

Character revealed through dialogue

Fearing the supporting players will wrest the story from their protagonist, writers sometimes create a cast of flat characters—in E. M. Forster's terms, types organized around "a single idea or quality" to flank a round central character, "capable of surprising in a convincing way."[16] While vividly rendered flat characters can be useful to a plot, a central character can only be persuasively revealed by another character who also possesses a capacity for surprise, a hidden inner life. We cannot take seriously the conflict of a son who can't make up his mind to rebel against a mother typed as a selfish tyrant, because she's incapable of triggering any real conflict in her child.

Dialogue offers the most direct means for exploiting one character to reveal the hidden inner life of another, to force inconsistency to surface in ways that have consequence. It must be structured as plot is structured, building tension around a central issue to arrive at a decisive shift. It must reveal character in ways that complicate the reader's understanding. And it must achieve figurative meaning, offering further clues to the story's subtext *as well as* generating the special kind of subtext that characterizes virtually all human conversation, in which intonation, word choice, and gesture inflect the task of communicating information. In order to generate a high ratio of subtext to text, dialogue must distill the meandering nature of real speech to a form that concentrates tension. Edith Wharton cautioned against "interlarding" dialogue "with irrelevant small talk, in the hope of thus producing a greater air of reality. But this is to fall again into the trap of what Balzac called 'a reality in nature which is not one in art.' "[17] It is disingenuous to defend as real or life-like flat dialogue in which characters say exactly what they mean and articulate their wants exactly as the writer wishes us to understand them. No matter how directly characters address their desires, the writer must plumb the material for subtext. Good dialogue engages the

reader in the kind of conjecturing about motive and implication and meaning that actually *does* occupy us in real life, at
least when we're listening carefully. Like all dramatic action, dialogue builds tension and reveals character by delivering partial,
piecemeal clues that are richly ambiguous, raising increasingly
refined questions about motive rather than answering them
at one go.

In composing dialogue you must first persuade your reader
that she is listening to a consistent individual. Sentence structure, vocabulary, and even punctuation can convey habits of
mind, and recurring constructions establish "signature lines" for
each character. (Consider the character qualities betrayed by con-
tinual reliance on sentence fragments.) Gestures and responses
to physical setting also reveal consistent qualities of character.
Yet these same strategies can alert us to dynamic inconsistencies. Discrepancies between what a character says and what she
does, between her thoughts and her actions or speech, or between
any of these and authorial telling can enable your reader to see
into internal contradictions, provided that you have the patience
to allow many kinds of clues to accumulate as the dialogue
progresses. A character who makes threats at one moment and
offers helpful advice at the next is merely indecipherable, because
inconsistencies of character that bob to the surface like flotsam,
apropos of nothing, will be dismissed as author error. What *will*
convince the reader is a host of strategies working in concert to
establish that a consistent pattern of behavior gives way *under
pressure*. When cumulative discrepancies are well handled, the
reader "composes" a coherent understanding of motive.

Unacknowledged or unstated motives can be betrayed in dialogue by many specific strategies, though just a few will be
enumerated here. Dialogue often represents a character's "story of
himself" (the beliefs he swallows whole), which is why cliché in
dialogue often strikes us as vibrant when elsewhere in a narrative
it can be deadening. To generate dramatic interest, you must supply clues to the value the speaker places on the story of himself.
Does the character sustain his course despite challenges, or does
he revise his story under pressure from his conversational part-
ner(s)? The "dead on" response, in which one speaker responds
accurately to the subtext of another's remark, alerts readers to
dissonance, often helpfully confirming, countering, or qualifying
speculative suspicions about the first speaker. If the first speaker

responds to dead-on accuracy with a "non sequitur," he's dodging the issue, while contesting a "dead-on" response betrays emotion he can't successfully repress. The strategic repetition of key words in dialogue, a different beast than the repetitiveness of real conversation, offers another clue to what lies beneath the surface of a character. In changing contexts, the connotation of a word or phrase can be altered so that by the end of the dialogue, it stands for something radically different than it did at the beginning. For example, in Hemingway's "Hills like White Elephants," the female character, pressured by her boyfriend to go ahead with an abortion, reiterates that things are "fine" until the word connotes her despair and lack of faith in him.[18] In varied configurations these strategies help readers to recognize when tension peaks and when it subsides.

Because Raymond Carver constructs brilliant dialogue, his short story "Careful" highlights how to exploit these site-specific strategies in the service of dynamic characterization. In the wake of his separation from his wife, Inez, Lloyd has moved to a miserable attic apartment, and the story opens as Inez arrives in the late morning. Lloyd is "trying to do something about his drinking," though he's still in his pajamas and must hide a liquor bottle in the bathroom before he answers the door. Inez has never visited Lloyd here, so he "somehow knew the visit was an important one," and we can guess that she has come to discuss their impending divorce.[19] But Lloyd's ear is clogged with ear wax, and he uses this problem to derail her agenda. He tells her that he's "in one hell of a shape," a plea for concern to which she simply answers, "It's eleven o'clock." So much more than a statement of fact, her non sequitur reference to the time simultaneously deflects his plea and hints at her exhausted patience. Lloyd immediately confirms her unspoken criticism by a defensive dead-on response: "I know what time it is."[20]

Lloyd continues, delivering his story of himself in a paragraph that illuminates how inconsistency can be dramatized internally in a character's speech as well as through an exchange:

> "But just now I'm about to go crazy with something. My ear's plugged up. You remember that other time it happened? We were living in that place near the Chinese takeout joint. Where the kids found that bulldog dragging its chain? I had to go to the doctor then and have my ears flushed out. I know you remember. You drove me and we had

to wait a long time. Well, it's like that now. I mean it's that bad. Only I can't go to a doctor this morning. I don't have a doctor for one thing. I'm about to go nuts, Inez. I feel like I want to cut my head off or something."[21]

Lloyd exaggerates his discomfort in terms vague enough to suggest a more potent cause—"go crazy with something." Exaggeration will become a signature of his speech, yet from the start this excuse absolves him of responsibility for his impaired state. Sentence structure provides clues to Lloyd's habitual mindset and even betrays inner conflict via the contrast between his melodramatic insistence and his questions and interjections. As Lloyd poses a problem that will keep Inez with him, at least temporarily, Carver gets out plot information in the wake of the character's strong desire. (Yes, folks, that's how it's done.) Lloyd not only gives the writer a chance to provide backstory but also makes a claim that translates roughly as "You took care of me once, and now you should do the same." He belies his earlier assertion of competence when he admits he doesn't even have a doctor; the need to persuade Inez she's his only viable option gets the better of him. This nice example of consistent inconsistency also illustrates cumulative corroboration, since it banks on earlier clues to Lloyd's disarray (the pajamas and the liquor bottle). With intense compression Carver also intimates the story's larger symbolic concerns and raises questions not yet answered: Does the clogged ear offer Lloyd an excuse to manipulate Inez or is he truly in desperate shape? How sympathetic can we—or Inez—afford to be toward a cunning drunk?

As a minimalist Carver uses physical details sparingly but gets the maximum effect from them. After Lloyd declares his problem, he sits down on the sofa and Inez sits down "at the other end." But "they were so close he could have put out his hand and touched her knee."[22] Even the conditional verb tense underscores Lloyd's longing *and* his long-standing failure to connect to his wife; the single unrealized gesture entwines key character traits that are in tension with each other. Next, by responding to the surface of his statements and not the subtext, Inez attempts to contain the conversation to the merely pragmatic: "What have you tried?" Lloyd deflects her unspoken intention with a non sequitur—"What'd you say?"—and in a rare metaphorical flight complains that he feels as if he's talking inside a barrel, and when she speaks, "it sounds like you're talking through a lead pipe."[23] These arresting images stand for a *shared* inability to listen and confirm the reader's instinct to read the dilemma figuratively. Inez persists in trying for containment, asking if Lloyd has Q-tips or Wesson oil to treat his ear, yet by pursuing the problem at all she is yielding ground.

Already Lloyd and Inez have activated core inconsistencies in each other that will drive the dramatic action, and the realized quality of each character informs that of the other, as in their next exchange:

> "Honey, this is serious," he said. "I don't have any Q-tips or Wesson oil. Are you kidding?"
>
> "If we had some Wesson oil, I could heat it and put some of that in your ear. My mother used to do that," she said. "It might soften things up in there."[24]

Lloyd has just won round 1. If Inez means to keep her distance, she betrays her vulnerability to Lloyd's tactics; the reference to her mother only enhances the reader's sense that unconscious emotions are now in play, and her hope that her tactic "might soften things up in there" renders her still-alive desire to reach Lloyd. Carver has plotted the story carefully so that we can read the dialogue in sections, as stages in the story's rising action, and a long narrative paragraph separates Lloyd's initial victory from the next skirmish. Once Inez finishes a cigarette and puts it out, she launches the next round: "Lloyd, we have things to talk about."[25] (Both characters tend to call each other by name—a device that beginners are normally warned to avoid—at those moments when they least expect to be heard.) If Inez reverts to her intended course here, the pressure of Lloyd's insistence has literal consequence. She will have to deal with Lloyd's ear before she can get him to listen, so she orders him to take a seat in the kitchen.

Dialogue gains dramatic potency from a literal task in which the characters must collaborate. Inez tells Lloyd she'll find a hairpin and some tissue paper to try to clean his ear, and Lloyd responds with alarm. Now the re-engagement he's solicited becomes problematic, an invasion. When he bleats a protest, their dialogue quickly delivers them back to Inez's intended announcement, employing strategies that clue us to subtext:

"What?" she said. "Christ, I can't hear you, either. Maybe this is catching." **[non sequitur response to Lloyd's alarm]**

"When I was a kid in school," Lloyd said, "we had this health teacher. She was like a nurse, too.... She said we should never put anything smaller than an elbow into our ear." **[determined sustained course]** He vaguely remembered a wall chart showing a massive diagram of the ear, along with an intricate system of canals, passageways, and walls.

"Well, your nurse was never faced with this exact problem," Inez said. "Anyway, we need to try *something*. We'll try this first. If it doesn't work, we'll try something else. That's life, isn't it?" **[sustained course, but conflicted; the reiteration of *something* betrays Lloyd's effect on her and also cues us that the writer is substituting the figurative for the literal]**

"Does that have a hidden meaning or something?" Lloyd said. **[dead-on response to her subtext]**[26]

Open diction lets figurative possibility in by the back door, supplying an increasingly ominous connotation for *something,* one that differs for each of them: Inez needs to escape Lloyd about as desperately as he needs to cling to her, yet neither wholeheartedly embraces his or her own desire. She still wants to fix him. He still feels crowded by intimacy, especially because it exposes him to judgment. In the next lines Inez trips over her own feet, simultaneously yoking Lloyd back to the literal and metaphorically telegraphing her intention to cut him loose: "It means just what I said. But you're free to think as you please. I mean, it's a free country." Round 2 goes to Inez, with this remark functioning as a climax for a passage that ends as Inez searches in her purse for a hairpin. She swears when she fails to find one, but Lloyd hears her words as if they're coming from "another room" and thinks: "They used to feel they had ESP when it came to what the other one was thinking. They could finish sentences the other had started."[27]

In this exchange plot has made its next advance both figuratively and literally: the characters encounter the next literal obstacle, and Inez's veiled declaration that she's done with him triggers Lloyd's keen awareness of their former closeness, impossibly idealized as a listening that didn't even require speech. Because of the discrepancy between this thought and Lloyd's visceral reaction to Inez working on his ear, we know, even if he doesn't, that this was never true. Had Lloyd been plausibly

reasonable about the minor irritation of his ear and Inez incapable of the outlandish proposal to go to work with a hairpin, the
story couldn't take off dramatically or begin to suggest figurative
concerns in which the reader too has a stake. Carver is accurate
about the dynamics of co-dependence, but the characterization
of both Inez and Lloyd far exceeds that of manipulative drunk
and accommodating enabler. Together they offer us an extreme
instance of the perilous complications of intimacy. In just three
pages of dialogue.

In each of the examples of characterization discussed here,
generating a consistently inconsistent character depends on
the writer's ability to pose increasingly refined questions about
motive. Contradictions cancel out previous impressions unless
the reader perceives some meaningful interplay, and when she
can't, she'll withdraw any investment in so approximate a cre-
ation. How does Carver help the reader to reconcile Lloyd's
manipulation with his genuine longing and fear? In the first
place, these character traits are often entwined; actions that
might otherwise forfeit our sympathies are paired with Lloyd's
hopefulness about managing his drinking. Second, the dialogue
is structured for revelation; the writer sneaks a hand on the scale
so that initially he emphasizes Lloyd's manipulation and emphasizes it as comic, which leaves room for a shift in our sympathy
and for revelation of an inner life that is anything but funny. (If
you want the reader to discover the hidden potential of character, as you did in the first draft, you may have to contrive when
you revise.) Third, the writer exploits the response of the other
character to modulate the reader's reaction. After Inez unsuccess-
fully searches in the bathroom for another implement to use on
Lloyd's ear, the reader registers that she has discovered the bottle
he hid there, but Lloyd is innocent of this. Whenever a writer
situates a reader so that she knows more than the character, this
can be misplayed as an invitation for the reader to condescend,
disrupting sympathy. Instead Carver exploits this to heighten
pathos as Lloyd resumes his efforts to engage his wife. When
Lloyd asks to use the bathroom before they work on his ear,
Inez doesn't accuse but only tells him, "Go ahead." *Her* insight
is ahead of the reader's and more sympathetic—she assumes he'll
sneak a drink and mercifully lets him do it.

Finally, the writer exploits the pressure of circumstances to
continue revealing new aspects of character that demand we

revise or qualify our feelings, not the facts of his nature. As Lloyd gulps from the bottle he stashed, he thinks about getting sober: "In the beginning, he'd really thought he could continue drinking if he limited himself to champagne. But in no time he found he was drinking three or four bottles a day. He knew he'd have to deal with this pretty soon. But first, he'd have to get his hearing back." Brought this close to the helplessness of addiction, forced to attend to the minute adjustments by which Lloyd cons himself into believing he'll get on top of this, the reader can't refuse her sympathy when he tries to con his wife. Only after he returns to the kitchen, where Inez is heating baby oil she borrowed from the landlady, does she reveal, "I found your stash in the bathroom."[28] Yet she is gentle as she pours warm oil into his ear in an effort to unclog it: "Don't be scared," she says.[29] The mystery of her character blooms at this moment. By her actions she confirms something real in Lloyd's nostalgia, the fact of her once deep attachment to him, and the contrast with her flat statement about his stash conveys what accusation could not: she's resigned herself.

Recrimination would have been the choice of a writer addicted to plausibility and to crude notions of drama; the unexpectedness of Inez's compassion rings true, in no small part because it serves to escalate Lloyd's fears rather than deflate them. He too recognizes something before the reader does: compassion has replaced her earlier irritation, signaling that she has achieved a more genuine emotional separation from him. She has really heard him, with this unanticipated consequence. As she ministers to his ear, Lloyd says, "If this doesn't work, I'll find a gun and shoot myself," and so many fears have coalesced around the desire to alleviate a trivial discomfort that this no longer seems like exaggeration.[30] Only now does the writer expose what has been strategically withheld. For the first time Lloyd can think past the immediate predicament, revealing the horror that his focus on his ear has masked—it hasn't been *just* a manipulative ploy. Worrying that his ear will get clogged again when he lies down to sleep beneath the sloping attic roof, "he began to feel afraid of the night that was coming. He began to fear the moment he would begin to make his preparations for bed and what might happen afterward. That time was hours away, but already he was afraid. What if, in the middle of the night, he accidentally turned onto his right side, and the weight of his head pressing into the pillow were to seal the wax again into the dark canals of his ear? What if he woke up then, unable to hear, the ceiling inches from his head?"[31] This passage seeds in the *reader's* subconscious the image of a coffin, again closing the gap between us and Lloyd, pulling us as close as possible to the profound emotional terror that fuels his drinking.

At the very end of this story, after the crisis has been resolved, after Inez has left, giving her phone number to the landlady in case "something happens," Carver treats us to one last delicious detail. Since Inez used the only available glass for the warm oil, Lloyd hastily rinses it so he can pour himself another drink. Of course, the drink doesn't taste right, and Lloyd dissects the flavor while he studies the film of oil on the champagne. It's hard to imagine a detail that could better compress a drunk's combination of frantic desperation and meditative distancing from his own compulsion. The tactile pleasure that writers take in such details proves to lie at the heart of characterization. Particularity delivers the singularity of selfhood—with relish. When it concentrates conflicting impulses, it delivers the mimetic illusion of a whole, complex personality. The hopefulness that Carver embeds in Lloyd's attempts to ration his drinking is very different from the beautiful image of the yellowed slippers by which Flaubert lets us glimpse a finer sensibility in Emma, yet both instances sound the right off-note. When we are convinced by qualities of character that we cannot entirely reconcile, we are in the presence of mystery.

6

Point of View Q & A

Pop quiz:

What is the difference between a central narrator and a peripheral narrator?

What is an undramatized narrator?

What constitutes a convenient shift in point of view?

Name the varieties of third-person narration and give an example of each.

OK. Has your eye begun to twitch? Are you experiencing any of the other nervous tics that afflict anyone who's ever been called on a point-of-view violation? This may scare you even more, but there aren't any rigid rules. When you write fiction, you have to consider the reader's take on things in relation to your own and in relation to the perspective character's and/or the narrator's, and point of view lets you play these off against each other to shape the stakes and lend texture to dramatic tension. In his classic text *The Rhetoric of Fiction* Wayne Booth speaks of this as "an implied dialogue among author, narrator, the other characters, and the reader. Each of the four can range, in relation to each of the others, from identification to complete opposition, on any axis of value, moral intellectual, aesthetic, and even physical."[1] A writer manipulates readers in an effort to "eliminate all distance between the essential norms of his implied author and the norms of the postulated reader."[2]

Simply put, point of view provides us with a means for messing with the reader's head: she might side with a character even when he's in the wrong, judge a situation in vastly different terms than a character does, or be pushed to reconsider her opinion thanks to a narrator's commentary. To eliminate *all* distance between the norms of the writer and the reader is probably impossible, and it implies that a writer marches the reader relentlessly toward a fixed conclusion. Dramatic tension more often derives from the reader wavering in relation to character, writer, or narrator for most of the way. Ideally, the reader will be left holding the bag, with a changed awareness of the difficulty of judgment. The true rhetorical aim of point of view is to complicate the question, not steer the reader to one answer or another.

Your choice of a perspective character situates the reader in relation to the action. This choice intersects with structure and characterization and even with style, since the voice of a narration is itself a persuasive means to modulate the relationship between reader and writer, character, or narrator. Mikhail Bakhtin's notion of heteroglossia is useful here, because it emphasizes that many voices are integrated in a work of fiction, which is a "system" of languages that can incorporate multiple speech types—authorial comment, interior monologue, the variegated speech patterns of a host of characters, philosophical statements, idioms that may be more or less distant from the narrator's.[3] A novel about a working-class boy infatuated with the manners of the rich can incorporate his mother's folk wisdom, his own street slang, and the diction of his wealthy employer, and contrasts among these voices will help readers to discern that the writer's stance on the matter differs from that of the characters. Fiction can modulate many tones in order to achieve subtle rhetorical effects, no matter what type of narration the writer employs: "Even in those places where the author's voice seems at first glance to be unitary and consistent...beneath that smooth single-languaged surface we can nevertheless uncover prose's three-dimensionality, its profound speech diversity."[4]

To distinguish between a central narrator and a peripheral one or to categorize types of third-person narration tells us very little about how to achieve this richness of effect, nor does it encounter the risks a writer takes as she strives to anticipate a reader's reaction and manipulate it. In responding to drafts of manuscripts, we should be less quick to hunt for rule violations and more ready to consider the dramatic problem that prompted them—and may justify them. Without having to resort to a blizzard of technical terms, we can reframe the typical questions we ask of a draft to ground them in flexible principle rather than set rules.

Whose story is it?

All you have to do is consider the multiple-perspective novel— *The Sound and the Fury* or *The Hours*—to see how the question "Whose story is it?" mistakes the terms even when a work is unified by a single narrator. The story of *The Great Gatsby* belongs, of course, to Gatsby, but the plot belongs to the narrator, Nick, whose understanding is challenged and changed by the events he reports. Even where both the story and the plot "belong" to a single character, this question can be more precisely framed if we ask how point of view shapes what's at stake. In practice this question often gets asked after the fact, since in a first draft you might go on instinct in choosing a perspective character and deciding whether or not she narrates her own story.

Your workshop readers can be more helpful if they understand a narrator's role and nature as provisional in a first draft and remain open to the many ways revision might address *either* end of the link between perspective character and plot. The plot problem is how to ensure the perspective character has *enough* of a literal stake in the outcome. The rhetorical problem is how the perspective character can filter events in ways that trouble or provoke the reader. Whose story is it? Ultimately, the reader's. In order for a perspective character's arc of change to instigate an arc of change in the reader, such a character needs to provide not a steady, grounded perspective but an unstable one, since this will engage the reader in genuine conflict about the meaning of events. Your task in revision is to figure out how and where plot can galvanize such instability rather than to succumb to demands for a thoroughly consistent orientation.

Some instrumental instability in perspective matters to the effects of plot. George Saunders's "The Red Bow" is narrated by a father whose little girl has been killed by a dog suffering from an unspecified malady much like rabies. After her death the girl's uncle, previously an unemployed couch potato, campaigns to kill all the animals in town because of the risk of infection, exploiting the sentimental symbol of the girl's red hair bow to work the entire town into a fever pitch of paranoia. Saunders pushes the envelope by treating the subject of mob thinking as comedy, and the story might be read as sly allegory for the Bush administration's campaign for the invasion of Iraq, with the collapsing World Trade Center as the "red bow." The story could have been told from the perspective of Uncle Matt, the instigator, but instead Saunders chooses the point of view of the girl's father. Because he's *nice*. Because a reader would be much less likely to identify with the uncle's crass opportunism and therefore much less troubled as he leads the town toward mob rule. Because the narrator's primary motive for cooperation elicits our sympathy.

Presumably Matt undergoes a more dramatic change in the story, but the narrator wins his job because his instability generates tension in the reader. A mild narrator given to sentimental platitudes is likely to be the most unstable when confronted by violence, and this narrator can't even bring himself to say how his daughter died: "It is like your kid is this vessel that contains everything good. They look up at you so loving, trusting you to take care of them, and then one night—what gets me, what I can't get over, is that while she was being—while what happened was happening, I was—I had sort of snuck away downstairs to check my e-mail." The comic tone is disconcerting, and it alerts us to the narrator's instability, confirmed when he betrays envy of Matt's clarity: "But losing her had, I suppose, made him realize for the first time how much he loved her, and this sudden strength—focus, certainty, whatever—was a comfort, because tell the truth I was not doing well at all."[5] The narrator's inability to name things both is and is not like Matt's cynical, if bumbling, use of euphemism to incite the mob: "Why do we live in this world but to love what is ours, and when one of us have cruelly lost what we loved, it is the time to band together to stand up to that which threatens that which we love."[6] Tension builds as the story closes the seeming gap between the narrator's mildness and his collaboration in accomplishing evil. As Robert Alter has noted, "Perspective is as essential to literary narrative as the use of words or the ordering of significant sequences of action into a plot," and "sometimes the combinations and permutations of perspective become the virtual subject of the fiction."[7] When perspective truly functions to shape the stakes, readers will not regard the characters as contesting with one another for ownership of the story.

Does point of view provide the best vantage point?

Whether or not we're privy to all his thoughts, a character's vantage point may well deliberately occlude the reader's view of the action. Any child narrator worth his salt readily demonstrates the dramatic value of an obscured view of events. What point of view obscures from the reader can contribute enormously to literal suspense. In Roberto Bolaño's *2666*, five literary scholars become friends because of their mutual obsession with the same writer; after they return from a conference, the omniscient narrator reveals that two of the men are infatuated with Liz, the sole woman in their group, and then reports, tongue-in-cheek, "As for what passed through Liz Norton's head, it's better not to say," and thus the question of how romantic entanglement might disrupt friendships remains suspenseful for the reader.[8]

A perspective character's blind spots matter vitally to suspense of a higher order. If the narrator of "The Red Bow" accurately suspected Matt of opportunism and self-aggrandizement, the reader wouldn't be provoked to question the narrator's desire to think the best of everyone or to view his inarticulateness as a moral problem. A change in tone would also change the stakes, since the comic discrepancy between euphemism and actuality fuels the story's power to disturb. Saunders could have chosen differently, but then something else would have to provoke the reader to waver in relation to the narrator.

In composing your own work, you may view an occluded vantage point as a plot problem rather than a rhetorical opportunity. You don't have to contort plot so your perspective character witnesses the important events if you can generate suspense from uncertain facts. And how bias distorts interpretation is one of the most interesting aspects of characterization, not to be avoided but embraced. You just have to make sure your reader is alerted to the possibility. "Authorial flagging," as critic James Wood so nicely puts it, "teaches us how to read" a perspective character of any stripe.[9] Applying different terms for the same principle, in *The Rhetoric of Fiction* Booth discusses techniques for correcting or supporting a character's report of events.[10] Granting access to a character's thoughts can help readers register his blind spots. A writer can contrast the character's perceptions with the evidence of scene or weld sympathetic feelings to unsympathetic actions (or vice versa), as Saunders does in "The Red Bow." Or the writer can allow other characters to confirm or counter the perspective character's views. When in "The Red Bow" a virtuous priest protests the slaughter of all dogs, we're encouraged to question the narrator's acquiescence to Matt's plans.

Yet we can't forget that point of view must serve dynamic characterization. Rather than helpfully clarifying at every moment the exact nature of a perspective character's blind spots, we want to use point of view to coax the reader to question at least some of the character's judgments and some of her own, at least for a little longer. The real aim is to keep the reader from being entirely certain. Although we can immediately read Saunders's narrator as mistaken, he is problematic (and compelling) because we continue to want to sympathize with him and because we can't reconcile his harmless sentimentality with wrongdoing. Often, when readers of a first draft feel that they don't know what motivates a character in a given situation, they will ask for more facts or unequivocal evidence when they really only need the writer to clarify the *questions* in play.

Has the writer established a consistent point of view?

Readers rightly mistrust a convenient shift in point of view when it delivers information that explains what the reader should have been able to infer from the action. We usually operate from the premise that once a point of view has been established, it must be sustained. But for third-person narration, we need to be more provisional. As is true for the choice of a perspective character, a shift in perspective justifies itself when it proves to shape the stakes of the work. Where the writer can provide a dramatic payoff, demands for consistency become moot.

Once, in response to a first draft of one of my stories, a reader lectured me on consistency and urged me to look to James Joyce as a model. Well, I took his advice, and I absorbed a very different lesson from "The Dead." Though Gabriel Conroy will be the perspective character for most of the story, we first see him from the perspective of Lily, the young maid of the household, and then only for as long as it takes him to enter his aunts' house, hand her his coat, and make brief small talk. Submitted to a workshop, this manuscript would meet immediately with a number of objections: Why start in a perspective to which you never return? Why can't the information be conveyed from Gabriel's perspective right from the get-go? Since Lily's perspective provides background on the socioeconomic status of the aunts, the style of their parties, and their reverential regard for their intellectual nephew, you could persuasively argue that all this information could be delivered via Gabriel. But perspective never delivers only information; it also captures tension. Unlike the later pages of the story, which hew close to the educated diction of Gabriel, the third-person voice of these initial pages employs Lily's vernacular: "They [the aunts] were fussy, that was all. But the only thing they would not stand was back answers. Of course they had good reason to be fussy on such a night. And then it was long after ten o'clock and yet there was no sign of Gabriel and his wife. Besides they were dreadfully afraid that Freddy Malins might turn up screwed."[11] Joyce's deployment of perspective brilliantly incorporates tonal contrasts, exploiting the heteroglossia Bakhtin sees as central to a fictional voice. And it accomplishes beautiful structural symmetry, shifting to Gabriel's perspective at a moment when he condescends to Lily: "Gabriel smiled at the three syllables she had given his surname."[12] (To pronounce it as "Con-a-roy" constitutes a class marker.) Having been locked inside Lily's provincial perspective, a reader is situated to have a more troubled response to Gabriel's condescension. What better way to introduce a character whose uncertainty about his superiority is at stake in the story?

What limits does a third-person narrator have to honor?

Not many. Workshop readers of a third-person narration will sometimes complain that they don't know whether information comes from the narrator or the character. When we read close third-person limited, it can seem impossible to parse the distinction. In Deborah Eisenberg's "Some Other, Better Otto," the cranky perspective character, Otto, poses such a high risk of being unsympathetic that the author counters by holding the reader close to his comically skewed perspective, adopting his diction and tone. Here are Otto's thoughts in response to his boyfriend's suggestion that they spend Thanksgiving with Otto's family: "It had taken him—how long?—years and years to establish a viable, if not pristine, degree of estrangement from his family. Which was no doubt why, he once explained to William, he had tended, over the decades, to be so irascible and easily exhausted. The sustained effort, the subliminal concentration that was required to detach the stubborn prehensile hold was enough to wear a person right out and keep him from ever getting down to anything of real substance."[13] Could you possibly pluck out even a phrase that you'd firmly attribute to the narrator, not the character? Yet switch to the first-person pronoun here, and you'd recognize that the narrator *is* filtering Otto's extreme slant. "He once explained" helpfully summarizes on Otto's behalf, and it also alerts us to the difference between Otto's predicament as he'd state it (a viable "degree of estrangement") and his predicament as he feels it ("wear a person out").

To fuss over maintaining some exact boundary line between narrator and character is to mistake for a fault what is actually a virtue, the flexible capacity for mediation between the two. All direct methods of characterization available in first-person narration, except that of a character-narrator who confides in the reader, are available in third-person narration, with additional options along a continuum from a narrator who is next to invisible to a narrator who directly addresses the reader. Figure 6.1 demonstrates the broader range of strategies available in third-person narration, which could even be plotted on this graph. A character's thoughts can be rendered directly (3) or mediated by the narrator (B) or some blend of the two (3B); even a description of a character's actions might be inflected because of the difference between the narrator's diction and a character's. Because third-person narration can also avail itself of first-person strategies, such as interior monologue, we must reconcile multiple ways of knowing a character, a terrific resource for complicating a reader's responses.

In third-person narration the camera does not have to be bolted to the floor, and it is not error if it moves closer to or farther from character, although judging *when* to do this does leave room for error. Though shifts in diction may provide only ambiguous "linguistic signals" to this transition, a narrator can close the psychic distance with character at will.[14] In *Madame Bovary* Flaubert executes just the tiniest shiver of a shift in psychic distance when he reports how Félicité, Emma Bovary's new maid, submits to her employer's efforts to "make a lady's maid of her" but privately resists: "The new servant obeyed without

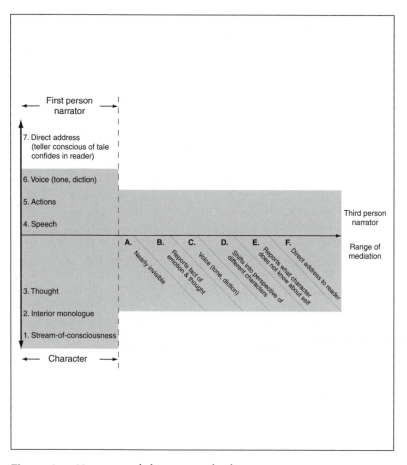

Figure 6.1   Narrator and character in third-person narration

The vertical axis represents direct methods of characterization, to which a first-person narrator is limited, and the horizontal axis represents strategies available to the third-person narrator only. The shaded area encompasses any of the possible permutations of direct and mediated characterization in third-person narration.

Illustrator: Alan Stonebraker

a murmur, so as not to be sent away; and as madame usually left the key in the side-board, Félicité every evening took a small supply of sugar that she ate alone in her bed after she had said her prayers."[15] In that one word *madame* we are momentarily admitted to Félicité's interior world. The flexible range of third-person narration means that you might effectively choose limits (as Eisenberg does) or exercise prerogatives (as Flaubert does) to achieve different dramatic effects. In the most liberally omniscient third-person narration, the writer can contrast what a narrator tells us with what is revealed of character via showing, setting us up to second-guess the character or to revise our judgment of him. This is why it's naïve to dismiss an omniscient narrator as old-fashioned, doing too much of the reader's work for her. On the contrary, in the right hands, such a narrator makes *more* work for the reader. (See Chapter 9 for a discussion of showing and telling.)

To give you a sense of the rich variety of effects available in third-person narration, I'd like to examine an instance in which the writer fiercely exploits the subtle difference between narrator and character. William Trevor sustains narrative distance for most of the way in "Sitting with the Dead." In doing so, he's exercising a prerogative available only in third-person narration, and he also offers a fine example of timing when to grant access to character. Two sisters, who have taken it as their Christian duty to sit with the dying, pay a visit to Emily, arriving too late, only hours after her husband has died. The two sisters are not named when they arrive, although the "quiet, sharp-featured sister" takes the lead when Emily answers the door:

> "We heard in MacClincy's," she said.
> "I'm sorry you've had a wasted journey."
> "It's never wasted." There was a pause, as if a pause was necessary here. "You have our sympathy," was added to that, the explanation of why the journey had not been in vain.[16]

Trevor even recruits syntax to convey the awkwardness of this encounter, thus situating the reader at a distance from all the characters. But we're asked fairly quickly to take another step back from the sisters, who "began to call her Emily, as if they knew her well," and have such decided ideas about their usefulness.[17]

We are also kept at a distance from Emily. Her husband as he exists in her thoughts is only gradually exposed to us. Had he been alive to receive these visitors, "he would have called her back as soon as she'd left them with him. He would have asked her who they were, although he knew; he would have told her to take them away. He'd never minded what he said—the flow of coarse language when someone crossed one of the fields, every word shouted out, frighteningly sometimes." "Not once, not ever, had there been violence," but Emily harbors a surprising yearning for it: "Yet often she wished that there had been, believing that violence would have been easier to bear than the power of his articulated anger."[18] Note how this sentence offers subtle signals that the narrator is keeping her at arm's length ("yet often," "believing that," diction that differs from the character's down to eschewing any contractions). This positions us to accept Emily's wish as certain fact, since it's the narrator who reports it. Because the narrator doesn't elaborate, we aren't any better equipped than her visitors to see inside Emily's perverse wish, but unlike them, we have been made aware of its existence. Thus, we grow increasingly distanced from the sisters as they persist in correcting Emily: "it wasn't so bad" counters the wish that it had been worse. When Emily hints at the isolation her husband imposed on her, Kathleen replies, "There's many a woman doesn't get out and about"[19]; when Emily mentions that because of her husband's debts she'll probably have to sell their farm, which she inherited from her aunt, she admits, "He married me for the forty acres," and Kathleen murmurs, "Ah, now, now... Ah now, dear."[20]

By sustaining narrative distance, Trevor achieves a lovely doubling of plot action in the story. Pressuring Emily to respect the dead by glossing over difficulties, the sisters goad her to counter with blunt statements: "I was a fool and you pay for foolishness" and "There's no grief in the house you come to."[21] It seems that tension derives from the sisters' refusal to allow Emily to admit her marriage was less than it should have been. But Emily's memories ultimately betray that her relationship with her husband was also *more* than she admits. About two-thirds of the way through the story the narrator finally grants us a glimpse of what lies beneath her wish for crude violence: "The time she began to paint the scullery, it frightened her when he stood in the doorway, before he even said a thing. The time she dropped the sugar bag and the sugar spilt out all over the floor he watched her sweeping it on to the dustpan, turf dust going with it. He said what was she doing, throwing it away when it was still fit to stir into your tea? The scullery had stayed half-painted to this day."[22] Sentence fragments and diction signal that we've moved closer to Emily's perspective for this key revelation. Because the narrator does *not* step in to confirm or to dissect her feelings, what is now shown to us is crucially ambiguous. This passage focuses our attention on unfinished consequence; if the reader, pulled closer, feels with Emily this terrorizing effect, he must also reconsider Emily's earlier blunt statements to the sisters. Honest protest or reverberation of her husband's talent for intimidation? The surface story may position her as partner in an ordinarily disappointing marriage, but the submerged story suggests a more insidious, still alive partnership. Trevor garners a huge payoff for what the narrator (not the character) has withheld for so long.

Without so much as a by-your-leave, Trevor heightens tension at the climax by shifting briefly to the perspective of the two sisters as they drive away from the house. Mistakenly locating horror in impropriety ("what they had heard had been all the more terrible to listen to with a man dead in an upstairs room"), the sisters deliver a false ending. The horror they actually witnessed was the continued life of this man in the reflexes that persist in Emily. The story closes with a paragraph firmly anchored in Emily's perspective. She no longer worries what the sisters might think—"nor did it matter if, here and there, they had not quite understood"—because the resistance they provoked in her has exposed her own complicity: "Hers was the ghost the night had brought, in her own image as she once had been."[23]

Things *are* more complicated when there are no hard-and-fast rules. Especially in relation to third-person narration, we can easily slip into the fallacy that more access to a character's thoughts is the preferred solution to any dramatic problem, when, as Trevor demonstrates, timing—sometimes choosing to withhold, sometimes to reveal—is everything. Shifts in narrative distance can contribute to suspense or they can give away too much too soon. But the possible permutations available to you are nearly infinite.

Is the first-person narrator plausible?

Particularly when you write first-person stories in the realist tradition, you may meet with protests from readers who don't believe a character's diction is appropriate to type. (A child narrator can provoke trivial quibbling over whether a seven-year-old's vocabulary would or would not include certain words.) Not only does this blur the useful distinction between first-person collo-quial (a narrator who intends to tell his story) and first-person "overheard" (a narrator whose diction does not have to be limited to what she'd use in speaking) but also it tends to impose a dreary uniformity, a "first-person sociological" point of view. Many first-person stories and novels published today sound alike because the writers subscribe to the reductionist idea that a narrator must be limited to speech patterns typical for his socioeconomic type and region. Overly scrupulous policing (especially in the work-shop, by nature predisposed to fault-finding) pressures writers to sacrifice vitality to narrow notions of veracity.

The truly credible first-person colloquial voice persuades us precisely because it is *not* like any other voice, even though it must integrate at least some markers of type to be fully convinc-ing. In *The Brief Wondrous Life of Oscar Wao*, Junot Díaz employs a first-person narrator who confounds strict notions of plausi-bility. Like Nick in *The Great Gatsby*, the narrator is ultimately transformed by his friendship with the hero, Oscar. Both are Dominican immigrants raised in New York City. Chapter 1 begins long before they met, when Oscar was a child, "something of a Casanova" and not yet a nerd:

> You should have seen him, his mother sighed in her Last Days. He was our little Porfirio Rubirosa.[4]
> All the other boys his age avoided the girls like they were a bad case of Captain Trips. Not Oscar. The little guy loved himself the females, had "girlfriends" galore.... The girls—his sister Lola's friends, his mother's friends, even their neighbor, Mari Colón, a thirty-something postal employee who wore red on her lips and walked like she had a bell for an ass—all purportedly fell for him. Ese muchacho está bueno! (Did it hurt that he was earnest and clearly attention-deprived? Not at all!)
> ... It truly was a Golden Age for Oscar, one that reached its apotheo-sis in the fall of his seventh year, when he had two little girlfriends at the same time, his first and only ménage a trois. With Maritza Chacón and Olga Polanco.[24]

Urban street slang nails the narrator's social milieu, and so do his easy transition from English to Spanish and his cultural reference points—"Captain Trips" is just one of many references to fantasy novels and comics.

But it is the narrator's inventiveness with his given idiom(s) that makes him a believable individual, capable of surprise—as in the metaphoric stretch of avoiding girls "like they were a bad case of Captain Trips" or the lexical stretch in his blend of colloquial and literary expressions (from "thirty-something" to "apotheosis"). We'd be less likely to accept this last stretch as plausible if Díaz did not play one tonality off another for satiric effect and if the diction did not situate his narrator as a closet geek, unable to suppress the urge to show off his vocabulary *and* his comics collection. The narrator's arch tone lets us know he's having fun with this range, but it also conveys uncertainty about whether to take his hero seriously. When he conflates the child's innocence with adult sexuality, idiom and tone also betray the narrator as burdened by macho values, and the writer links this stance with politics the narrator condemns. In the footnoted reference to Porfirio Rubirosa, a henchman for the Dominican dictator Trujillo, Rubirosa is described as "the original Dominican Player, [who] fucked all sorts of women."[25] The true challenge in first-person colloquial is to betray though idiom character traits germane to the conflict.

How are we able to distinguish Díaz's strategy from sloppiness about the vernacular? In the first place, the writer foregrounds the question of narrative authority. The narrator refuses to stay in the box of first-person colloquial narration, appropriating the privileges (and vocabulary) of a traditional omniscient narrator, as in this announcement: "Our hero was not one of those Dominican cats everybody's always going on about."[26] The narrator also blithely assumes the authority to report events he could not have witnessed, to enter the consciousness of other characters, and even to footnote the text for a reader presumably ignorant of Dominican history. His "plausible" identity as a young man who befriends Oscar is shot to smithereens by these choices, yet in concert such strategies alert us that perspective serves as the "virtual subject" of this novel. Just as the narrator is a hybrid of first-person colloquial and omniscient narration, his language nimbly hybridizes English and Spanish, street patois and political analysis, obscure references to literature and to comics: "What is it with Dictators and Writers, anyway? Since before the infamous Caesar-Ovid war they've had beef."[27] These strategies bear fruit in the form of provocative defamiliarization: "You really want to know what being an X-Man feels like?

Just be a smart bookish boy of color in a contemporary U. S. ghetto."[28] This capacious, syncretistic voice *is* the point, a quintessentially American voice borne of the narrator's struggle to embrace multiple allegiances and to invent a language inclusive enough to accommodate his doubled (enriched) cultural experience.

Is the first-person narrator reliable?

To question the accuracy of reporting in third-person narration is to accuse the author of error: when the narrator tells us a character is afraid, we trust we'll get confirmation from scene, and if we don't, we're just plain confused. But with respect to a first-person narration, this questioning is the name of the game: we're meant to read between the lines of a first-person narration, looking for clues to lies, misjudgments, or self-protective distortions of fact. Yet too often, when readers in a workshop spot a slip-up on the part of a first-person narrator, they leap to judge the narration unreliable as a whole. This amounts to throwing out the baby with the bath water. First, an unreliable narrator is more narrowly defined as someone who speaks from values that are not those of the work; if the writer succeeds, we'll eventually oppose what this narrator declares to be right. An unreliable narrator does not necessarily earn our dislike—as Wayne Booth observes, in *Huckleberry Finn,* "the narrator claims to be naturally wicked while the author silently praises his virtues behind his back"[29]— and his unmasking is usually not the point of the work. His ability to disturb us is. The unreliable narrator of "The Red Bow" doesn't forfeit our sympathy even as he cooperates with Matt's vigilante-ism, and we do not doubt that he accurately reports events even if we might not agree that his neighbors' readiness to follow Matt evinces "deeply moving" grief for his daughter, as if "somehow they had come to understand how good she had been, how precious."[30] Second, our fluctuating sympathy for and wavering trust in any first-person narrator is an essential part of dramatic tension, so to assume that a narrator can ever be fully reliable misconstrues the dynamic, inherently unstable function of point of view in relation to plot. Sometimes we call a narrator unreliable when actually we mistrust the *writer* for failing to make us feel this fluctuation as intentional.

A third-person narrator may be a nearly invisible nub of a crea-ture, but the first-person narrator possesses all the advantages of a realized character, who is a jumble of contradictions and incon-sistencies that shift in response to pressure. A reader's feelings about a first-person narrator can be as complicated as hers about her world. We might judge her to be an accurate observer but a biased interpreter of events, trust her opinion of politics but wince at her views on romance. Of course, there is no collective *we,* only a motley crew of readers, each of whom might quarrel with the narrator on different issues.

A writer can never assert absolute control over the range of possible interpretations, but be consoled. *Some* range is essen-tial to a satisfying read. Such indeterminacy constitutes a central dramatic virtue of first-person narration: slant is at the heart of the conflict. As a character, a first-person narrator engages the reader via self-betrayal *and* persuasive distortions, both of which cajole a reader to arrive at a truth that usually lies somewhere between her biases and those of the narrator. Imagine your story is told by a thief: some readers will bring to the table a moral-istic view, while others may be inclined to ally with an outlaw. You must qualify both these possible readings by ensuring that either kind of reader will identify with the narrator along some axis for at least part of the way and by dislodging both from any settled position. As a manipulative third-party to this rela-tionship, you can use a reader's inclination to sympathize with a first-person narrator in order to lure the reader outside her moral comfort zone. Though you may supply support or correc-tion only through direct methods of characterization, you have more opportunities to exploit voice—to pair the seductive vitality of the vernacular with dicey opinions or to betray a narrator's bias via some discrepancy between his tone and the actions reported. These techniques not only help readers to gauge when to trust a first-person narrator and when to doubt him but also to discern the difference between writer and narrator. Readers will grant a first-person narrator far more moral leeway when they do not confuse his failings with those of the writer.

Like many of Alice Munro's short story collections, *The Love of a Good Woman* is united by craft as well as thematic concerns. In this primer on point of view, Munro tests how perspective contributes to coherence and demonstrates that point-of-view rules readily give way to this principle.[31] One of the stories, "My

Mother's Dream," also offers a wonderful example of how a writer can exploit a narrator's unstable reliability. In this story, set just after World War II, a pregnant war widow is forced to move in with her husband's mother and two sisters, Ailsa and Iona. Dependent on her in-laws, Jill feels increasingly threatened by the prospect of raising a child, which may force her to sacrifice her ambitions as a concert musician. But hold on to your hat, because this story is told by the baby she's carrying, a flagrant violation of the rule that a first-person narrator can report only events she has witnessed. Roughly half of the action takes place before the birth of the narrator, and with the exception of the epilogue, the rest of the action occurs in the first few weeks of her life. The narrator portrays herself as an agent even while still in the womb; when Jill moves in with the relatives, she notes, "I joined them too, being large and lively inside her."[32] Either we reject the story as implausible or we accept it as a retrospective reconstruction of events the narrator has been told about throughout her childhood. By referencing the speculative nature of the tale telling ("the story is," "the truth may be"[33]) and appending an epilogue that confirms it as retrospective, Munro cajoles the reader to buy in to her risky premise.

The action takes the form of a pitched battle for supremacy among Ailsa, Iona, and Jill: the domineering Ailsa enforces a confining social respectability; the tremulous Iona gains the upper hand once the squalling newborn refuses to be comforted by anyone but her; and Jill's will to rebel is shattered by her baby's hostility to her. The story begins out of chronological order, with the narrator recounting a dream of Jill's in which she makes an agonized search for her lost baby. Not only does this declare the narrator's outrageous prerogatives from the start but also it situates the reader to grant sympathy to Jill when for most of the story the narrator is at war with her. In other words, Munro begins by supplying correction for her narrator's extreme slant. The narrator then circles back in time to recount Jill's courtship with George and his death soon after their wedding. Although early in her pregnancy Jill continued to perform, once she moves in with her husband's family, she quits practicing violin for the stated reason that "her fingers had got too puffy now."[34] The narrator freely exercises the prerogative to dip into Jill's perspective or Ailsa's or Iona's in order to depict each woman as helpless before fate. Even Ailsa is sometimes referred to as "poor Ailsa," because she sacrificed her own ambitions to send her brother to law school, and "then he flouted her—he signed up; he went off and got himself killed."[35]

The events of the story are defamiliarized not only by the narrator's flippant tone but by her mediation of other voices, from George's reported disdain for his sisters to the cant of respectability. Although this story represents an unusual case, it illustrates nicely how even a first-person narration subsumes "heteroglot voices" that, in Bakhtin's words, provide the author with "the background necessary for his own voice, outside of which his artistic prose nuances cannot be perceived, and without which they 'do not sound.'"[36] The *writer's* voice sounds against a murmuring background of condescension toward virtuous women and platitudes meant to deny loss and terror (as when the narrator borrows Ailsa's explanation for Iona's past mental breakdown, a result of "being a bit too thin-skinned and the supervisor's being a bit too hard on her").[37] By selecting for this background, Munro provides a yardstick for evaluating the narrator's determinism about the necessity of female sacrifice. From the narrator's perspective, but not the author's, some iron law of nature prevents Jill from practicing, requires Ailsa and Iona to sacrifice their schooling for their brother's sake, and so on. Amusingly, only the newborn baby has a choice, but she's as unaccommodating as Mother Nature appears to be: "I refused to take my mother's breast....So Iona mixed up a formula and took me out of Jill's arms where I stiffened and wailed....Iona's arms and the nipple that she was in charge of became my chosen home."[38] Iona is the perfect slave, in contrast to Jill, who tries practicing the violin again only to have the baby scream in order to shut her down: "My crying is a knife to cut out of her life all that isn't useful. To me."[39] Munro convincingly demonstrates that the reader can readily sift one kind of narrative reliability from another: if the narrator is wildly mistaken in attributing gender constraints to natural law, she's able to impart, with dead-on accuracy, how these constraints force women to compromise their own desires.

The implausible narrator proves to be the only narrator who could shape *this* story. As the catalyst that shifts the balance of power among these women, the narrator speaks from the standpoint of a devouring ego, inviting us to qualify where she will not, and her unsteadiness as an informant is compounded by her shift from the role of a peripheral narrator to that of a central one. At the story's climax the exhausted Jill, left alone with the screaming baby, shaves a few grains of a sleeping pill to add to the baby's bottle, and when the rest of the family returns home, Iona takes one look at the limp infant and screams that Jill has murdered her. Now the narrator makes a crucial choice: "To me it seems that it was only then that I became female.... when I decided to come back, when I gave up the fight against my mother...and when in fact I chose survival over victory."[40]

If Munro dismantles so many presumed rules about point of view (including the expectation that a narrator will remain either peripheral or central), she beautifully demonstrates the overriding justification for doing so. The baby makes the best narrator for this story *because* her view of events is occluded: dramatic tension springs from this impediment rather than from narration that grants us the clearest line of sight. Munro's example thus informs the work of writers who don't push the limits of plausibility to the same extreme. At some point in any provocative work of fiction, the reader will be asked to read events against the grain of the narration, a feat accomplished by the writer's orchestration of voice as well as plot. In this case, because we are privy to the baby's devouring egotism and because her slant highlights distortions in the norms of her social world, we have room to respond sympathetically to Jill's nearly murderous impulse to stifle her screams, to be troubled by Iona's slavish devotion, to acknowledge that even Ailsa has made painful compromises for the sake of survival. When we plot our fiction, we should consider carefully how a perspective character's *disadvantages* can be instrumental in generating this enriched experience of ambiguity, be alive to the potency of what she cannot tell us accurately or clearly.

7

Synecdoche and Metonymy in Setting, Staging, and Dialogue

When the early works of the Impressionists were routinely rejected by the Paris Salon, Ernest Meissonier commanded extravagant prices for small portraits executed in minute detail, making him wealthy enough to afford an opulent estate just outside Paris. Ambitious to secure his reputation as the greatest painter of his day, Meissonier turned to painting historical subjects, and in 1863 he began work on *Friedland,* a large canvas commemorating Napoleon's 1807 military victory on Prussian soil.[1] In the painting Napoleon, seated on a white horse, accepts a salute from his triumphant cavalry. Fanatical about historical accuracy, Meissonier borrowed the actual saddle used by Napoleon and even had a tailor make an exact copy of the coat Napoleon had worn.[2] The painter also aimed for an absolutely correct representation of the charging cavalry. Before the advent of stop-action photography in the 1870s, no one understood how horses moved at a gallop, since the naked eye can't process so fast a motion. Even the equine anatomy courses Meissonier had taken at a veterinary school were no help here. But Meissonier was obsessed and he had resources. On his estate he built a minia-ture railroad track and installed a small carriage. While a man on horseback galloped alongside the track, Meissonier kept pace in this carriage so that he could repeatedly sketch the mechan-ics of the horse's motion. In the finished painting the horses were complete down to the veins beneath their skin, but this excruciating care ultimately detracted from realism rather than heightening it.[3] Accuracy of detail could not compensate for the fact that Meissonier's galloping horses did not *look like* galloping horses.

Meissonier's example demonstrates that copious detail does not constitute convincing detail. Careful selection not only creates a more vivid impression than a catalogue of information but also persuasively conveys a particular gestalt, a way of viewing the world. We don't want empirical objectivity from art; we want to enter a world distinctively colored by a sensibility that enhances our seeing. The convenient comparison between Meissonier's horses and those of his Impressionist contemporary Edgar Degas emphatically confirms this. With far less detail Degas not only conveys some essence of horse-in-motion but also by manipulation of perspective and line engages the viewer in supplying any missing details. In other words, Degas offers us an *experience* of a horse, not an anatomical illustration. As Matisse once declared, "Exactitude is not truth."[4]

Writers commit the "Meissonier error" when they employ a notion of setting common to genre fiction and travel guides—a "voiceless" delivery of logistical facts of place utterly severed from the distorting, but authenticating, influence of perspective. If truth can't be located in a comprehensiveness that flattens all detail with equivalence, the key may be to treat the partial glimpse as a virtue rather than a limitation. As the poet Louise Glück suggests, "All earthly experience is partial. Not simply because it is subjective, but because that which we do not know, of the universe, of mortality, is so much more vast than that which we do know. What is unfinished or has been destroyed participates in these mysteries. The problem is to make a whole that does not forfeit this power."[5]

Synecdoche and metonymy as principles of selection

Like painters, writers must determine how to suggest with the fewest possible brushstrokes both the fullness of reality and a highly particular take on it. The generative principles for achieving this are those of metonymy and synecdoche, tropes fundamental to human perception and to artistic rendering of perception. A trope, or figure of speech, involves some deviation from the ordinary connotation of a word; metaphor and simile (tropes of comparison) link two unlike things to surprise us with unexpected likeness, while synecdoche and metonymy (tropes of substitution) proffer one related thing in place of another. Synecdoche substitutes the part for the whole, as in "give us this day our daily bread," in which *daily bread* stands for *food*. Metonymy substitutes some attribute of a thing for the thing itself, as in "these radicals spit on the flag," where *spit* stands for *express contempt* and *flag* for *patriotism*. As many rhetoricians acknowledge, we can't always distinguish between these two closely related tropes, but most of us readily decipher substitutions in a text.[6] Consider this example from Toni Morrison's historical novel *Jazz*, a sentence about jazz music of the twenties: "Songs that used to start in the head and fill the heart had dropped on down, down to places below the sash and the buckled belts."[7] We don't have to parse the distinction between metonymy and synecdoche to recognize that *head* substitutes for *thought*, *heart* for *romantic emotion*, and *places below the sash* for *sexual impulses*. These tropes have the power not only to compress but also to inflect the tone of a narrative—to convey a particular sensibility. "Places below the sash," for example, firmly connotes primness.

Metonymy and synecdoche, like metaphor, function not only to render rather than describe experience but also to compress a great deal of unstated information and emotion into a relatively short compass. As a way of processing experience, these tropes are natural to us, and most writers use them instinctively. Although it can boost your street credibility to drop these terms in a craft conversation, you don't need to master terminology in order to make use of the principle. What matters is to recognize the ubiquitous nature of substitution and its figurative power; T. S. Eliot's roomy term, the objective correlative, covers actions, images, and gestures that partake of the qualities of these and other tropes.

Toni Morrison's trope-dense style also illuminates how metonymy and synecdoche operate as principles of selection, enabling the writer to substitute for generalities the sensory specifics of individual experience. (This is entirely in accord with story logic, which borrows from dreams a propensity for substitution.) Morrison's novel *Jazz*, set in Harlem in 1926 and told by an omniscient narrator, is centered on an older married couple, Joe and Violet Trace, who were part of the historic migration of blacks from the harshly segregated rural south to northern cities. Early in *Jazz* Morrison incorporates a flashback to Joe and Violet's trip north on the train, a trip that will stand for the migration of thousands. How does she make this more than generic emblem? In part, by looking to the periphery. When the young couple boards the train (to ride in the "colored section"), Morrison emphasizes the novelty of the experience for two people who've spent their lives as field hands. Joe and Violet stand instead of sitting down, so they can better feel the "trembling" of the train as a "dancing under their feet."[8] The next scene opens as a train attendant moves through their passenger coach to announce, "Breakfast in the dining car." A perfectly ordinary detail until Morrison focuses the reader's attention on a key metonymy. Having crossed the Mason-Dixon line, the black passengers are no longer prohibited from entering the dining car, "if only they would. If only they would tuck those little boxes and baskets under the seat; close those paper bags, for once, put the bacon-stuffed biscuits back into the cloth they were wrapped in, and troop single file through the five cars ahead on into the dining car, where the table linen was at least as white as the sheets they dried on juniper bushes; where the napkins were folded with a crease as stiff as the ones they ironed for Sunday dinner; where the gravy was as smooth as their own, and the biscuits did not take second place to the bacon-stuffed ones they wrapped in cloth."[9]

The freedom to enter the dining car is metonymic, but so are the items in the (synecdochic) list that Morrison supplies, each trailing a story not on the page. (For example, people accorded second-rate public accommodations are well-versed in the refinements they supply as servants.) Having provisioned themselves for the Jim Crow South, most of the passengers don't set aside the food they packed for the journey, just as they cannot simply shed the humiliating accommodations of the past—or the inner reserves that helped them to endure. The train ride north may be an obvious choice for this novel, and the choice to mark the culture shift by the freedom to go to the dining car merely a good one, but emphasizing the reluctance to waste the good food these country people packed at home is a brilliant stroke.

As principles of selection, metonymy and synecdoche inform many of the essential tasks of the fiction writer. By definition a work of fiction substitutes a part—a single, particular plot—for the whole, the entire story implied by that plot. In Raymond

Carver's short story "Careful" (discussed in Chapter 5), when Lloyd's wife, Inez, visits him to discuss their impending divorce, he can't hear well because his ear is stuffed with wax. The metonymy of the clogged ear suggests an inability to listen, and the action of the plot, Lloyd's efforts to solicit his wife's help in clearing his ear, also functions as synecdoche, standing for his desire to re-engage her on many levels. In selecting what details of setting to include in a story, you must consider how this will synecdochically convince readers of place; in staging a story you must consider the metonymic suggestions of setting a scene at dusk or at dawn, in a confined space or a wide-open one; in writing dialogue you attempt to explore a topic that metonymically suggests the stakes.

Suggestive setting

Synecdoche and metonymy provide a key to suggesting the fullness of reality, especially of physical place, enabling you to con the reader into believing that a stage backdrop of building façades hides a complete interior rather than resting on naked scaffolding. So what goes wrong when setting still falls flat despite your reliance on these key tropes? The illusion of fullness—of setting and of character—depends on the right partial glimpse. If selection is merely a means to winnow information to a sizeable chunk, it can't convince your reader of *essential* qualities of the environment. If the facts are irrelevant to a character's experience of a place (for example, how many miles a city is above sea level, which is akin to Meissonier's anatomical knowledge of horses' veins), then they won't hold a reader's attention or launch rich associations. And not just any trope will do. The city of San Francisco won't come to life if a writer chooses a synecdochic list of the Golden Gate Bridge, hippies on Haight Street, and Fisherman's Wharf. Setting must also serve tension, have some signal relationship to character more buried and devious than the broad conception of character in harmony or in conflict with environment. As Eliot noted for the objective correlative, the problem lies in finding the right detail—organic to the story, firmly literal in ways that metonymically suggest. Setting does not have to take up much space in order to matter to plot. In Hemingway's "Clean, Well-Lighted Place," set in a café, we are given almost no details of place beyond spare, recurring references to cleanliness and light, which metonymically narrow our focus to the small solace possible in an existentially barren world. Just once, Hemingway references the setting beyond the café window; as a soldier walks by with a girl, "the street light shone on the brass number on his collar."[10] Out of all the details Hemingway might have chosen, he gives us one that depends on light, a designation of rank that subtly hints at the futility of striving for status.

To explore in greater detail how setting functions in relation to plot and meaning, let's consider Tessa Hadley's "Sunstroke." The story's omniscient third-person narration dips into the perspective of various characters at will, an unusual, rule-breaking decision. Rachel and Janie, both of whom have fallen into the traditional role of staying home with their young children, are tempted to sexual dalliance by the unexpected arrival of a family friend, Kieran, at the seaside resort where Rachel's and Janie's families are vacationing together. The story opens with a paragraph that focuses on setting:

> The seafront really isn't the sea but the Bristol Channel: Wales is a blue line of hills on the other side. The district council has brought sand from elsewhere and built a complicated ugly system of seawalls and rock groins to keep it in and make the beach more beachlike, but the locals say it'll be washed away at the first spring tide. Determined kids wade out a long way into soft brown silt to reach the tepid water, which barely has the energy to gather itself into what you could call a wave. It's hard to believe that the same boys and girls who have PlayStations and the Internet still care to go paddling with shrimping nets in the rock pools left behind when the tide recedes, but they do, absorbed in it for hours as children might have been decades and generations ago.[11]

The writer takes care of literal business: one could find this beach on a map and diagram its key features down to the gradual slope of the shoreline. Hadley even establishes depth perception with the "blue line of hills on the other side." Because the kids have "PlayStations and the Internet," era is established in just a phrase.

But the interesting thing about any depiction of setting is where the writer chooses to embellish detail, where not, in order to situate the *reader* in relation to the setting. Without the writer having to say so, we recognize this as a low-rent resort, with an

ugly but workable system of seawalls to make the beach functional, murky silt beneath the water rather than crystalline sand,
and only the feeblest suggestion of surf. Not a beach for lovers
or adventurers but for kids who paddle and dig and poke around
in tide pools, indifferent to the aesthetic value of their tame surroundings. From the very first sentence, in which "the seafront
really isn't the sea," this paragraph generates tension around the
question of seeming. The manufactured seawalls and "sand from
elsewhere" "make the beach *more beachlike*" (even if the seawalls
might be "washed away at the first spring tide"), and the "tepid
water" can hardly gather itself "into what you *could call* a wave."
Even the children's industriousness is "hard to believe." Setting
already functions metonymically via its suggestion of manufactured structures that tame unruly nature but may or may not offer
reliable support.

In the next paragraph the camera pans the populated waterfront: "The high street is festive with bunting and flowers; the toy
shops have set out their metal baskets of buckets and shovels and
plastic flags; the cafés are doing good business selling cream teas
and chips." Particularity is achieved through slant rather than
comprehensiveness. Hadley enables us to get the quick fix that
cliché offers but complicates information by her presentation.
The synecdochic emphasis on the tawdry trappings of a low-end
resort mirrors the depressingly make-do quality of the natural
environment, and her compressed list highlights the irony of
"festive" by ending with "good business." Next she transforms
information about setting from static to dynamic by offering a
vivid visual of people in action: vacationers, "pink-skinned in
shorts and sunglasses, with troops of children," "change twenty-
pound notes into piles of coins and lose them all in the machines
in the amusement arcades."[12] In depicting gambling as tame
activity rather than risk in this setting, Hadley demonstrates that
not just any part can stand for the whole, and not just any
substitution can conjure a particular concept.

When Hadley introduces Janie and Rachel in the next paragraph, she places them in a "messy family camp of bags, cardi-
gans, plastic water bottles, discarded children's tops," settled
"half in and half out of the dappled shade of some kind of ornamental tree that neither can identify," and both women lie on the
grass, staring "dreamily up into the delicate lattice of its twigs
and leaves, stirring against the light with an effect like glinting

water." "Some kind of ornamental tree" elaborates the emphasis on seeming so that it incorporates difficulties in discerning.
Because "water" reminds us of the description of the sea, we can
make another connection here. The "delicate lattice" of the tree
leaves "glinting" in bright light is in tension with its counterpart, "ugly system of seawalls," an exquisitely spare reference that
will generate large effect. Hadley often establishes setting via a
"motion shot" focused on gesture or action—sea walls that might
wash away, kids wading in silt, people exchanging cash for coins
as if it's their duty to be amused, Janie and Rachel watching leaves
shift in light. In this last instance Hadley exploits a perspective
character's response to setting as a means to characterize, creating
a subtle dissonance between the lyrical slant of this phrase and
the jaded ironic tone of the narrator's depiction of the waterfront.
Although in their generic role the women "hardly interrupt their
conversation to dole out what's needed" by their children, their
dreamy sensitivity immediately alerts the reader to their potential
for deviating from expectation.[13]

For a genre writer cliché serves to depict setting as an inert element, but Hadley renders setting as pocked with unreadable or
unresolved qualities. The metonymic allusion to structural stability is both confirmed—leading us to trust the author—and left
suspended, since we can't yet see how freely either Janie or Rachel
might operate within the confines of their traditional functional
status. We don't know yet how plot might bear out the figurative
implications of the tension between seeming and real, between
structures dense and structures delicately woven, between the
appearance of tameness and the underlying reality.

A good writer also incorporates cultural context as setting, in
an equally economic way. Janie and Rachel have taken their children to the beach in part to escape their husbands for a few
hours. Both women do only "a token amount of work outside
the home." Janie's husband, Vince, is a set designer, and Rachel's
husband, Sam, is working on a novel, artistic leanings that challenge the women's absorption in "the warm vegetable soup of
motherhood, which surprisingly resembles their own mothers'
lives, thirty years ago."[14] Rachel tells Janie that Kieran dropped
in recently when Sam wasn't home, and she confides that even
though Kieran seems "such a serious sort of intellectual—you
know, only interested in talking about Habermas or Adorno
or something"—he helped her bathe her children and seemed

smitten by her domestic competence.[15] The staging of this dialogue matters: in time-honored female tradition, mothers confide secrets within earshot of their children, who interrupt them to make demands, yet Rachel's arch intellectual allusions offer a pointed kind of distancing, and a woman of her mother's generation would never dream of her maternal role as a sexually alluring novelty. As Rachel casually contemplates an affair with Kieran, she's ensconced in a setting that belies the ironic stance she shares with Janie. That's a provocative inconsistency.

The women return home to discover that Kieran has made another surprise visit and will spend the night. Because of a sick child, Rachel has to bow out of an adult trek to the local pub, leaving Janie, titillated by Kieran's attentiveness to Rachel, with the opportunity for sexual adventure. Hadley galvanizes details of setting as the story reaches its climax. Instead of being disappointed at her missed chance, Rachel savors the solitude in which to gloat over Kieran's interest in her. Having put her children to bed, she steps out into the garden: "The light is draining imperceptibly out of the sky; the velvety plum color of the copper beech is drinking up darkness. Yellow light from inside the house glitters on the stone flags of the patio." It's a nice trick to defamiliarize sexual arousal via a character's response to setting, and Rachel's feelings are evident in her intense awareness of color at this moment and in the acute attention she pays to infinitesimal stirrings of life: "Moths come visiting Rachel's chive flowers and nicotiana in a pale blur of movement. A bat stirs the air with a beat of its leathery wings."[16] Reinforced by the slow transition from dusk to dark, the delicate refinement of her perceptions echoes the earlier description of the "lattice work" of the leaves.

In a contrast heightened by sequencing, when Janie and Kieran fall behind Sam and Vince as they walk home from the pub on an unlit road, they are "plunged into a darkness deep and complete and astonishing to these city folk." "Walking into that darkness," Hadley tells us, "feels as counterintuitive as walking into a wall."[17] What a pay-off for the opening image of the massive sea walls, and what a contrast with Rachel's response to nightfall. At this moment, when they can't even see each other, Janie and Kieran impulsively kiss; what they have really plunged into is relief from the need to discriminate between seeming and real. But their simplifying, coarse sensual pleasure is in tension with Rachel's lyrical discernment of fine gradients of sensation only a page earlier. That one woman can so easily be substituted for another also brings to bear the story's repeated allusions to historical eras, to the sameness that coexists with impermanence and change.

Setting proves useful in the resolution too. Rachel lies awake still savoring "a glorious abundant tide of secret possibility," while in an echo of "messy family camp," Kieran lies awake feeling repelled by the smells, sights, and sounds of Rachel's domestic life, "wondering how families manage in this awful perpetual twilight of false sleep."[18] Especially at the beginning and end of the story, Hadley has been careful to select for those elements of setting that will have synecdochic and metonymic force, helping her to focus the reader's attention yet open up the questions that the story asks about the deceptive patterning of both desire and domestic tameness, about what might be washed away by the "glorious" tide.

You could simply superimpose Hadley's strategies on a story you're composing or revising, and the setting would be dynamically in play with other elements of story. Open with a few paragraphs depicting setting. Via metonymy, single out one aspect of setting and then a second one that is in tension with the first. Include a "motion shot" that involves your perspective character. At the climax of the story or chapter, exploit another element of setting that echoes the opening but doesn't reuse the same details, and in the last paragraph include at least one word or image associated with the description in the opening paragraphs, as Hadley uses *tide* and *twilight*. In practicing these strategies you'd be exploiting principles that apply to any dramatic configuration of setting and story. "Motion shots" can reveal your characters *and* their inconsistencies through their interaction with setting. Metonymy and synecdoche can be used not just to compress information but to cue readers to hidden tension, especially if you focus on details that possess a tension orientation—that tap into the contradictions and friction inherent in the plot.

Staging and subtext

An artist I know currently teaches sculpture to animators at a well-known film-animation studio. She was hired because the studio's animators tended to draw cartoon figures that floated oddly against the background on film. They were failing to take into account the need to convey volume in space—how the pressure on a weight-bearing foot compresses flesh and distorts perspective, how surface resistance and gravity affect motion in three dimensions, and so on. A writer also must emphasize how the character leaves an imprint, where environment resists her as she moves. The dynamic interplay between character and setting depends on staging, as when Hadley contrasts Rachel's contemplative solitary scene in the garden with Janie and Kieran's impulsive kiss in the dark. In *The Art of Subtext* Charles Baxter defines staging as "the poetry of action and setting when it evokes the otherwise unstated," and its theatrical connotation is appropriate to the sensually realized world of fiction: "Staging in fiction involves putting characters in specific strategic positions in the scene so that some unvoiced nuance is revealed. Staging may include how close or how far away the characters are from each other, what their particular gestures and facial expressions might be at moments of dramatic emphasis, exactly how their words are said, and what props appear inside or outside.... Certainly it involves the writer in the stagecraft of her characters just as a director would, blocking out the movement of the actors."[19]

In Gina Berriault's short-short story "The Woman in the Rose-Colored Dress," staging focuses the reader's response without calling attention to itself as artifice. Told by a young girl, the story is set at a party she attends with her parents; Mary discovers that her father is having an affair with a woman she meets at the party and must contend with knowing what her mother does not. The story does not have section breaks, but its scenes are staged to allude to hidden tension. In the first scene Mary's mother encourages her to pretend that this is a party for her own thirteenth birthday, "one only we two knew about." The daughter might, at least unconsciously, chafe at playing pretend; she wanders away from her mother and goes "alone into the rooms where the strangers were."[20] Mary registers that she's getting looks from men, but she doesn't know how to respond; the game of flirtation, still mysterious to her, parallels the childish game her mother wanted her to play. When her father arrives late to the party, Mary holds his hand and wanders around with him until they settle in a room by themselves. Then a young woman enters the room "timidly, as if she needed to ask a favor," and though the father introduces her to his daughter, he orders Mary to leave.[21] But she can't, just as he can't hide his sexual feelings for the young woman who sits beside him on the sofa, a startlingly quick shift in the power dynamic of *this* game of seduction. Vanquished, the father strides off, leaving Mary to take his place on the sofa and sit in silence with his young mistress. When Mary goes in search of her mother, she finds her in a crowd that has gathered around a pianist playing a tune about lovers who meet with one ridiculous disaster after another. The adults, playing a childish game of sing-along, are "laughing on cue," ranged against the antisocial nature of passion, and in the story's last sentence Mary responds to this collective posturing: "no matter how many joined together at that piano and everywhere else to belittle lovers, I knew that all attempts would end in failure."[22]

In the course of just four pages, staging subliminally enacts the question of shifting allegiance so beautifully surfaced in the story's last paragraph. Figure 7.1 diagrams this staging of scenes

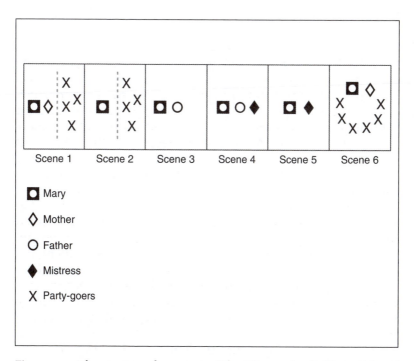

Figure 7.1 The staging of scenes in "The Woman in the Rose-Colored Dress"
Illustrator: Alan Stonebraker

and suggests how it helps to shape subtext by emphasizing exclusive pairings, ending with the daughter's attempt to rejoin her mother (ostensibly her fellow victim) in a circle of adults, which triggers the realization that her allegiance lies with the lovers. Berriault could not have earned the big statement of her ending without such careful staging of pairs, which complicates the daughter's choice by fluidly aligning her with each member of the love triangle, superimposing the roles of protected child, betrayed innocent, and sexual transgressor before it deposits her in the circle of social consensus. When you're stuck with a story or chapter, try a diagram like the one in Figure 7.1. Because non-verbal arrangement of your materials defamiliarizes your process, it can lead to unexpected insights. And it exercises your mimetic muscles because it focuses your attention on enacting meaning.

Staging dialogue

In order to generate a high ratio of subtext to text, dialogue must be synecdochic—compressed in ways that suggest developing conflict, past history, and so on—and metaphoric or metonymic, with its stated topic substituting for an unstated one with which it is entangled by powerful associations. If you choose the right explicit topic as a starting point, your dialogue will naturally open onto figurative possibility. To return to the example of Carver's "Careful," Lloyd's clogged ear poses a problem that engages his wife despite her intention to keep her distance, substituting for the whole of her past entanglement with his addiction, and their negotiations trigger her recognition that she can't solve the underlying problem. When you get stalled in writing dialogue that explicates your characters' desires, try giving your characters some concrete task to distract them and the reader from the real issue at stake. If the task is well chosen (metonymic) and well staged, it will suggest what remains unspoken. And it will root your characters in their bodies, so that they are not merely talking heads issuing balloons of speech.

In the beach dialogue between Janie and Rachel in Hadley's "Sunstroke," tension is heightened by staging—they discuss sex within earshot of their children, surrounded by the expected paraphernalia of mommyhood. Toni Morrison's *Jazz* offers another fine illustration of how a writer can exploit staging and props in dialogue. The novel opens shortly after Violet has appeared at the funeral of a teenaged girl, Dorcas, and stabbed the corpse in its open casket. Not only was her husband, Joe, having an affair with Dorcas, he murdered her in a fit of jealous rage; though there were witnesses, no one in his community has been willing to turn him in to the police. In the wake of the murder Joe's grief and remorse only deepen Violet's heartache and bitterness, and the novel explores the rift between them and their efforts to heal it.

In chapters 3 and 4 of *Jazz,* Morrison records a series of visits that Violet has made to the home of Dorcas's guardian, Alice Manfred, in the months following Dorcas's funeral. If it strains credulity to imagine that Alice would open the door to the woman who defaced her niece's corpse, Morrison enters Alice's perspective in chapter 3 to explore the core instability that motivates Alice. The middle-class Alice holds both Joe and Violet in contempt ("And Alice Manfred knew the kind of Negro that couple was: the kind she trained Dorcas away from. The embarrassing kind."[23]), yet she has failed to keep Dorcas from Joe. Because her notions of right behavior are challenged by Violet's impulse to violence as well as Joe's, she has been scouring the newspapers for tales of women who, unlike Alice, act out their rage: "Black women were armed; black women were dangerous and the less money they had the deadlier the weapon they chose."[24] Alice has compelling reasons to hear what Violet has to say.

In her first few visits the slowly unraveling Violet appears with her clothes in tatters; prim distaste prompts Alice to mend the unsightly hem of Violet's coat. At the conclusion of chapter 4, their last encounter depends on props for its full effect. On this visit, depicted from Violet's perspective rather than Alice's, Violet arrives as Alice is ironing clothes, a task that, like sewing, metonymically suggests traditional female work (emotional as well as physical mending) and literally reinforces the reader's awareness of the distance between Alice and Violet, who came of age doing a man's work. A prop launches conversation when Violet, watching Alice iron, says, "I used to love that stuff," and Alice automatically registers that Violet used to chew the crunchy starch used for ironing. Next, the iron "hissed at the damp fabric," a simple indication of the passage of time (in an awkward silence) and a reminder to attend to the dangerous implement in Alice's hand, another metonymic touch.

If dialogue is often conceived of as a battle for control, it just as often culminates in connection, and in either case, the writer needs to sustain tension about which direction the conversation will ultimately take. The props in this scene—the iron, the starch—underscore the distance between Alice and Violet, and yet we also witness via the same props the potential for connection. Only after the iron hisses does Violet venture another observation: "You iron like my grandmother. Yoke last." When Alice responds, "That's the test of a first-class ironing," she's giving ground, which leads Violet to offer a confidence about her youth that references class distinctions: "We picked cotton, chopped wood, plowed. I never knew what it was to fold my hands. This here is as close as I ever been to watching my hands do nothing." Whatever their differences, both women have been made idle by loss, the emotional or literal absence of the person they meant to care for, and this metonymic allusion provokes Alice to answer with what seems to be a threat about Joe: "He'll do it again, you know." "In that case I'd better throw him out now," Violet says, but Alice roughly reminds her of the empty-handedness of their mutual bereavement: "Then what?"[25]

Because of the shift to Violet's perspective for this chapter, dramatic tension peaks at this moment. A few pages before, Violet recalled her mother's suicide, and her own struggle not to succumb to the same passive despair crucially informs her response when Alice urges her to forgive Joe: "You got anything left to you to love, anything at all, do it."[26] Incredulously, Violet asks, "Don't fight?" and Alice launches into a list of all the future mistresses Violet might have to attack, women just as poor as Violet, just as vulnerable as the orphaned Dorcas and the assailants Alice has read about in the newspaper. In the midst of this rhetorical flight, Alice notices Violet staring and looks down to see that she has burned a black and smoking stain into the collar of the shirt she's ironing. "Shit!" Alice yelps, and both the unladylike vulgarity and the ruined shirt dramatize how far Violet has drawn her outside herself.[27] Then the two women begin to laugh. The staging of this brief passage of dialogue makes maximum use of props to convey the passage of time, portray the characters in physical proximity, metonymically suggest what's at stake in ways that heighten uncertainty about outcome, and literally trigger that outcome.

To underscore the usefulness of synecdoche and metonymy in constructing setting, staging, and dialogue, I'd like to return to the analogy with Degas's horses. The job of the artist is to give us a horse that we recognize—but as we've never seen it before. If we compare Morrison's *Jazz* with Fitzgerald's *Great Gatsby* we recognize commonly handled signifiers of setting in the music, the speakeasies, the fashions. Both writers honor objective reality. But the particularity of each writer gives us on the one hand the Jazz Age of a work-worn Harlem resident and on the other, that of a man striving to imitate the hedonistic upper-class, and in this we discover the multiplicity of truth, a patterning of experience, a glimpse of reality that is valid *because* it's slanted. Partiality, in both senses of the word, is crucial to artistic persuasion.

8

Patterns of Imagery

Story logic demands a particular kind of precision. The writer's task can be compared to that of a photographer immersing photographic paper in a tray of developing fluid. Slowly the picture begins to develop. If the photographer removes the paper too soon, the picture she gets is a murky blur. But if she leaves it in for the "exactly right" time, she gets a photo in which every single detail is clearly delineated. The fiction writer, unlike the photographer, has to yank the paper out of that bath somewhere between these two poles, at the "inexactly right" moment when the reader can intuit whatever's missing or blurred based on those details that *have* emerged in sharp relief. Because a single image can suggest so much that isn't there on the page and exponentially more associations when we connect it to other images and to the action, patterns of imagery help writers to hint at the hidden tension enacted by plot.

The first effect any image exerts on a reader is to call for a particular kind of attentiveness. Poet Robert Hass has pointed out that the image isolates an aspect of reality and consequently always has "a sense of absence about it...as if, the more palpable it is, the more some immense subterranean displacement seems to be working in it; as if at the point of truest observation the visible and invisible exerted enormous counterpressure."[1] In "Barn Burning" William Faulkner depicts the main character's father, a poor sharecropper, dressed in a "formal coat of broadcloth which had once been black but which had now that friction-glazed greenish cast of the bodies of old house flies."[2] The sensual accuracy of the image denotes a vivid visual reality, which is more than enough, yet the density of the image also offers "subterranean displacement," evoking qualities and emotional tones not visible. The formal coat might metonymically suggest a preacher. Its worn condition references an ongoing process, not just a static visual, with "friction-glazed" suggesting the wearing effects of this man's life. The metaphor that compares the coat's color to the "greenish cast" of houseflies transfers connotations of staleness and decay. All these associations are held in the mind simultaneously, and though we can trace them, we don't have to in order to feel the power of the image.

An image invokes first an emotional response and second a tentative and exploratory questioning of the qualities conferred by the writer's choices. Faulkner takes advantage of both metonymy and metaphor to achieve this. All tropes have the useful capacity to compress many associations, and metaphor and simile serve Hass's principle of visible and invisible exerting "counterpressure" by stressing an unexpected likeness. As Stephen Dobyns suggests in "Metaphor and the Authenticating Act of Memory," "every metaphor is based on withheld information that the comparison given by the metaphor tries to uncover. Implied in each metaphor is the question of how the image is like the object. In the act of answering this question the reader becomes a participant by authenticating the comparison from his or her own memory and/or imagination."[3]

Every image comes equipped with a built-in paradox, because it both aims the reader's attention in a highly specific way and generates a profusion of implications and associations. The power of a single image is exponentially increased by its recurrence or its relation to a set of images; both strategies enable the writer to downplay certain associations and emphasize others. For example, in "Barn Burning" Faulkner employs recurring images of the sharecropper's formal black coat until his righteousness becomes firmly linked with that of a fire-and-brimstone preacher.

More than mere ornamentation, imagery contributes to the dynamic effect of plot, tugging and pulling at literal meaning in ways that contribute to the sine qua non of fiction, the cumulative building of tension. Because we are intuitively metaphoric and metonymic thinkers, readers will register the impact of images that cluster according to common areas of reference even when they don't stop to analyze exactly how this colors the literal action. In Raymond Carver's story "What We Talk about When We Talk about Love," four people sit drinking at a table as daylight dwindles, and even the most sparing references to the failing light imbue their encounter with connotations of dimmed vision. Images of encasement proliferate in this story, focusing attention on the question of how each of the characters assumes some defense against the risks attendant on love. Part of the fun of reading the story lies in registering how subtly the images align with one another to form sets—a beekeeper's suit, a knight's armor, and a body cast all provide protection, for example—and in being provoked by the ways in which these correspondences reconfigure the associations we bring to the story, since the knight in shining armor is ordinarily associated with the ideal of chivalric love, not vulnerability or immobility. Cumulatively, these images of encasement interact with the images of dwindling light to suggest decline. The images not only speak to each other but also confirm the tension implicit in the action, in which a character who professes confusion at how medieval knights contended with the weight of their armor can also speak enviously of the beekeeper's suit.

Patterns of imagery enable a writer to recombine figurative implications in infinitely varied ways. In their relation to the action, such patterns can underscore the tension of literal events or generate implications that counter the literal tension. Where the images in Carver's story reinforce building tension, degenerating from knights in shining armor to beekeeper's suits as the character's defenses increasingly fail them, imagistic and literal tension diverge in James Joyce's "Araby," with sacramental images and allusions supporting the young narrator's notion that he is on a quest for his beloved even as he moves toward the revelation that he is merely making a trip to a shabby bazaar in search of a tawdry souvenir to bring her. When images cluster in sets, they also interact with other sets of images to shape an opposition or continuum the reader would not have foreseen, transfer qualities from one set to another, or enforce parallels between seemingly unlike things.

How patterns of imagery inform literal tension

A more detailed analysis of a specific short story can illustrate the complex interaction between patterns of imagery and plot. In Helena María Viramontes's magical realist short story "The Moths," the child narrator recounts the death of her grandmother from stomach cancer. This rebellious girl gets cursed at and beaten by her father for her reluctance to attend Mass (so she can save her "goddamn sinning soul"), and she fights constantly with her sisters, who behave in more suitably feminine ways. Because of her clumsiness at female tasks and her readiness to use her fists, the girl is saddled with the nickname "Bull Hands." Whenever she goes to the local market, the narrator is drawn to the chapel across the street, yet she rebels at her parents' demand that she attend Sunday Mass and detours to her grandmother's house, where she's enlisted to help crush roasted chiles in a *molcajete,* a delightfully aggressive substitute for the emblematic domestic task of cooking a meal. She also helps her grandmother plant cuttings of avocado, sweet potato, cilantro, hierbabuena, and chayote vines, started off in Hills Brothers coffee cans before being transplanted to the yard. At her grandmother's house the girl gratifies her desire to strike out at the world by puncturing drainage holes in the bottoms of the coffee cans with a hammer and nail; under her grandmother's eyes, one gray and one brown, the narrator feels "safe and guarded and not alone. Like God was supposed to make you feel."[4]

In the present action the narrator spends her visits caring for her dying grandmother, who has nursed the girl through several ailments with folk remedies, once rubbing her hands with a balm made of "dried moth wings." Her grandmother touches and points rather than talks; her mother talks only when she's so sad or angry that she's crying; and the narrator repeats these grievances to herself "like rosary prayers."[5] When Abuelita dies, the narrator is alone with her in her house. Ceremoniously, "with the sacredness of a priest preparing his vestments," the narrator prepares to wash the body.[6] Finally, she lowers her grandmother into a tub of steaming water and rocks her body as moths emerge from the woman's mouth.

The images in this story cluster around certain common areas of reference: eyes, hands, mouth, church, and plants and folk cures. Yet each of these categories "cross-references" or overlaps with others, something like the Venn diagrams children study in grade-school math, in which separate sets of numbers share at least one element with another set. (For example, only some odd numbers are divisible by three.) Figure 8.1 roughly approximates the image sets in "The Moths" in the form of a Venn diagram.

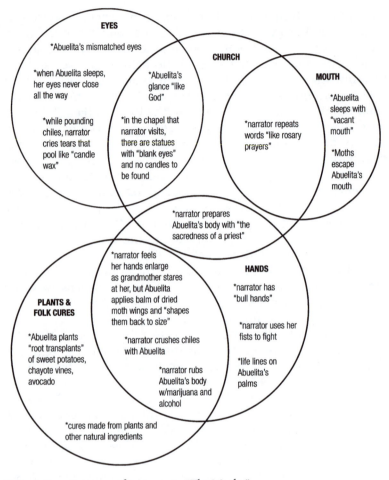

Figure 8.1   Patterns of imagery in "The Moths"
Illustrator: Alan Stonebraker

As the diagram suggests, images can't be neatly peeled off from actions. Many of the images in "The Moths" are embedded in actions that betray the narrator's conflict between rebellion and submission. This tension is implicit within each image set. The narrator has trouble meeting Abuelita's "mismatched" grey and brown eyes, yet Abuelita is the only adult who makes her feel safe. The images that cluster in the church set suggest the narrator's resistance to the solace it offers, yet she mirrors religious ritual in her handling of her grandmother's body. The greatest degree of tension is embodied in the images of hands, which have the power to inflict hurt or to heal.

The correspondences between sets of images complicate literal tension in many ways. Folk cures for the body, associated with the plants Abuelita grows, and church cures for the soul constitute separate sets, yet these are linked by the "hands" set, so closely identified with the narrator. (The "laying on of hands" literally embodies the church's symbolic power to cure the soul.) Figurative tension is heightened by overlaps that belie the surface opposition between the two sources and kinds of healing (the two cultural traditions). Abuelita does not offer consoling words but conveys sympathy in assigning her granddaughter the task of crushing the chiles, which the girl feels she can "scrape hard to destroy the guilt" for disappointing her parents.[7] If the older tradition might accommodate a fierce female, it can't make her guilt disappear. When the narrator repeats her mother's grievances "like rosary prayers," the simile links her mother's helplessness with the church and colors the narrator's action. She is testing not only this kind of solace but also her affinity for her mother. Fighting against constraints jeopardizes connection, and there's no longer a simple dichotomy between rebellion and submission.

At the end of the story the flurry of moths escaping from Abuelita's mouth reconfigures the relations among the image sets. Creatures of the dark even if they are drawn to light, they revise and disrupt the images that link vision with spiritual clarity. They are not only a symbol of the soul departing the body but also an embodiment of female muteness—the unspoken sorrows of the grandmother, of the narrator's mother (whose husband blames her for her rebellious daughter), and of the narrator herself. Although the fluttering moths evoke strong identification with her female forebears, this does not resolve the problem of muteness. The story's tension is coiled in its final image, in which the *visible* beauty of moths "fluttering to light" strains against the *invisible* reality of their metamorphosis, which depends on a destructive feeding, the capacity to "slowly eat the spirit up."[8]

In the best fiction, patterns of imagery heighten this sense of the relationship between the visible action and its invisible meaning(s), and they do so through subtle associations, seeming to occur at the periphery of the reader's field of vision, so that their cumulative effect is an ah! response of astonished recognition. A pattern of imagery can accomplish what a single image cannot in terms of suggesting the unspoken, much like a jazz musician's elaborations and riffs can teasingly evoke a familiar melody by incorporating just a few bars, sounding the notes the musician doesn't actually play.

Chekhov's story "Gooseberries" offers an elegant example of this and a nice contrast with "The Moths," because its images, rather than suggesting submerged continuities, strike dissonant notes and seem to unravel the implications of the plot. The story begins as Ivan and Burkin, on a trek through the countryside, take refuge at the estate of their friend Alekhin when it begins to rain. After they have bathed in the river and settled comfortably in Alekhin's house, Ivan tells his friends a moralistic story about his brother Nikolai, who became so obsessed with his dream of owning an estate where he could grow gooseberries that he sacrificed every last scrap of human feeling to achieve this aim. While Ivan talks, the beautiful servant girl Pelagea wanders in and out of the room, provisioning the guests. Ivan goes on to say that all human happiness depends on the silent misery of others, and "there ought to be a man with a hammer behind the door of every happy man to remind him by his constant knocks that that there are unhappy people."[9] He finishes by urging his friends to take action: "Don't *you* let your conscience be lulled to sleep!...Do good!"[10] But in the cozy room his friends find it "dreary" to listen to him. At story's end Ivan and Burkin share a bedroom; there's a "strong smell of stale tobacco" from the pipe Ivan left on the table, but Burkin lies awake a long time, wondering "where the stifling smell came from." In the last line, "The rain tapped on the windowpanes all night."[11]

Over the course of the story the actions and images counter and qualify one another, like counterpointed melodies that fail to deliver anticipated harmonies. Even the sour gooseberries Nikolai cherishes can't be read as an unequivocal symbol of the unsavory outcome of his selfish dreams, for his brother Ivan suffers as much or more from a bitter rejection of Nikolai's delusion. The rain that forces Burkin and Ivan to take shelter with Alekhin acquires a specific history within the story. As they arrive at Alekhin's estate, the two men observe workers going about in the rain holding sacks over their heads, an image that prefigures Ivan's diatribe about the will to ignore misery, yet the action counters this association when the three men bathe in the river and Ivan turns up his face to the rain to shout repeatedly, "Ah, my God!"[12] While the rain conjures specific associations with the misery of life, it also plays a part in Ivan's unpolluted joy as he swims, and so this duality leads the reader to question the moral of Ivan's story. For those who might stubbornly persist in taking Ivan's tale at face value, that bitter smell haunts the ending, forcing the reader to cast back over the story in search of buried clues.

In Figure 8.2 a Venn diagram of the imagery in "Gooseberries" reveals a different structural pattern than that of "The Moths." (The risk in supplying a Venn diagram for either story is that it might seem to reduce complexity to a systematized neatness; these diagrams are meant to offer a tool for investigating what operates subliminally.) Rather than a series of roughly equivalent sets with small areas of overlap, this diagram shows many seemingly self-contained image "subsets." Only by abstracting some common qualities suggested by the images can we derive two larger, *implicit* sets (images associated with misery, images associated with pleasure) that intersect with each subset. It is no accident that each subset is united by one of the five senses: the body's unconflicted response to sensual pleasure is at issue in the story. Yet even sleep and wakefulness, both bodily necessities, conform to this polarity. The "gravitational pull" of each larger set is countered by the stubborn coherence of each subset, so that the stability of either is called into question.

The critical key to this disequilibrium is literally peripheral, seen out of the corner of the eye, in mere phrases that note the reappearance of Pelagea. She is a literal, if minor, actor in the story, yet she also functions as a *visual* image, thus invoking the fifth sense as well. Recurring images offer what amounts to an exact rhyme, and they occur in this order: "The beauteous Pelagea, looking very soft and delicate, brought them towels and soap"[13]; "the beautiful Pelagea, smiling softly, stepped noiselessly over the carpet with her tray of tea and preserves"[14]; "the fair Pelagea was now going noiselessly to and fro"[15]; "There was a pleasant smell of freshly laundered sheets from the wide, cool beds which the fair Pelagea had made up for them."[16] In the unstable force field of this story Pelagea never appears without her stable honorific, and Chekhov twice emphasizes the *noiseless* movements of a servant girl in a story in which Ivan declares

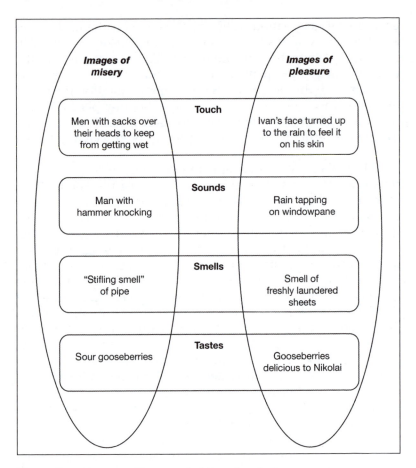

Figure 8.2   Patterns of imagery in "Gooseberries"
Illustrator: Alan Stonebraker

that "those who are happy can only enjoy themselves because the unhappy bear their burdens in silence, and but for this silence happiness would be impossible."[17] Allusions to silent misery *and* beauty coalesce around the figure of Pelagea. In addition, the writer draws our attention to the appealing scent of freshly laundered sheets just before the story's closing moment, when Burkin notes a "stifling smell." Sequencing matters hugely in the arrangement of images just as it does in the order of the events of a plot. Here, it establishes strong tension between beckoning pleasure (associated with the sleep Ivan begs his friends to resist) and a nagging disturbance.

The story's pattern of imagery counters any reductionist either/or reading of the action. Is the source of the bad smell Ivan's moralistic tale or the indifference of his listeners? Does conscience demand from us a bitter clarity? Does Ivan's tale trouble us because it fails to account for the joys of life—the sensual pleasure of swimming in the rain or watching beautiful Pelagea—that do *not* depend on the misery of others? But what might Pelagea's silence hide? Does our love of comfort hinder us from grappling with moral responsibility? But isn't the body a conduit for both? Just as Pelagea moves "to and fro" between seemingly exclusive states, images of rain also counter antithesis. If the rain tapping on the windowpanes at story's end echoes the knocking of the man with a hammer, it offers a disruptive off-rhyme because of the gentle sound that it makes. It spans both Ivan's pleasure during his swim and the misery referenced in his tale, offering a natural reminder, not a human interpretation, of their coexistence. A rich and provocative reading of the story is made possible by the duality of its images and by their interplay, dependent on both dissonant notes (off-rhymes) and sequencing.

Permutation in patterns of imagery

Although the principles remain the same, patterns of imagery accrue still more figurative detritus over the longer course of a novel's plot. Changed contexts and configurations enable images to weld the literal consequences of the plot to the progression of its thematic concerns, linking the formula of conflict-crisis-new crisis to idea. The central concern of *The Hours,* by Michael Cunningham, can be illuminated by tracing the evolution of the imagery in three key parallel actions. The novel's title is taken from the working title of Virginia Woolf's novel *Mrs. Dalloway.* Its plot dramatizes just a few hours in the lives of three women, each living in a different era: Virginia Woolf; a fifties housewife named Laura Brown; and a contemporary New Yorker, Clarissa, nicknamed Mrs. Dalloway after the character in Woolf's novel. Virginia begins a novel in her few hours, Laura bakes a cake for her husband's birthday, and Clarissa plans a party in honor of her friend Richard. Within each strand of the plot, a suicide takes place or is contemplated; each of these women in some way contends with the dilemma of living *as if* life has meaning in the face of death.

The three key scenes link the three strands of the plot by reworking figurative images and diction so that we can read the action as symbolic. In the first scene Laura bakes a cake for her husband's birthday, squeezing from a pastry tube a border of yellow rosebuds and then writing "Happy Birthday Dan" in white icing. But she feels disappointed with the result of her efforts: "She'd hoped (she admits to herself) it would look more lush and beautiful, more wonderful. This cake she's produced feels small, not just in the physical sense but as an entity.... Its clumsy aspects (the scattering of crumbs caught in the icing, the squashed appearance of the 'n' in 'Dan,' which got too close to a rose) are part of its charm."[18] Unable to talk herself into feeling contented ("Why did she put the roses on first, when any idiot would have known to begin with the message?"),[19] Laura eventually dumps the cake and makes another attempt. Because this novel is replete with allusions to another novel, the reader readily recognizes why the cake receives so much attention: within the proscribed limits of domesticity, Laura strives to arrange something with an artist's impulse.

The second scene occurs in the very next chapter, sequenced so that a reader will readily register connections. Virginia Woolf's sister, Vanessa, pays a visit with her children, who have found a dying bird. Vanessa's daughter, Angelica, insists on holding a funeral for the bird, and Virginia becomes absorbed in helping her niece arrange "a bed in which the thrush can die."[20] They make a mound of grass and arrange yellow roses along its circumference, "a rough circle of rosebuds, thorny stems, and leaves." This image echoes the trim of yellow rosebuds on Laura's cake, and figurative diction also reinforces the concern with second-guessing a possibly disappointing arrangement: Virginia "almost protests that the bird should be laid down first, the roses arranged around its body."[21] The dead bird "seems to have wanted to make the smallest possible package of itself. Its eye, a perfect black bead, is open, and its gray feet, larger than you'd expect them to be, are curled in on themselves."[22]

This second scene is linked to the first by quiet repetition of certain elements (including an emphasis on smallness), but the imagery also permutes the suggestions of the earlier scene by incorporating new comparisons. In emphasizing death, the image of the bird in its circle of roses offers a pun on Laura's devotion to baking a cake for a *birth*day. The desire to arrange is now connected with death as well as aesthetic impulse and balanced against the longing to retreat or surrender: Virginia would "like to lie down" on this "modest circlet of thorns and flowers; this wild deathbed."[23] But her niece, once the arrangement is complete, "wants to dispatch the bird as quickly as possible and go hunting for its nest."[24] Is this beautiful deathbed a means of contending with death or a self-deluding gesture, one that the healthy child dismisses as a diversion while her aunt lingers to contemplate it?

The third scene in this trio, occurring much later in the novel, asks us again to revise our understanding of both its predecessors. Clarissa's friend Richard, suffering from AIDS-induced dementia, jumps from a window to his death. Clarissa descends several flights of stairs to the light well where the body lies, passing through a "stale yellow box of a room" where a door bears a "Grateful Dead decal, a skull crowned with roses." Obeying the impulse to restore Richard's dignity, she tugs at the robe that has flown up over his head to expose his nakedness—she *rearranges* what she has found. Like the bird, Richard has grey feet, shod in "grey felt slippers," and when Clarissa tugs at his robe, she exposes an open eye set in the shattered, bloodied mess of his skull, a brutal rewriting of the still, peaceful image of the dead bird. Richard lies not on a bed of grass but on a "pallet of concrete" "amid shards of glass," the remnants of a shattered beer bottle.[25] This scene offers a sly recombination of shared ingredients—the yellow rosebuds, the grey feet and open eye, ugly vs. beautiful arrangement—as well as comic allusion in the Grateful Dead skull. Here Cunningham artfully counts on our anticipation of notes he doesn't play. He doesn't have to repeat the verb *arrange* because recurring images and figurative diction accomplish it for him, and "pallet" (a small hard bed) conjures its near-synonym, "deathbed."

If our attention is narrowed to the signal qualities of arrangement, birth/death, and smallness, successive permutations complicate our interpretation of these elements. The disturbing mix of comic and degrading details in this last scene counters the solemnity of Virginia's funeral rites for the dead thrush and revives the threat of triviality suggested in Laura's concern with the cake. Sequencing matters here too, since Cunningham describes Virginia's dignified funerary ritual *before* depicting Richard, landed on a heap of trash rather than a beautiful bed. This image calls into question the truthfulness of Virginia's arrangement for the dead bird and insistently hisses the possibility that death is simply meaningless. (The novel offers a lovely bridge between these two images when Virginia, some time after she has arranged the bird, imagines her husband dumping the dead thrush in the garbage.) The impulse to arrange is reinforced by related images but also revised by them, lent the presumptive glory of art by Virginia's response and the insignificance assigned to domesticity by Laura's, while Clarissa quite literally attempts to cover up something horrible. In any case, what is the efficacy of this impulse?

Because these permutations sustain tension rather than reconciling it, the reader must at least momentarily live within the realm of conflict. Since the plot of the novel bears out these figurative effects, the cleverness with which shared elements are rearranged isn't simply cleverness, though Cunningham's gamesmanship does raise the thorny question of when enough is enough. If the reader registers a pattern of imagery as too obvious or too neat in its symmetries, the writer sacrifices the essential power of the image, which weds emotion to perception and radiates meaning in many directions, not just one.

Thinking in images is the necessary prerequisite for contemplating their relation to one another. In fact, as Italo Calvino has noted in his essay "Visibility," images tend to engender other images, a process that engages the analytic mind as much as it does the imagination:

> In devising a story, therefore, the first thing that comes to my mind is an image that for some reason strikes me as charged with meaning, even if I cannot formulate this meaning in discursive or conceptual terms. As soon as the image has become sufficiently clear in my mind, I set about developing it into a story; or better yet, it is the images themselves that develop their own implicit potentialities, the story they carry within them. Around each image others come into being, forming a field of analogies, symmetries, confrontations. Into the organization of this material, which is no longer purely visual but also conceptual, there now enters my deliberate intent to give order and sense to the development of the story.[26]

This "field of analogies, symmetries, confrontations"—an acti-vated, alive pattern of imagery—comes about when you pay deeply receptive attention to your work. You're in the business of imbibing the open-ended associative logic of story, not trans-lating image into a closed logical system. This applies even to revision: if you impose tidy correspondences at this stage, the result will be overexposed symmetries or none at all.

In fiction writing, thinking concretely is the coin of the realm. So when you explore connections among images, don't abstract them too soon but be guided by the physical properties the images hold in common or in contrast. Confuse these physical properties with emotional ones. Look to the periphery for images you didn't trouble over in the first draft. Pursue multiple points of connection, as Cunningham does; in a *field* of analogies connec-tions radiate along many axes—vertical, horizontal, or diagonal. Savor images that *don't* fit within a set; they're useful to the array too. Keep questioning the draft: re-read its images, not its action, in order to pursue secrets that remain hidden from you. Take this advice literally, even if you have to color code images and figura-tive diction that bear some close relation to each other. Sketching a Venn diagram of your own work can be helpful too, because it defamiliarizes process by diverting your attention (momentarily) from linear narrative to schematic configuration. Your aim is not to affix labels but to work with something far more evanescent, the charge that images give off in relation to one another and to plot. Ultimately, even for the writer some qualities of story should remain mysterious.

9

Showing and Telling

In nearly every workshop I've taught, whether the students were gathered for a writing conference, taking creative writing as curious undergraduates, or enrolled in a graduate writing program, I have asked how many class members are familiar with the dictum "show, don't tell" and been answered with a unanimous show of hands. Nearly everyone agrees with this rule in principle, and nearly everyone routinely violates it in practice. Why does the almost universal awareness of this dictum fail to stem the tide of rampant telling in student stories? Even if it sometimes takes the form of cheating, the impulse to tell springs from a gut recognition of the genuine difficulties of storytelling. Virtually no good fiction writer does without telling in some shape or form. Even Hemingway, often credited for fostering an aesthetic of showing, relies easily and casually on telling:

> Nick loved his father but hated the smell of him and once when he had to wear a suit of his father's underwear that had gotten too small for his father it made him feel sick and he took it off and put it under two stones in the creek and said that he had lost it.[1]

> They had a sound basis of union. Margot was too beautiful for Macomber to divorce her and Macomber had too much money for Margot ever to leave him.[2]

In the first example a simple bit of telling firmly establishes a contradiction; consider how much space Hemingway would have to devote to showing unequivocally that Nick loved his father and how much force he gains by pairing this with a visceral hatred of his smell. More than economy is served by the close link between two sure statements that are difficult to reconcile; we're primed to read for tension in the showing that follows. In the second example the juxtaposition of the first sentence and the second generates irony: a "sound basis of union" must, it seems, be a situation in which both parties are trapped. Good telling does not merely summarize information but shapes its unstated implications, just as good showing does.

Joseph Conrad once said that his aim as a writer was to "render the highest kind of justice to the visible universe, by bringing to light the truth, manifold and one, underlying its every aspect." While a writer must make a primary appeal to the senses, this may not be enough to bring to light what lies beneath the surface, "the stress and passion within the core of each convincing moment."[3] Since no writer can assume a reader's automatic sympathy for his view of things, the practical difficulty of determining what to show is compounded by the technical challenge of knowing when telling might counter a reader's habitual responses and direct her attention to "the stress and passion within the core." Remember Chekhov's precept that the proper inclination of a work of fiction is to trouble judgment, not to dictate it—to formulate the question correctly for this jury of one.[4] When telling violates the unspoken rules governing this manipulation, a reader will resist it. You can try any tactic you can get away with in an effort to get the reader to enter the uncharted waters of ambiguity. But no writer who wants to be taken seriously can adopt the same techniques in order to stack the deck.

Regardless of the constraints of a particular point of view, the same principles govern the relationship between showing and telling. In judging when and whether to show or tell, the one absolute rule is that you cannot tell your story's secrets but must dramatize what lies at the heart of the conflict. Because of the primary virtue of economy, direct telling that enables a writer to establish quickly the dramatic focus is effective telling. We can legitimately be told that a narrator hates her mother so long as this premise does not serve to explain the issue at stake. But while telling can economically fix meaning in this way, it can also provide the writer with the means to amplify the literal stakes in a story. Good telling tries to pass itself off as a wolf in sheep's clothing by relying on concreteness and on figurative diction and imagery; purposeful ambiguity in the telling engages the reader in exactly the kind of speculation that good showing elicits. As a further refinement the reader can be asked to reconcile discrepancies between what is shown and what is told. The meaning of a work of fiction must be the product of the reader's effort to interpret, and any possible combination of showing and telling that serves this aim is valid. Since a writer can conceivably avoid telling and rely almost exclusively on showing, even to convey unstated emotion, the interesting question is, what are the virtues of sophisticated interplay between the two?

Telling to establish intimacy with character

One of the primary virtues of telling is that it grants us privileged intimacy with a character. Readers respond to effective telling of a character's thoughts much as they do to showing, taking it as evidence of how the character perceives the world rather than as instructions from the writer. For example, this passage, which occurs early in A. L. Kennedy's third-person novel *Day*, depicts Alfred, a World War II vet haunted by traumatic memories of serving in a Royal Air Force bomber crew:

> If you couldn't keep control and stay wary, you might think anything, which was exactly the one freedom you'd avoid. You could dodge certain thoughts, corkscrew off and get yourself out of their way, but they'd still hunt you.
> *You have to watch.*
> This morning he could feel them, inside and out, bad thoughts getting clever with him, sly. They lapped like dirtied water behind his face and outside him they thickened the breeze until the surface touching him, pressing his lips, was far more quick and complex than only air. Today it had the smell of blue, warm Air-Force blue: the stink of drizzle rising up from wool and everywhere the smell of living blue: polish and hair oil and that sodding awful pinky-orange soap and Woodbines and Sweet Caporal and those other cheap ones, the ones they gave away after ops: Thames cigarettes, to flatten out the nerves.[5]

In the first paragraph we are *told* the nature of Alfred's struggle to dodge his horrific memories. Without this telling, we might not register the details provided in the third paragraph as a torment that Alfred cannot stifle—in other words, we wouldn't yet understand his dramatic predicament. And while the telling establishes this, it does so indirectly. "Corkscrew off and get yourself out of their way" offers a vivid metaphor for a frantic helplessness, and it remains to be shown why the freedom to "think anything" is dangerous. The telling in the first paragraph not only offers us an intimacy with character that could not be achieved any other way but also serves as dramatic trigger for compressed showing of the first order. The list of items equated with "Air-Force blue" stands for the oppressive memories of Alfred's war service and reiterates their randomness, suggesting how unbearable emotion fractures his ability to recollect the past in coherent terms. In this passage showing and telling are not polar opposites but an integrated method for enacting emotion.

Tension between what is told and what is shown

Even when an omniscient narrator employs telling as a firm anchor for the reader, it requires electrical charge from its relation to showing. Artfully handled, this kind of telling actually enables our further imaginative engagement in the text. We're so used to assuming that showing is the only and best way to duplicate experience that we overlook the ways in which telling can also set us up to experience dynamic contradictions in character. In *Middlemarch* George Eliot first introduces us to Fred Vincy on a morning when he has overslept, thereby keeping his mother and the servants waiting, trying to keep his breakfast warm. The omniscient narrator tells us in no uncertain terms that this young man is self-centered and lazy, "the family laggard, who found any sort of inconvenience (to others) less disagreeable than getting up when he was called."[6] But when Fred finally comes to the breakfast table, his conversation with his mother and his sister, Rosamund, is charming. They grill him about the new arrival in town, a doctor named Lydgate, whom he has recently met. Wittily, Fred frustrates their mutual desire to imagine Lydgate as an eligible suitor for Rosamond. When Fred describes Lydgate as a prig "who wants to show that he has opinions," his mother remonstrates that "doctors must have opinions." Fred retorts, "Yes, Mother, the opinions they are paid for. But a prig is a fellow who is always making you a present of his opinions."[7]

Before we know it, and against our better judgment, Fred has charmed us, and we have to adjust our initial impression of him as just a selfish, lazy creature. Eliot's telling places the reader in this dramatically potent position. Setting aside the issue of economy, one might argue that Eliot could have shown all this. However, showing would not guarantee the initial perception of Fred as a laggard (perhaps the reader also has a hard time getting out of bed in the morning), and consequently wouldn't, with certainty, place the reader in the position of having to amend an initial *judgment*.

Whenever a writer makes use of the tension between what is told and what is shown, telling functions dramatically. Conversely, telling that merely specifies the effect of dramatic showing remains inert. If a normally peaceable character argues with her mother and then rages at a driver who cuts her off in traffic, the author doesn't need to tell us "she was still so angry at her mother." Telling shouldn't be used when other strategies of indirection will do; in this instance, sequence already supplies enough clues, and furthermore, this telling closes off interpretation rather than fueling it. Not only is a reader robbed of the chance to guess accurately about the connection between the two arguments, she's deprived of the room to guess at other motives too. As we struggle with a first draft, we can get anxious about providing enough of the right clues to hidden tension, with the result that we inadvertently resolve tension that needs to remain open. Smart writers in particular fall prey to this, out of a responsible concern for the reader that they must learn to suppress. In the example from *Middlemarch* Eliot is willing to let the reader's feelings about Fred Vincy remain unresolved. A "helpful" writer might spoil everything by filling in some connection on the reader's behalf: "Fred was charming despite his laziness" or "Since charm cost him nothing, it was consistent with Fred's disregard for others."

Telling to raise the stakes in scene

Showing and telling can be orchestrated to amplify literal tension, and to examine how this informs the whole action of a work of fiction, we can turn to Nadine Gordimer's "Safe Houses." This third-person story opens with two paragraphs that establish the circumstances of the main character, a white South African revolutionary who has gone underground to evade prosecution by the apartheid government. We are told the ironies of his circumstances:

> Underground: this time, as at other times, he's aware of how unsuitably abstract a term that is. To hide away, you have to be out in the open of life; too soon and easily run to ground, holed up somewhere....
>
> ...Reading a newspaper with its daily account of the proceedings at the group trial where he is a missing accused, worrying about these comrades in arms, he tries not to feel self-congratulatory at his escape of arrest, a form of complacency dangerous to one in his position, sitting there in a bus among people he knows would be glad to hand him over to the law; but he can't suppress a little thrill, a sort of inner giggle. Perhaps this is freedom? Something secret, internal, after all? But philosophizing is another danger, in his situation, undermining the concept of freedom for which he has risked discovery and imprisonment yet again.[8]

Gordimer quickly summarizes the uneasy fit between the absolute ideals of the revolutionary and the entirely human giddiness at getting away with something, telling the premise for her story and implicitly directing our attention to the detachment her perspective character cultivates.

While riding the bus to while away his useless hours in hiding, this man comes to the rescue of a well-dressed woman he immediately identifies as "a misplaced person"; forced to take the bus home because her car broke down, she doesn't even know how to purchase a ticket from the conductor.[9] She is a member of the wealthy class he's bent on destroying, and yet when they get off the bus at the same stop, he accepts her offer of a drink as thanks for his assistance. Immediately, we are *shown* that he impulsively gives in to the "thrill" he schooled himself to "suppress" in the first paragraphs. Within the secure, gated compound of Sylvie's vast house, this man provides a false name (Harry) and makes a game of fleshing out a persona as a construction engineer who travels for his work, as Sylvie's husband does: "So he was free to transform his experience of guerilla training camps in Tanzania and Libya, his presence in the offices of an exiled High Command in cities deadened by northern snows or tropical heat, to provide exotic backdrops for his skyscrapers."[10]

The freedom that Gordimer so neatly bifurcated in the story's opening—political ideal versus personal license—now must be worked out as dramatic problem.

Because of her husband's convenient absences, Sylvie and Harry can embark on an affair. Irony is layered over irony: Sylvie complains about her husband's secretary ("I can't stand subservient people, can you—I mean, I want to shake them and get them to *stand up*—"[11]) to a man acutely aware that her luxurious life depends on brutal oppression. She presumes that Harry's circumspection, like her own, derives from purely personal motives for secrecy. Harry's assumptions about her are in turn challenged when she responds to his cover story with feeling, asking if his life is lonely and if he has a wife and children somewhere. At the end of their first meeting she asks for his phone number and then takes his hesitation as evidence he's involved with another woman: "Her gaze changed; now she was the one who was put in her place."[12] Elsewhere willing to report Harry's thoughts copiously, Gordimer relies only on showing when she depicts Harry's response to Sylvie's embarrassment. Though it also breaks the rules of living underground, he agrees to take her number rather than provide his own: "He found a ballpoint in his trouser pocket but no paper. He turned his left hand palm up and wrote the seven digits across the veins showing on the vulnerable inner side of his wrist."[13] The gesture speaks for itself, and the contrast between this showing and the telling of Harry's ironic condescension allows us to read his response as instinctive or unconscious. In other words, we glimpse his inner life. We can continue to read his behavior as thrill seeking, but motive is compounded by the carefully chosen sense detail. Through sexual intimacy Harry *will* write Sylvie into his skin, but this sexual attraction is tinged with vulnerability; his moment of sympathy neither fits within the confines of his ideology nor constitutes mere personal license.

Throughout this story showing gives us the sensuality of their affair and its satisfactions, contravening what we are told of Harry's ideological antipathy toward Sylvie's privilege. But even then the dramatic action does not mirror a bifurcated notion of freedom; tension builds as the mutually exclusive categories of political and personal prove to overlap, undermining the stable ironies by which Harry tries to live. The interplay between showing and telling in this story allows Gordimer to keep open the question that Harry believes is already firmly decided. However he might distance his life from Sylvie's, he is repeatedly forced to recognize parallels; for example, her vigilance about the affair being discovered by the servants or her husband parallels his vigilance about being underground.

Because a reader might view their affair as isolated incident that alters nothing *or* believe intimacy can conquer any division between two people, Gordimer uses telling to insist on the problematic coexistence of public and private identities for both Sylvie and Harry. At a key moment late in the story this tension peaks:

> Like him, she had her erratic moments of anguish, caused by conflict with the assertion of reality—her reality—rising within her to spoil an episode outside her life, a state without consequences. These moments found their expression as non sequitur remarks or more often as gestures, the inner scuffle breaking through in some odd physical manifestation. One night she squatted naked on the bed with her arms round her knees, clasping her curled feet tight in either hand. He was disturbed, and suppressed the reason that was sending a sucker from the root of his life: after interrogation in detention he had sat on the floor of his cell holding his feet like that, still rigid with his resistance against pain.[14]

Just as A. L. Kennedy does, Gordimer closely entwines showing with telling. "Like him" places the reader in Harry's position, acknowledging likeness across the gulf that divides them, yet the rest of the first sentence underscores his desire to dodge the full brunt of this understanding. The coldness of "odd physical manifestation" is immediately countered by the image of Sylvie clasping her curled feet; the interplay of showing and telling pulls the reader's sympathies back and forth too. Abstract idea and sensory detail are commingled when Harry's response to Sylvie squatting naked is metaphorically intensified as "a sucker from the root of his life" and paired with the parallel image of him in a detention cell. Finally, it is no accident that the word *suppressed* is used here, showing (yes, showing) that Harry has come a long way from the opening paragraphs, in which he suppressed "a little thrill." The telling that provided a premise in the initial paragraphs of the story further justifies itself by this delayed effect, which the writer has been so careful to exploit. The difficulties of reconciling personal and political reality are never resolved in this story; at the end, when Harry has been caught and awaits trial, he wonders if Sylvie would recognize him from his picture in the paper and then remembers he never saw newspapers in her house, where she thought herself "safe from the threat of him and his kind."[15]

The key to the success of telling in this passage is its density: though in many ways the telling precisely frames the situation for the reader, it never reports the obvious emotion and it steadily generates rich implication. If we are told what causes Sylvie's "erratic moments of anguish," we must infer the power of the intimacy against which Harry believes himself to be guarded, since in his presence her pain can surface unbidden. Once we discern that "state without consequences" stands for their affair, we must regard this as ironic, since the affair not only poses the literal risk of discovery for Harry but even in this moment evinces huge consequences. That Sylvie's private domestic misery can call up his suffering as a political prisoner (in descriptive lines paired in their length and in their spare detail) and thus evoke emotion that springs from the "root" of his life flies in the face of the facts by uniting these two dimensions of his existence— sympathetically. The telling in this passage could not impress us if the showing were not so good, while the full dramatic effect of showing could not be realized without telling that highlights the dissonance between a nonverbal connection (which by definition can admit no lies) and the social identities that work against connection.

As a counterpart to showing, good telling asks the reader to do yeoman's work in interpreting clues, especially by highlighting strategic gaps that the reader must fill in imaginatively in relation to other clues provided in the text. Like an evocative image, effective telling simultaneously narrows our attention and deepens it, intensifying the dramatic predicament yet refining the terms on which we understand it. Both Gordimer's example and Eliot's suggest we can test the effectiveness of telling in our own work by considering whether it resolves or complicates tension for the reader.

Summary as set-up for effective showing

In first-person narration, telling follows the same principles as for third-person narration but offers particular technical challenges.

Because a writer can use inaccuracies in telling to reveal what a narrator does not consciously admit, she must contend with the corollary temptation to tell too much and the risk of confusing a narrator's perceptions with those of the author. Telling by a first-person narrator underscores how carefully this strategy must be balanced with showing in any point of view and how effectively tone can generate dramatic interest.

The first chapter of Tobias Wolff's novel *Old School* is devoted almost entirely to summary, with the retrospective first-person narrator setting the stakes and providing background for the story he's about to tell before he zeroes in on a flashback. The chapter's structure demonstrates the value of summary to story and shows how a writer can employ it to foreshadow the stakes of a novel as a whole. In the very first paragraph the narrator, a scholarship student at a prestigious, progressive boarding school, establishes era in ways that expose him from the get-go:

> Robert Frost made his visit in November of 1960, just a week after the general election. It tells you something about our school that the prospect of his arrival cooked up more interest than the contest between Nixon and Kennedy, which for most of us was no contest at all. Nixon was a straight arrow and a scold. If he'd been one of us we would have glued his shoes to the floor. Kennedy, though—here was a warrior, an ironist, terse and unhysterical. He had his clothes under control. His wife was a fox. And he read and wrote books, one of which, *Why England Slept*, was required reading in my honors history seminar. We recognized Kennedy; we could still see in him the boy who would have been a favorite here, roguish and literate, with that almost formal insouciance that both enacted and discounted the fact of his class.[16]

Via the narrator's tone, a mix of sincerity and posturing, Wolff wittily defamiliarizes the political candidates who are judged by the terms of high-school popularity. The intensity of this summary stems from its ability to compact romanticism and shallow immaturity; showing would have diluted this effect over several different scenes.

Like many of his classmates at this literary-minded school, the narrator is "book-drunk," and over the course of the novel Wolff dissects the literary ambitions of these boys and troubles us with the ways in which their idealism is tainted by crude ambition, naïveté, and the need for attention. By the second page the narrator declares the code of his school: "absent other distinctions,

you were steadily giving ground to a system of honors that valued nothing you hadn't done for yourself. That was the idea, so
deeply held it was never spoken; you breathed it in with the smell
of floor wax and wool and boys living close together in over-
heated rooms."[17] This telling is cloaked as showing, thanks to
the concrete detail and even the choice of verbs; "giving ground"
implicitly references a struggle to surrender self-interest to the
ideal.

Immediately on the heels of a paean to his English teach-
ers, the narrator describes three schoolmates with whom he's
contending for a school literary prize; Frost, who has agreed to
serve as judge, will grant a private audience to the winner. Wolff
simultaneously devises a clever way to introduce us to the main
characters and to *show* us the contradictions at the core of his narrator and his plot, generating dramatic tension precisely because
the narrator is crudely sizing up the competition. If this were
delivered in scene, most readers would be bored by the minutiae
of an adolescent male contest for supremacy. Instead, in summary the narrator's tone provides dramatic interest, comically
overlaying literary terminology with slang ("You could tell, reading George's poetry, that he knew his stuff. His lines scanned, he
used alliteration and personification."[18]) and exposing the boys'
self-parodying efforts to emulate their chosen masters. Summary
enables the writer to lay bare, with great economy, how the narrator's knowingness is bound up with vulnerability, as when he
recounts his peers' attempt to be cynical about their hero wor-
ship of Hemingway: "We even talked like Hemingway characters,
though in travesty, as if to deny our discipleship: That is your
bed, and it is a good bed, and you must make it and you must
make it well."[19]

Summary allows for another kind of compression too: the
three main competitors for the prize represent a cross-section
of the school's socioeconomic makeup, and if the narrator has
admitted he's a scholarship student, he withholds from us exactly
how he has fitted himself into the social hierarchy of the school.
Wolff skillfully weaves in snippets of scene that offer opportunities for us to question some of the narrator's judgements. He
recalls being invited out for dinner by the father of his literary
competitor Bill, which led to the discovery that Bill was Jewish,
something Bill has never admitted. The fact that Bill has kept
quiet confirms the narrator's assumption that to be Jewish is a

social liability at their "dream" school. But afterwards Bill "gave no sign of feeling compromised by my knowledge that he was not who he seemed to be. That made me wonder if he'd never meant to seem not Jewish.... I didn't really believe that, of course."[20] The writer exploits the reflexiveness of this disbelief to establish the distance between his stance and the narrator's. In taking Bill's reticence for "further artifice" (because "that's how I would've carried it off"), the narrator betrays himself as someone readily capable of dissembling and pressured to do so by fears of inadequacy. Aware of "the problem of class," he is divided between his desire to believe in the school's ideals ("It was a good dream and we tried to live it out") and his need to manipulate them to secure his own status.[21]

As soon as he nails this core instability, Wolff turns quite baldly to scene: "From my first days there I grasped and gratefully entered the dream but at the same time behaved as if I knew better, as in the following instance." The flashback that follows on this announcement puts every bit of the summary to dramatic use. It begins with a preamble of its own: the summer before he came to the school, the narrator worked in the kitchen of a YMCA camp, where the chef, Hartmut, protected him from older guys who "rode me pretty hard."[22] Five or six weeks into the school year, the narrator climbs the stairs whistling a tune he picked up from Hartmut, and it happens that he's following on the heels of the school janitor, Gershon, who turns and harshly demands his name. Summoned to the dean's office, the narrator fears he's about to be lectured on his poor grades (such an interesting aside) and discovers instead that Gershon, a Holocaust survivor, has accused him of deliberately whistling a Nazi song to torment him. It takes several pages of dialogue to show the dean as an honest, compassionate man, ascertaining that the narrator didn't realize he was whistling the "Horst Wessel Song." Though for other reasons he deserves the lecture he anticipated, the narrator cries because he has been "unjustly accused."[23]

When the dean comforts the boy, saying he believes in his innocence, the narrator confides, "But *how* did he know? How could he, in the face of such an inconceivable coincidence? Surely some doubt remained. I had the means to prove myself, but already knew I'd never make use of it."[24] So much is accomplished implicitly by this fragment of telling: the narrator's doubt in his own integrity is now in play, reinforced by the shock that the reader experienced along with him. (We too were prepared to admire Hartmut for protecting him.) Furthermore, the writer provides a teaser that arouses our curiosity about fact and motive. By what means can he prove himself? When the dean sends the boy to explain himself to Gershon, who does not believe his disavowal, for the second time the boy decides not to provide his "proof": his own father is Jewish, though he has kept it a secret. Why not play this "trump card"? Because "I'd let Gershon think the worst of me before I would claim any connection to him, or implicate myself in the fate that had beached him in this room. Why would I want to talk my way into his unlucky tribe?"[25]

At this moment all the strands of narrative laid out in the summary are knotted together: we revise our understanding of the dinner with Bill and his father; "trump card" again betrays the narrator's anxiety to scramble for position, but now with larger stakes; even at this school where the dean honorably opposes overt discrimination, the narrator senses it as an undercurrent; as with Hartmut, appearances cannot be trusted. Not just prejudice but perceived hypocrisy becomes "a shadow on my faith in the school." We've witnessed the narrator's cowardice in the clearest kind of showing, bearing out earlier hints of duplicity, but the pressures that might enforce this behavior have also been exposed, thanks to the slant of the telling. The narrator concludes that "other boys must have felt the same intimations. Maybe that was why so many of them wanted to become writers. Maybe it seemed to them, as it did to me, that to be a writer was to escape the problems of blood and class."[26] No amount of showing could have linked the narrator's literary ambition with his class consciousness so precisely, yet no amount of mere telling could have convinced us that this proposition entangles an authentic idealism with the narrator's baser instincts. By interweaving showing and telling, Wolff fosters identification with a narrator whose actions will challenge the school's code of honor.

Wolff employs telling more than another writer might in a first-person narration, but the degree to which a writer relies on telling doesn't by itself determine skill or effectiveness. In whatever proportion, when showing and telling are functionally interwoven, the sum total is a "show," a plump ratio of subtext to text that situates the reader in a problematic, active relationship to the work. Apprentice writers often regard telling as a convenient means of getting unpleasant narrative business out of the way—fitting in background information in a compressed fashion or quickly labeling a character's feeling in the moment. Or telling constitutes an aside to the reader, a self-contained statement of meaning rather than one that depends on some interaction with showing for its full effect. But once you understand that you must conceive telling and showing as entwined methods of indirection, you're in a position to discover rich strategies for amplifying meaning. When you read the drafts of other writers in workshop, you will be less likely to clamor for scene, scene, scene, because you will recognize that a summary, which offers opportunities for artfully leaving out, might be the more evocative choice. In evaluating a given instance of telling in a manuscript, you will ask whether it contributes to a whole effect greater than what could have been accomplished by showing or telling alone. Is it redundant, spoiling what might have been deciphered entirely from showing? Does it provide a premise that proves essential to an understanding of the stakes? Does it stand alone as a statement of meaning or are its implications dependent on what is shown? Does it cumulatively complicate the act of judging characters' actions?

Just because every writer is forced to speculate on the assumptions a reader brings to a text, you will probably always need readers to help you ascertain where telling is unnecessary or when it's too directive. The beginning and ending of any manuscript usually deserve the closest scrutiny, because you can easily err on the side of providing unnecessary preamble or on the side of summing up implications that should remain subterranean at story's end. But if readers can spot delayed effects for telling that occurs at the beginning of a narrative and if at the end they cannot fully reconcile the telling with a paraphrase of the story's meaning, chances are good that the writer has put telling to dramatic use.

Telling deserves to be liberated from the negative connotations that it has acquired since the early twentieth century, when Western writers, responding to the larger cultural uncertainty about absolute values, began to back away from anything that smacked of authorial intrusion. It is constructive to consider Raymond Carver's eventual disillusionment with reliance on showing almost to the exclusion of telling. Near the end of his life, this minimalist writer began to explore in his stories the possibilities of telling more, of conveying more information about the inner lives of his characters. He even revised earlier stories to conform to this emerging æsthetic.[27] There is a poignancy and truth to the earlier stories in which the inarticulate characters could not grasp some principle of meaning by which to navigate their lives. There is another kind of truth, still difficult and painful, in the later stories, in which Carver grants his characters a greater capacity for insight into their circumstances without any added power to change them, an effect he could not achieve without relying on telling.

The pursuit of effective ways to dramatize the full complexity of our experience ultimately justifies telling in a work of fiction. And here, the argument is no longer about technique, no longer about tactics that can be learned. Artistic telling serves to surprise us, so that we may vicariously experience life and see into the order of the world in a way that we could not on our own. This is, as E. M. Forster has said, one of the great pleasures of reading fiction. In life we can know others only from what we can observe, only from surfaces, but a character belongs to "a world where the secret life is visible, to a world that is not and cannot be ours, to a world where the narrator and the creator are one."[28] It takes sensibility to imagine this secret life with a complexity that doesn't merely confirm a reader's experience but broadens it. Since sensibility can't be taught or acquired, it's only too tempting to fall back on the standard, safe advice to "show, don't tell." But when a writer never tells, she risks being bound by those assumptions she already shares with the reader, including reflexive ways of seeing. Beyond this one absolute—in which all dramatic effects must be achieved by showing—exists a rich variety of ways in which a writer may balance showing and telling, all of them equally capable of granting us access to a world where the secret life is made momentarily, luminously visible.

10

The Sentence as a Touchstone of Style

When I was just starting out as a writer, I was in a Faulkner phase, completely enamored of long, labyrinthine sentences and Latinate words. His patience sorely tried, my workshop instructor finally hauled me aside and said, "Stop trying so hard to have a style." I think he might have let me have my head, working all the Faulkner out of my system until what was left was mine, and I never warn my students away from similar infatuations, since I trust that they'll work through it—and that it's good to fall in love. Yet I'm happy to grant the point of my exasperated instructor: style emerges from a writer's natural inclinations and habits of mind. Freed of the burden of "having a style," you must take up another, a sentence-by-sentence effort to embody the principles of story logic in grammar and syntax.

"Human speech," Flaubert wrote, "is like a cracked tin kettle, on which we hammer out tunes to make bears dance when we long to move the stars."[1] Rather than evincing untroubled proficiency, a stylist strives to work the flawed but seductive material of language to its capacity, to recruit the reader's emotions as well as to generate subtext by any means available, including diction, which subsumes both our word choice and our syntax. When Robert Frost distinguishes between "grammatical sentences" and "vital sentences," he locates the effort to make the reader see new—to defamiliarize—in syntax itself.[2] Unlike a merely grammatical sentence, a vital sentence recruits form in the service of sense. As poet Aaron Shurin points out, negotiating between these two poles is fraught with risk: "Poetry is that literary form in which both the depth function and the surfaces of language are

activated, and, pleasures abounding, you are constantly threatened with being in one at the expense of the other." To illustrate,
Shurin cites a speech by Oberon in *Midsummer Night's Dream*: "I
know a bank where the wild thyme blows,/Where oxlips and the
nodding violet grows,/Quite over-canopied with luscious wood-
bine,/With sweet musk-roses, and with eglantine." In this passage
the nearly delirious tension between content and the intensified
sensory appeal of music threatens to "undo coherence."[3] But if
Shakespeare didn't bump up against this limit, we'd get nothing
but information. As Wallace Stevens once said, style *is* the subject.

Prose writers may be a little more earthbound than poets, but
as a resource for enacting feeling and idea, the sentence offers
boundless mimetic possibilities in a work of fiction. In Joseph
O'Neill's novel *Netherland*, the first-person narrator is a Dutch
transplant to Manhattan whose British wife has recently left him,
taking their young son back to England with her. Riding a com-
muter train, the narrator discovers in his briefcase a gift from a
friend, a booklet entitled *Dutch Nursery Rhymes in Colonial Times*.
O'Neill capitalizes on some of the tactics of poetry by incorporating in his text a verse from the booklet, with a blank where the
child's name should be sung:

> *Trip a trop a troontjes*
> *De varkens in de boontes,*
> *De koetjes in de claver,*
> *De paarden in de haver,*
> *De eendjes in de water-plas,*
> *De kalf in de lange gras;*
> *So groot mijn kleine* _____ *was!*[4]

Nonsense syllables for the reader, if not the narrator, but to
sound them out instantly fires kinesthetic memory. By giving us
syllables of sound rather than sense, the writer awakens recall,
drawing us back to our own childhood, when most of us would
have experienced the beat of nursery rhymes in a bodily way,
bouncing on the knee of a loving adult. Humming the song, the
narrator taps his knee, imagining his son's weight on his thigh,
his memory triggered too, and his longing for his child is intensified for readers because feeling has been recruited before content
is specified. Right down to the visual blank on the page, we are
made to miss this child.

In the next paragraph the narrator thinks of his last visit with his son Jake: "He wore his purple quilted jacket, and his thermal khakis with an inch of tartan turnup, and his blue ankle boots with the zip, and the blue sweater with the white boat, and—I knew this because I had dressed him—his train-infested underpants, and the red T-shirt he liked to imagine was a Spider Man shirt, and Old Navy green socks with rubbery lettering on the soles."[5] The *syntax* holds on to the absent child in this sentence elongated by adding *and* between every item of Jake's apparel and, wherever possible, just one more appended detail.

Because grammar poses such heady possibilities as this, Gertrude Stein could rave that grammar is so "very exciting," adding that diagramming sentences is "completely exciting and completely completing."[6] The study of grammar and syntax has gotten a bad name because too often it centers on error correction, which pressures apprentice writers to limit the strategies they're willing to try rather than engage joyfully with the limits of language. Correctness counts, but to be merely correct is tantamount to entering a plow horse in the Kentucky Derby. In "Guy de Maupassant," Isaac Babel's narrator dismisses a translator who "took pains to write correctly and precisely, and all that resulted was something loose and lifeless." If correctness is insufficient, so is a flagrant violation of the rules; as Babel noted, "A phrase is born into the world both good and bad at the same time. The secret lies in a slight, an almost invisible twist. The lever should rest in your hand, getting warm, and you can only turn it once, not twice."[7]

To look at just one or two sentences by a writer gives us only a partial glimpse of her style, but style is forged sentence by sentence, and a close analysis focuses our attention not on the burden of "having a style" but on the attitudinal stance and resourcefulness a good writer brings to the table. The sentences discussed in this chapter were chosen because their syntax is beautiful, offering a pleasure that threatens to undo coherence, exploiting every resource of language to intensify meaning by enacting it.

Like Gertrude Stein, I think sentence diagrams are a marvel, illuminating the architecture of a sentence, but they demand a detailed vocabulary and long practice, so I've tried to keep to a streamlined terminology and schematics here. An independent clause contains its own subject and verb plus an object if the verb takes one. (As a grammar geek, I have to point out that forms of the verb "to be" take a subjective complement in the "object slot.") This core syntax can form a sentence by itself or be joined to another clause. Coordinate clauses are joined by a semi-colon, a colon, or a coordinating conjunction (*and, but, for, or, nor*): The cat scratched the door, *and* the dog howled. A subordinating conjunction (*although, while, even though, because,* and others) links clauses in a way that makes one dependent on the other for meaning—subordinate to it: *While* the cat scratched the door, the dog howled. The independent clause "the dog howled" can survive on its own as a sentence, but the subordinate clause "while the cat scratched the door" cannot. We can also tuck one clause inside another. A noun clause can serve as a subject (*that she wished for love* was understood) or object (she knew *that he'd be ready*), or a relative clause can be tucked in to function like an adjective or adverb. (The hat *that he left on the table* was lost.) A relative pronoun (*that, which, who, whose, whom*) or relative adverb (*when, where, why*) links in a relative clause but can be left out where its presence is understood (the hat *he left on the table*). When we consider a sentence in terms of the relationship between core syntax and any embellishment, we can ask useful questions about how a writer organizes information into recognizable chunks and whether she works with or against the inherent linearity of syntax.

A sentence might incorporate any number of clauses of any kind and can, in theory, run on forever, because syntax also allows for adding embellishment (such as adjectives, adverbs, and modifying phrases) in every syntactic slot. Contrary to the breezy notion that a comma indicates a pause, it serves a logical function, though it can be exploited to enhance rhythm. A comma separates items in a series and indicates whether any addition that interrupts core syntax is necessary (restrictive) or not (nonrestrictive). If the addition is nonrestrictive, it is set off by commas. (The red hat, *which he left on the table*, belongs to me. Because the adjective *red* already specifies which hat, the addition is nonrestrictive.)

A writer can play with the order of any of these materials in a sentence for multiple effects, employing sentence strategies known as schemes to depart from the expected or strictly utilitarian order of words. For example, the schemes of alliteration and assonance involve a word order that intensifies sound effects, and the scheme of polysyndeton deliberately inserts extra conjunctions, as in the passage from O'Neill's novel. Whatever syntactic strategy you might try in a given sentence, its effect will be dependent on *circumstance,* on content and word choice; polysyndeton in O'Neill's sentence has a clinging quality because he strings together noun phrases that signify the absent child, but if you were to employ this strategy for an unadorned string of verbs, you might instead lend forceful emphasis to a sequence of actions.

George Eliot, *Middlemarch*

> You will hardly demand that his confidence should have a basis in external facts; such confidence, we know, is something less coarse and materialistic: it is a comfortable disposition leading us to expect that the wisdom of providence or the folly of our friends, the mysteries of luck or the still greater mystery of our high individual value in the universe, will bring about agreeable issues, such as are consistent with our good taste in costume and our general preference for the best style of thing.[8]

In this sentence George Eliot describes the optimism of young Fred Vincy, a charmer who's hard-pressed to pay off gambling debts he incurred by pretending to a gentlemanly style beyond his means. "You will hardly demand," an almost contentious beginning, signals that the narrator will correct an impression she has already generated in the reader (thus repositioning our sympathies). We are carefully steered through the three independent (coordinate) clauses of this sentence, laid out in the sentence diagram in Figure 10.1. (The only time I'll indulge, I promise.) The second independent clause repeats "confidence" and refers back to it with the comparative "less," and the pronoun "it" that serves as subject of the third independent clause also refers back to "confidence" (its antecedent). Although Eliot disguises this for the sake of rhythmic variety, the second independent clause really reads "we know *that* such confidence is." So the diagram shows that the independent clauses are roughly parallel in structure: subject + verb + noun clause in the object slot of the sentence. The third independent clause offers a changeup (with the noun clause as the object of a verbal phrase) but repeats the emphasis on the object slot of the sentence. Punctuation (rather than a conjunction) links the independent clauses, helpfully framing

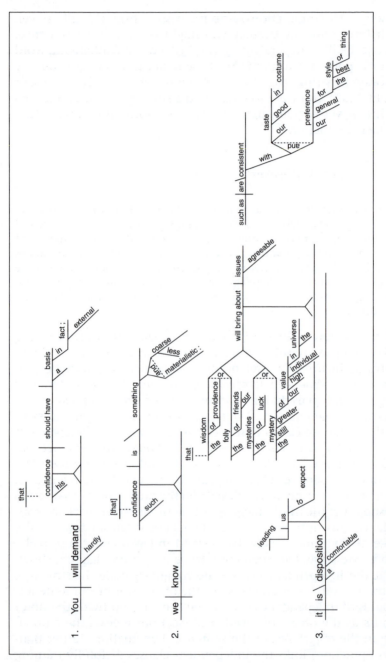

Figure 10.1 Diagram of a sentence from George Eliot's *Middlemarch*

them as a series of restatements, with the colon serving as a fulcrum at which the sentence shifts from general statement to illustration. A very tidy organization.

The last noun-clause-as-object ("that the wisdom of providence...") makes up the bulk of the *entire* sentence, a surprise heightened by the hitherto regular syntactic pattern. The four parallel subjects of this noun clause are treated as two pairs rather than a single series (*a* or *b*, *c* or *d* versus *a*, *b*, *c*, or *d*):

> the wisdom of providence
> *or* the folly of our friends,
>   the mysteries of luck
> *or* the still greater mystery of our high individual value in the universe

Eliot's use of pairs heightens the contrast between a set of objective and a set of highly subjective reasons for optimism, thus injecting tension, since reason hardly ever cleaves so neatly from self-interest. And when the long last item unfurls, it wittily mimes the distorting grandiosity of ego. Eliot ends the sentence with a flourish, shifting from the formal "agreeable issues" to the colloquial in one last effective pairing, "our good taste in costume and our general preference for the best style of thing." This phrase comically deflates what has preceded it, and by its deliberate imprecision ("best style of thing") enacts the sentiment of the opening clause: "such confidence" is not grounded in hard facts but has the pleasant vagueness of vanity. The shift to the colloquial nails a nice dramatic tension between objective certainties about human nature and sympathetic identification with some of the impulses we were so ready to judge a moment ago.

So much can be accomplished by a writer who employs parallelism strategically. By treating like items in like grammatical manner, parallelism often enables us to compress information. Correctness provides clarity and efficiency but also poses opportunities to enact meaning. A lot would have been lost if Eliot had written "Someone with a comfortable disposition might count on the wisdom of providence. The folly of his friends might work in his favor, or he could get lucky. Sometimes he might count on the mystery of his high value in the universe." When parallel items are similar in length as well as structure (the scheme of isocolon), the writer capitalizes on syntax *and* sound to influence sense.

Because parallelism imposes grammatical equivalence, a writer can use it to imply content equivalence, even among items that might not seem obviously alike. In any series, two items make a pair, which lends itself to antithesis (to tension), whereas three items or more suggest profusion, often synecdochically standing for many instances. Which structure works better in relation to content? Consider how much more Eliot was able to imply about human myopia when she contrasted reason and wishes in terms of two pairs rather than four undifferentiated items.

William Faulkner, "Barn Burning"

> The boy, crouched on his nail keg at the back of the crowded room, knew he smelled cheese, and more: from where he sat he could see the ranked shelves close-packed with the solid, squat, dynamic shapes of tin cans whose labels his stomach read, not from the lettering which meant nothing to his mind but from the scarlet devils and the silver curve of fish—this, the cheese which he knew he smelled and the hermetic meat which his intestines believed he smelled coming in intermittent gusts momentary and brief between the other constant one, the smell and sense just a little of fear because mostly of despair and grief, the old fierce pull of blood.[9]

Where Eliot works with the linearity of core syntax, Faulkner's methods are interruptive, with chunks of modifying information proliferating seemingly at every opportunity, a highly varied pattern of "nesting" modification. The subject of the first independent clause is modified before we even get the verb. In the next independent clause, the object ("shelves") is modified by an adjective trailing a prepositional phrase, in turn modified by a relative clause, in turn modified by the "not...but" construction, which even contains its own aside. Faulkner loves the "not...but" construction as much as Eliot loves the colon, probably because this parallel construction emphasizes simultaneity. Figure 10.2 illustrates his intricate nesting.

At the dash the sentence circles back to "this" (to the initial emphasis on the sense of smell) and is jammed with appositives, alternates for a noun or pronoun that occupy the same syntactic slot. "This" takes as an appositive "cheese" and "hermetic meat," each trailing a relative clause. The "other constant one" is then modified by an appositive, "the smell and sense," in turn modified by another appositive, "the old fierce pull of blood." To

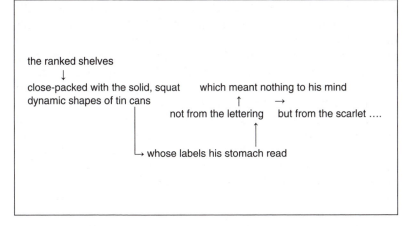

Figure 10.2 Nesting modification in Faulkner's sentence

help you see how Faulkner is combating the inherent linearity of syntax, here's another visual:

this		the other constant one
the cheese	coming … between	the smell and sense
the hermetic meat		the old fierce pull of blood

It's all legal. Although Faulkner strains the limits of syntax by inverting the order of nouns and adjectives, by inserting relative clauses within modifying phrases, and by stacking up appositives, the whole loopy process obeys the rules of grammar. Where George Eliot's sentence proceeds in stately, compartmentalized fashion, Faulkner's is designed to create a lovely interplay between sensory and perceptual information as it works its way incrementally toward interiority. Syntax brings the reader as close as possible to the boy's perceptual process, with structure literally amending initial impressions.

Any writer could profit from studying the strategies that enable Faulkner to do this. The core syntax of the sentence is simple, concise, and literal—*the boy knew he smelled cheese,* and *he could see the ranked shelves*—and we get it up front, so that the embellishment occurs after perspective and physicality have been established. Closely related verbs (*knew, meant, knew, believed*) anchor highly varied information, as do parallel constructions, aided by repetition. Relative clauses are an ordinary grammatical convenience, but when Faulkner packs them in and packs them with perceptual "adjustments," he entwines sensation with internal response. Where Eliot's pronouns always reference a clear antecedent, Faulkner often supplies a pronoun (such as "the other constant *one*") before providing the noun for which it stands, which reinforces interiority by intentionally breaking a rule of formal usage. As further reinforcement, Faulkner provides the emotional tenor of the "constant one" (fear, despair, grief) before he specifies its actual nature (blood ties). Amazing in its own right, this sentence from the first paragraph of "Barn Burning" also enacts the central conflict of the story as a whole: the boy's hunger (for justice) competes with his allegiance to his vindictive father.

Faulkner's sentence illustrates the fine distinction between economy and efficiency. The phrase "intermittent gusts momentary and brief" could be more efficiently recast as "brief, intermittent gusts." Aside from the fact that this arrangement could not be so pleasing as the "mirror" stresses on either side of the noun (**intermit**tent/**mo**mentary), the seeming redundancy of *intermittent* and *momentary* draws out the process of perception so that the reader might feel with the boy the pang of pain returning. So it's necessary, but it strains correctness, especially since one could presumably defend a wordy sentence by a similar rationale. There is, as Babel tells us, a slight twist, often only the faintest distinction, between a brilliant move and an ineffectual one.

Efficiency matters greatly in fiction, and syntax can help us to sequence closely related actions, provide spatial orientation, and establish pacing. Yet efficiency does not always equate with economy, which has to do with getting the most bang for the buck regardless of how many words are actually on the page. As effective as elaborate modification is in Faulkner's sentence, the converse is also true: deliberately choosing not to link corollary information can generate equally powerful, if different, effects. In either case the skillful writer demonstrates Babel's maxim: "No iron can stab the heart with such force as a period put just at the right place."[10] Consider the deliberately choppy structure of this passage from Denis Johnson's "Car Crash." In the wake of a horrific car crash, the pill-popping narrator observes a dying man being loaded into an ambulance: "He was still alive, still dreaming obscenely. The blood ran off him in strings. His knees jerked and his head rattled."[11] Here is an efficient, smoother rewrite: "Still alive, he was dreaming obscenely, the blood running off him in strings, his knees jerking, and his head rattling." But Johnson needed sentences that would capture the jerky perceptual state of his narrator, and the whiff of perverse envy in the phrase "dreaming obscenely" would have been diminished if he'd appended anything else before the period.

Virginia Woolf, *Mrs Dalloway*

> For heaven only knows why one loves it so, how one sees it so, making it up, building it round one, tumbling it, creating it every moment afresh; but the veriest frumps, the most dejected of miseries sitting on doorsteps (drink their downfall) do the same; can't be dealt with, she felt positive, by Acts of Parliament for that very reason: they love life. In people's eyes, in the swing, tramp, and trudge; in the bellow and the uproar; the carriages, motor cars, omnibuses, vans, sandwich men shuffling and swinging; brass bands; barrel organs; in the triumph and the jingle and the strange high singing of some aeroplane overhead was what she loved; life; London; this moment in June.[12]

The full impact of sentences is felt only in context, and this pretty pair of sentences illuminates the principle. Sentence 1 contains three coordinate clauses: "For Heaven...afresh"; "but the veriest frumps...for that very reason"; and "they love life." Sentence 2 gives us one long independent clause. Like Proust, Woolf often generates sentences that have the quality of litany, with isocolon lending a sonorous cadence. In these sentences Woolf precisely characterizes the feeling of joyful aliveness in Clarissa Dalloway, recently an invalid, as she sets out on an errand in London. In sentence 1 the first clause posits Clarissa as central actor, the source of this feeling, so it is no accident that at the end Woolf piles up a parallel series of *ing* verb forms (*making, building, tumbling, creating,* all gerunds, or verbs-as-nouns) or that each of the items begins with a strong stressed syllable. This stress pattern recurs immediately in the second clause, with the parenthetical "**drink** their **down**fall" striking the reader as a pleasing aural ornamentation, though its allusion to ruin has bearing if

we remember Clarissa's recent illness. The shift of focus to specific others also links the upper-class Clarissa with "the veriest
frumps."

This first sentence closes with a simple forceful statement
("they love life") that echoes the more convoluted first clause,
in which love of life is posed as a mystery, thus setting us up to
anticipate some resolution. Because the next sentence inserts a
long list of objects for the preposition *in* before we ever get a subject or verb, structure heightens our anticipation of grammatical
as well as content completion. Only things, but such an active
inrush of them (thanks to sheer number and the stress on the
first or only syllable of each noun) that this sentence reverses
the proposition of the previous one: Clarissa exists in a state of
receptivity. If the first sentence began by emphasizing the act
of making, the second emphasizes the profusion that feeds this
sense of aliveness via sight *and* sound, especially because the syntax inverts conventional order; instead of the direct, active "she
loved what was in," we get the subject ("what she loved") last.

If we arrange the second sentence in the form of a list, we
can see how Woolf exploits sound strategies and the visual aid of
punctuation to heighten our awareness of the musicality of her
phrasing:

> In people's eyes,
> in the swing,
> > tramp,
> > and trudge;
> in the bellow
> > and the uproar;
> > the carriages,
> > motor cars,
> > omnibuses,
> > vans,
> > sandwich men shuffling and swinging;
> > brass bands;
> > barrel organs;
> in the triumph
> > and the jingle
> > and the strange high singing of some aeroplane overhead
> was what she loved;
> life;
> London;
> this moment in June.

The rhythm of the list of nouns is not mechanically uniform; some strings of nouns are alliterative, and the preposition *in* recurs three times, entwining the pleasure of rhythmic variation with meaning, since it reminds us that the grammatical construction is not yet complete. Departing from convention, Woolf even uses the semi-colon, "stronger" punctuation than a comma, to mark rhythmic units within this list; where a semi-colon is used to separate single words, each item stands out in its cherished particularity. After the subject of sentence 2 is finally provided, the long list that preceded it is recast as a series of three nouns, echoing the stress on an initial syllable and landing on a final stressed beat, which resolves the sound pattern without supplying an explicit reason for this mysterious joy.

One could say that readers recognize rhythm in prose by a process that is the inverse of that for formal verse: against a pattern with a high degree of variation in its stresses, any rhythmic regularity stands out, as does any cluster of stressed syllables. Like Woolf, Faulkner and Eliot also reinforce meaning with sound strategies. With "the **wis**d̲o̲m o̲f **pro**vidence or the *f*o̲lly o̲f our *f***riends**," Eliot exploits alliteration, assonance, and meter (pattern of stresses) to reinforce the isocolon, and Faulkner closes his sentence with a forceful string of successive stresses in one-syllable words: "the **old fierce pull** of **blood**." Even a writer bent on capturing the sound of spoken English can exploit rhythmic change-ups in ways that lend emphasis without violating the naturalness of speech. Lending insistence and metricality to a colloquial sentence, Grace Paley leads off with a pattern of initial stresses that is echoed later: "**Still** and **all**, in **spite** of the **qua**lity, it was a mean present to give a woman you planned on never seeing again, a person you had children with and got onto all the time, **drunk** or **so**ber, even when everybody had to get up early in the morning."[13]

Gabriel García Márquez, "The Last Voyage of the Ghost Ship"

Figure 10.3 shows the beginning of "The Last Voyage of the Ghost Ship," a short story written as one sentence.[14] Although analysis of any work in translation is at best approximately accurate, this passage offers provocative insights into how a fiction writer exploits syntax and grammar to manage time,

NOW they're going to see who I am, he said to himself in his strong new man's voice, MANY YEARS AFTER he had FIRST seen the huge ocean liner without lights and without any sound which passed by the village ONE NIGHT like a great uninhabited palace, longer than the whole village and much taller than the steeple of the church, and it sailed by in the darkness toward the colonial city on the other side of the bay that had been fortified against buccaneers, with its old slave port and the rotating light, whose gloomy beams transfigured the village into a lunar encampment of glowing houses and streets of volcanic deserts every fifteen seconds, and even though AT THAT TIME he'd been a boy without a man's strong voice but with his mother's permission to stay very late on the beach to listen to the wind's night harps, he could STILL remember, as if STILL seeing it, how the liner would disappear when the lights of the beacon struck its side and how it would reappear when the light had passed, so that it was an intermittent ship sailing along, appearing and disappearing, toward the mouth of the bay, groping its way like a sleepwalker for the buoys that marked the harbor channel until something must have gone wrong with the compass needle, because it headed toward the shoals, ran aground, broke up, and sank without a single sound, even though a collision against the reefs like that should have produced a crash of metal and . . .

Strategies that help to clarify chronological sequence:

Boldface = subordinating conjunctions to link clauses

Boldface and underlined = coordinating conjunctions to link clauses

CAPITALIZED = adverbs, nouns, or prepositional phrases that reference time

Highlighted = verbs that vary from the verb tense used for the present action

Figure 10.3   The beginning of "The Last Voyage of the Ghost Ship"

the key ingredient of any narrative. García Márquez does so with the added challenge of depicting a ghostly ocean liner that only the boy protagonist can see, and then only intermittently. To manage so complex a sentence, García Márquez clarifies sequence by employing inter-related strategies. Because the story's present action is told in the past tense, a shift to past perfect (*had* plus a verb) alerts us to a shift to a previous event, after which a writer can revert to past tense in narrating the event. Verbs also cue us to habitual or recurring action ("how the liner *would* disappear . . . and how it *would* reappear") and to speculative time, which exists only in the imagination of the protagonist. ("Something *must have* gone wrong," and a collision *"should have* produced a crash.") Five distinct representations of time are marked by as many verb tenses or moods, exquisitely coordinated in relation to one another not only to clarify chronology but also to lend psychological nuance. For example, the subtle difference between "he *could* still remember" and "he remembered" conveys the intensity of the boy's vision of the ship, granting access to his inner life.

In establishing chronology, verbs often require contextual reinforcement. Past perfect does not specify how much time has elapsed between a present moment and a past one, and the helping verb *would* might reference either habitual past action or future intended action. Even in a sentence that makes fewer demands on a reader than this one does, writers should not distract a reader with unnecessary literal confusion. For this reason García Márquez doesn't balk at reinforcing verbs with explicit references to time ("many years after," "at that time").

For a story about obsession, a sentence that can't escape itself and keeps doubling back makes a perfect choice. To weave so long a sentence, García Márquez must use subordinating as well as coordinating conjunctions to sew clauses together, and his methods underscore the compacting effect of subordinate clauses, which reinforce our orientation in time or space and may also establish causal sequence. His use of subordination helps readers to segment this long sentence into chunks that are more or less closely related. This is a carefully reiterative style but not a redundant one. Where a subordinating conjunction will precisely seam closely related actions, García Márquez supplies no further cues. When he makes a leap back in time or "sideways" to interiority, he reinforces the subordinating conjunction, as in "*and* **even though** *at that time he'd been* a boy." In this instance you can see that García Márquez also uses the subordinating conjunction to convey slant—to make us aware of the slight pressure of the boy's obsession on what he reports. The clause could logically and efficiently be written without the inclusion of "even though," but something of the boy's perceptual state would be lost in this version. Instead we get a hint, reinforced immediately ("he *could still* remember, as if *still* seeing") and throughout the story, of the boy's *insistence* on the accuracy and validity of his perceptions. As with parallelism, the conventional use of subordination comes under pressure in fiction: a logical syntactic structure is employed subversively to privilege the associative logic of emotion. Subordination, in other words, is put to use in the service of mimesis.

Ernest Hemingway, "The Short Happy Life of Francis Macomber"

> Then watching the object, not afraid, but hesitating before going down the bank to drink with such a thing opposite him, he saw a man figure detach itself from it and he turned his heavy head and swung away toward the cover of the trees as he heard a cracking crash and felt the slam of a.30-06 220-grain solid bullet that bit his flank and ripped in sudden hot scalding nausea through his stomach. He trotted, heavy, big-footed, swinging wounded full-bellied, through the trees toward the tall grass and cover, and the crash came again to go past him ripping the air apart.[15]

Whether a writer dodges the merely grammatical by stuffing a sentence like a roast turkey or by pruning it of expected logical links, style announces itself by tweaking conventional patterns in order to enact meaning. As markedly as Faulkner disrupts linearity with nested modification, Hemingway insists on linear structure and eschews syntactic hierarchy, rarely tucking clauses within clauses or using subordination to supply logical links. In these two sentences from "The Short Happy Life of Francis Macomber," a story of a safari in Africa, Hemingway momentarily dips into the perspective of a lion, a choice guaranteed to raise a few eyebrows. In the first sentence the lion reacts when a hunter emerges from a car on the other side of a stream. Hemingway characteristically uses polysyndeton to link actions in an undifferentiated linear chain ("*and* he turned his heavy head *and* swung away ... *and* felt"). His choice dodges correctness, which would automatically privilege a more compact sequencing in time ("turning his heavy head, he swung away ... and then felt"), but because *this* slight twist provides mimetic payoff, we recognize intention, not error. Once the lion sees a threat, no commas interrupt its consecutive actions; commas are not employed even where strict observance would require it. Hemingway *does* employ a subordinating conjunction here ("*as* he heard a cracking crash"), but a restrictive one to denote simultaneity at a crucial turn in the action, when the bullet slams into the lion. Where the period is placed underscores this turn.

In the next sentence we are made to feel how the wound impedes the lion's progress by the string of modifiers following "he trotted," *all* demarcated by commas. Verbs and verb forms dominate the diction of both sentences: the verbs of their core syntax are simple—*saw, turned, swung away, heard, felt, trotted, came*—but the pace of the action is quickened by a wealth of verb forms jammed in elsewhere: *watching, hesitating, going down, cracking, slam, bit, ripped, scalding, swinging, wounded, ripping.* Main verbs emphasize the simple, clear lines of instinctual response, while corollary verbs and verb forms enact shattering violence, often onomatopoeically. Though we tend to view Hemingway's style as poles apart from Faulkner's, both writers structure sentences that imitate sensation. Using syntax to defamiliarize, they deconstruct conventional patterns of organization in an attempt to give us experience direct and to shape it beautifully—to perform what Gertrude Stein calls "the creating it without naming it."[16]

You don't have to be stylistically like any of these writers in order to imbibe their avid interest in what syntax can be made to yield. Go forth and play. Like Eliot, generate a regular syntactic pattern and then slip in a surprise, or end a sentence with a noun clause so weighty it threatens to topple the whole structure. Like Faulkner, nest modification so that your syntax will mimic the process of perception. Like Woolf, arrange the syntax of a sentence so that it generates suspense, or exploit punctuation to reinforce rhythm and even insinuate subtext. Like García Márquez, seam together a sentence at least a page in length so that you can practice managing chronology and consequence, and use the link of a subordinating conjunction to convey slant. Like Hemingway, use syntax to slow or speed narrative time and exploit verbs as the spine of a sentence. Like all of them, pay attention to the sound of sense.

Fiction is written sentence by sentence, and the habit of thinking about syntax as a dramatic element should be part of your composing process, not just a task reserved for revision. Despite all the advice books that recommend settling for a sloppy first draft and trusting to revision, a practice of indifference toward syntax usually means a writer will rely on conventional arrangement of words to order conventional ways of seeing. One sentence leads to another, and a bad sentence leads to another like itself.

Focusing on the crafting of a sentence can help you solve dramatic problems because it inculcates the "half attention" that allows the subconscious to go to work on the material. When you focus *here,* you can gain effects *there.* Reordering a sentence to make a depiction of action more efficient can often isolate an error in sequencing, pose a new opportunity to generate subtext by omission or repetition, or expose mimetic possibilities in syntax of which you were initially unaware. And in revision, when the sentences seem to have hardened like cement, sometimes you must force your hand, experimentally recombining sentences on the page so that information is woven into different syntactic arrangements, forging one kind of link and then another and another. Recasting sentences not only improves clarity and economy but helps you move to the *next* sentence in a very different way, so that in both stages of the drafting process you can make discoveries. If so much of what stylists achieve derives from instinct, from the impulse to wallow in language like a pig in mud, Chekhov advises us never to forget that striving is required too: "Have you noticed Tolstoy's language? Enormous periods, sentences piled one on top of another. Don't think that it happens by chance or that it's a shortcoming. It's art, and it only comes after hard work."[17]

Exercises

These exercises are intended to foster your willingness to play—to defamiliarize the writing process in order to cultivate different ways of paying attention, to impose constraints that will force invention, and to give you practice at techniques that will help you to solve dramatic problems. Although the exercises are organized by chapter, in practice many of them address the dynamic interplay of more than one craft element. For some of the exercises, you are asked to write a complete story or scene according to the parameters provided, and I recommend a page limit of two to four double-spaced pages for scenes and five to ten double-spaced pages for stories. The asterisked exercises can be applied to a work you're composing or revising; in revision these exercises may help you to perceive your draft as workable clay once more, and they may give you a new way to approach trouble spots in the manuscript.

1 Story Logic

Essences

For the main character of a work you're composing or planning, write out a list of ten questions you'd ask in the game of "Essences." (What kind of car are you? What kind of bird?) Write your character's answers. Incorporate at least three of these answers as metaphors in your draft.

2 The Elusiveness at the Heart of Story Structure

The Hitchhiker Story

To explore how literal tension can function as an objective correlative for hidden tension in a plot, you will tell a version of the hitchhiker story discussed in this chapter.

A husband and wife, driving at night, pick up a hitchhiker. The wife is sometimes dissatisfied with her husband because she feels he is stingy, but he doesn't seem aware of this. During the drive, the husband tells an anecdote. The climax occurs when the hitchhiker, about to get out of the car, asks for money. Whether the husband hands over his last twenty dollars or grudgingly provides a few coins, this will provoke the wife to decide to leave him. And she will do so because she has misread her husband's capacity for generosity until now. But you cannot directly say so.

Choose one element from the first list and one from the second:

Who comes along for the ride:	*Response(s) to the husband's anecdote:*
a young and charming female hitchhiker	story amuses wife and hitchhiker
a menacing, scruffy male hitchhiker	hitchhiker believes story, wife doesn't
a young and charming male hitchhiker	wife believes story, hitchhiker doesn't
ravaged older female hitchhiker	story bothers wife but not hitchhiker
	story bothers hitchhiker but not wife

*Realignment

Rework the climax of a current story or chapter in imitation of one of the writers discussed in this chapter, with the aim of reconfiguring of what has come before.

- After the climax insert at least two paragraphs of resolution that depict the main character's thoughts before she takes an action that calls this "epiphany" into question ("Wants").
- Add a flashback just before the climax of the story and try to accomplish the resolution in no more than a sentence ("Fiesta, 1980"). Think of the flashback as a device for imbuing the literal action at the climax with figurative meaning; try using an indefinite pronoun or a noun that links the flashback and the climactic action.
- Insert a lyrical description that immediately precedes harsh or brutal action at the climax ("Light Is Like Water"). (Or you can insert a brutal statement just before a lyrical description of the climactic action in order to heighten tension at this moment.)
- At the climax incorporate two new sentences that echo the last lines of two previous scenes or sections in order to suggest a new connection between them ("Fathers"). (You might choose to change the last lines of preceding scenes so you can achieve this alignment.) Reinforce surprise by adding at least three unexpected adjectives.

3   Chapter Structure and Shapeliness in the Novel

*The Looming Event

Novelists need to take advantage of the roominess of their form to explore character in moments that are *not* pitched at crisis. Yet no matter how quiet the moment, it should be imbued with tension, and often this tension is "borrowed" from a previous event or an anticipated event. Write a scene in which the main character of your novel travels on foot or by train or car through a familiar place. This journey occurs immediately after some crisis or dramatic conflict that has not been resolved. The scene must conform to these parameters:

1. The recent dramatic conflict may be referenced in the narrative but its import and emotional consequences may *not* be declared.
2. The character observes and responds to the setting; this response should betray something of his emotional state at this moment.
3. At least once the character observes another human (or living creature) in the setting and reflects on the observation.
4. An object—in the possession of the character or a part of the surroundings—triggers a flashback. (The flashback should be a realized sensory memory, not summary, and it should be a memory of an event that has not yet been explored in the novel.)
5. Some unnamed response to the recent dramatic crisis informs the main character's emotional state and actions at this moment, and not until the last sentences of the passage does this surface, though all the preceding elements should offer the reader clues that suggest its existence.

*Permutations

Take any chapter that occurs in the second half of your novel. Rewrite the chapter to incorporate at least five separate references to an event that took place in the first half of the novel. Only one of these may directly describe the event; the others should reference an image associated with that event, employ words or phrases important to that event, or reference another event in the novel that is also connected with it. Now change at least five other sentences in this chapter to capitalize on these additions.

4   Three Key Strategies of Story Logic

A Winter's Day

This exercise is intended to heighten your consciousness of working within the constraints of form; it imposes strict rules and requires you to employ recurrence. Write a complete story (with rising action, climax, and resolution) following these parameters:

1. The story must be told by a first-person narrator.
2. The narrator has wronged someone and seeks forgiveness.
3. It is snowing, but the present action takes place inside a room.

4. You must use two key terms in this piece: *violin* and *lock*.
5. You must choose a third key term from the list below:

   window, photo, knife, train, ring, hammer, hat, apple, vodka, church

6. The form of the story requires that you use these key terms in a certain order, as follows:

   Violin must appear in the first sentence.
   Lock must appear in the third sentence (for the first time).
   The third key word that you choose must appear in the fifth sentence.
   Violin must be repeated in the eighth sentence.
   Lock must occur in the tenth sentence.
   Either *violin* or *lock* must recur in every third sentence after that.
   The third key word and *violin* must appear in the last sentence.
   None of the key words should occur in any other sentences.

Be forewarned: following these parameters will disrupt your composing process in frustrating ways. Remember that what doesn't kill you makes you strong.

This exercise is adapted from a theater exercise.

*7/8 of the Iceberg

For a story you're about to revise, follow these parameters:

1. Single out an image, object, or gesture that seems peripheral, and open your second or third scene with it. You must include the same image, object, or gesture at the beginning or end of at least one other scene and in the ending.
2. Set aside the ending. For the other two scenes where you've inserted this image, object, or gesture, cut the existing five lines on the other side of the space break—the last five lines of a previous section or the first five lines of the next. Rewrite the new ending of a prior scene or new beginning of a following scene so that something happens "in the space break."

5   Captured in Motion: Dynamic Characterization

Kissing a Thief

Write a scene or story in which your main character arrives home to discover a robbery in progress. The scene ends with the main character kissing the thief. Your goal is to stretch the reader's notion of the plausible—to make him believe the character would take the action she does.

*Method Acting

When an actor takes on a role, he devotes time to considering how he will inhabit his part physically—how he can use his body to convey qualities of character by nonverbal means. For example, Hamlet might strike us as more or less decisive if the actor playing the part uses expansive, emphatic gestures or walks haltingly and stammers. If fiction writers can't exploit an actual physical presence, they can compensate via tone and metaphor. For this exercise, you'll put the main characters from a work-in-progress through their paces in situations that may not be a part of your plot but may help you to gain a stronger awareness of your characters' physicality and signature gestures.

1. Write four to five sentences describing your main character as she carries out each of the following actions, and for each task include at least one simile or metaphor for the gestures or physical attributes of your character.

   - getting dressed
   - making a meal
   - jostling for place in a line of people trying to board a bus

2. Repeat the process for another key character in the same novel or story.
3. Now put these two characters together, and in *two* pages, show them responding to a dilemma that requires physical action—moving a sofa up three flights of stairs, responding when a pot on the stove goes up in flames, changing a flat tire in the rain, and so on. Import into this passage at least one simile or metaphor and at least one gesture from steps 1 and 2.

*Either/And

This exercise aims to help you locate the core instability of a consistently inconsistent character. Choose a scene from a chapter or story in which your main character takes a decisive action. Rewrite the scene so that the character makes the opposite or an alternate choice. That is, if in the original she locks her drunken husband out of the house, this time she lets him in. Do this *without* changing what the character says or thinks (if you have reported her thoughts), though you may add actions, thoughts, or details to account for this different choice. Go back to the original version, and when you revise, incorporate at least three of these additions.

6   Point of View Q & A

Doubting Thomas

Write about an appealing character from the perspective of a character who doubts and distrusts this attractive creature. You may choose any of these scenarios:

- The perspective character resists when the other asks for a loan.
- The appealing character is hosting a noisy party, and the perspective character, a neighbor, wants the noise to stop now.
- The characters are involved in a car accident in which one of them is at fault.
- The perspective character catches the other lying about a recent event.

As the scene unfolds, the reader must come to a *different* judgment than the perspective character does about the genuinely appealing qualities of the other character. (Or you may reverse the dynamic: your perspective character is infatuated with this appealing creature, but the reader comes to have serious doubts.)

Ripped from the Headlines

Choose one item from this list of articles that appeared in tabloid newspapers:

- A newspaper reporter is visited by an angel who predicts the end of the world.
- A widow finds that the face of her dead husband has miraculously appeared on her scarf.
- A cheerleader is arrested for participating in an armed robbery of a convenience store, committed with three friends, all from well-off families.
- A middle-aged heart transplant recipient believes that her personality has altered to resemble that of the reckless young man whose heart she received.

Write a dramatic monologue (a conscious address to a listener) from the perspective of one of these characters, describing the given dramatic situation. Follow these parameters:

1. You are not allowed to condescend to your narrator.
2. The events the narrator describes must generate some conflict for him. He must convey information that he is not conscious of imparting, revealing unacknowledged motives or desires.
3. The narrator must also be persuasive, so that by the end of the monologue the reader has to grant some validity to the narrator's claims about events.

Forbidden Zone

From a work-in-progress choose a passage that has given you difficulty and excise all sentences that zoom in for a close-up of the character's thoughts and feelings. Leave an asterisk where these passages occurred. Now rewrite the scene, and treat each asterisk as if it marks a forbidden zone. For each asterisk, you must add a new passage *elsewhere* in which you move closer to character. If a sentence from the original sticks in your memory, you may re-use the material in a new location, but you should rewrite it, not simply reinstate excised passages. Now compare the two versions to consider when the choices to move in close have greater strategic value, and incorporate at least three of the changes in your next draft.

7   Synecdoche and Metonymy in Setting, Staging, and Dialogue

Everybody's Got a Job to Do

Write a dialogue between two people in a romantic relationship. One is about to leave the other. They are forced to collaborate on a necessary task (plug a leaky faucet, fix a computer problem, contend with a bleeding dog that their car has just hit). The dialogue should conform to these parameters:

1. Don't tell the reader the nature of the emotional conflict between the characters. Allow it to emerge from their difficulties as they negotiate a mutual task.
2. In describing how the characters carry out their task, use an object or tool necessary to the task as a prop that triggers some exchange between them.
3. Do not include any direct references to the fact that one character intends to leave the other.
4. End the dialogue at a culminating, decisive moment when a crisis has been averted or invited. This moment must involve the prop.

Mapping the Terrain

Take another shot at exploiting setting in a work-in-progress. You might start by diagramming this space or listing its key features. Freewrite for at least two pages and then select for those details that possess a tension orientation. Follow these parameters:

1. In your opening paragraph, depict this space from a distance; imitate Tessa Hadley's "panoramic shot" of the beach and resort town at the opening of "Sunstroke."
2. In the second paragraph, zoom in to the location where your main character is situated.
3. In the third paragraph, depict your main character engaging with the environment. In this "motion shot" your character must behave in some way that "reflects" tension in the depiction of setting in the previous paragraphs.
4. At the end of your story or chapter, reference at least two details from these early paragraphs. But be tricky about it. Just as Hadley used "tide" figuratively to remind us of her opening description of the sea, you might choose a word that only alludes to the literal setting or single out details of setting different from those you emphasized in the opening paragraphs.

Staging the Scene

Block the scenes in a chapter or story as if you were converting this material to the form of a play. For each scene, write a paragraph of stage directions. How is the stage laid out? What props are required? Where are characters situated in relation to each other and to the stage set? By considering the staging of your fiction, you may be able to discover patterns that you can exploit to suggest subtext.

8 Patterns of Imagery

Scavenger Hunt

For a work-in-progress you will import imagery from one of the assigned areas of reference to inform the literal tension. Your choices are as follows: a constellation in the night sky, bird migration, beekeeping, a Greek myth, the craft of weaving, or the DNA strand.

1. Conduct research on the Internet, which may lead you to narrow down the area of reference—say, from any constellation to the Pisces constellation.

2. Compile a two-page list of phrases and details (images) from your research. Don't worry about what might be useful in relation to your manuscript; just note things that appeal for any reason.
3. Insert phrases or details from this research in at least four different places in your draft. Phrases might be taken utterly out of context, so that the reader would never guess the area of reference, or you might pursue this material as a metaphor for your character's predicament.

Your primary goal is to see how these details can generate some figurative yield, to transfer their qualities onto human relationships. (Figurative diction and recurring phrases or constructions will help you with this.) Remember that *unexpected* likenesses bear the best fruit, and allow the assigned area of reference to force your hand as you write.

*Venn Diagram

Re-read the draft of a work-in-progress and underline or circle key images and figurative diction. Make a two-column list. In the left-hand column, quickly sketch out the action in your draft, writing a phrase or two for each scene. In the right-hand column, list any key images that occur in this scene. Next, try arranging the images in a Venn diagram. Can you identify image sets and any overlap or tension between them? Create one Venn diagram, then create another; more than one way of conceiving sets is possible. Does either diagram help you to perceive hidden tension you might exploit further? Try these strategies:

1. Move at least two images from one scene to another in order to reinforce or counter what's happening in the plot.
2. Incorporate new images (or a recurring image) in at least two places so that you're adding to the image sets suggested by your Venn diagram.
3. On at least two different pages, use figurative diction so that it reinforces qualities suggested by the imagery.

9 Showing and Telling

Excuses, Excuses

About to go on vacation in Las Vegas with a lover he wanted to impress, F. borrowed three hundred dollars from C., a hard-up friend. F. was confident about repaying the money, because F. is usually lucky at gambling. Instead, F. lost all the money. C. now needs the money to make this month's rent and has asked F. to repay the loan. On the way to C.'s apartment, F. thinks about how to break the news.

Expand this paragraph to two pages in which you *tell* F.'s thoughts as he makes his way to C.'s house. Your aim is to garner the reader's sympathy for F.'s unsympathetic actions, given these constraints:

1. You must not use the words *sorry, ashamed, trust,* or *regret* or any synonyms for these words.
2. You must not tell anything about F.'s feelings of friendship for C. but can only *show* evidence of this.
3. You may use no more than two sentences to tell the reader what F. anticipates about C.'s response to this news.
4. Otherwise, you may only tell how F. felt when he was in Las Vegas.

*Reverse the Proposition

Choose a scene from your draft in which two characters are in conflict. By incorporating at least five additional sentences in which you tell the perspective character's thoughts, suggest a closeness that is belied by their apparent antagonism or distance. Or conversely, in a scene in which two characters apparently come to an accord, employ telling to suggest antagonism or alienation. In at least two of these additions, rely on metaphor to convey emotions that are in tension with what is shown. You may not reference the immediate conflict in any of these instances of telling.

10   The Sentence as a Touchstone of Style

*The Sincerest Form of Flattery

Choose two pages from a work-in-progress. Rewrite the descriptive passages (but not dialogue), choosing one of the options below:

- In imitation of George Eliot, tell the reader more about your main character's predicament. Add at least five sentences that employ a colon as a fulcrum between the initial statement and what follows. In each of these sentences include a long noun clause as the object of a verb and use paired parallel items. Bonus points if abstractions used in the initial statement are recast in concrete terms after the colon.
- In imitation of Faulkner, use nesting modification, rearranging existing sentences or adding to them; make sure you end up with fewer, longer sentences. Think about how you might "hook" perceptual

information on to sensory detail, especially in the form of a relative clause ("not from the lettering *which meant nothing to his mind* but from the scarlet devils and the silver curve of fish"). Bonus points for using the "not … but" construction.

- In imitation of Woolf, explore the possibilities for using lists within this passage, which may require you to rearrange material or add items to flesh out a list. In at least two consecutive sentences, incorporate lists in *different* syntactic slots (subject slot, verb slot, or object slot). How can you exploit this to generate subtext, as Woolf does?
- In imitation of García Márquez, rewrite the two pages as one single sentence, adding coordinate or subordinate conjunctions to link the clauses. Consider how a subordinate conjunction, which implies a dependent link, can help you to suggest a close relationship between two actions or be used unconventionally to suggest emotional stance or tone.
- In imitation of Hemingway, rewrite sentences so that verb forms and their sounds mimic the pace or the emotional tenor of the action. At least once, employ polysyndeton where you want the reader's attention to *linger* over an impression.

*Pure Artifice

As Mario Vargas Llosa points out in *Letters to a Young Novelist,* "Literature is pure artifice, but great literature is able to hide the fact while mediocre literature gives itself away."[1] In relation to style this means that the sound and the sense reinforce each other. By paying attention primarily to sound rather than sense, you can discover meaning you haven't yet uncovered in the material. Try exploiting some of the strategies of poetry to achieve this.

1. Choose a paragraph from your draft that is in some way problematic—awkwardly worded, unclear, or lifeless. Break it out in the form of a poem, with one line for each clause.
2. Change the order of the words in at least three clauses/lines for the sake of rhythm. Can you make any items parallel (even use isocolon)? Do you see any opportunities to begin or end consecutive lines with the same word or phrase for the sake of emphasis?
3. Change at least six words to capitalize on possibilities for assonance or alliteration. (Use a thesaurus if necessary.) Emphasize either long vowels (moon, screen, ought) and soft consonants (l, m, s, sh) or short vowels (ox, rat, bet) and harsh consonants (f, g, k, t, p, z).
4. Substitute at least three new verbs for existing ones, and be sure the verbs connote a visual ("corkscrew" away from an idea rather than

"avoid" it). Where do the most forceful or key verbs fall within a line? Can any be shifted to the prime location of first or last word?

5. Limit your diction. Repeat at least three key words. Cut at least three adjectives or adverbs.

6. Read the piece aloud, and see if you can spot any opportunities to substitute a word of different syllables or stresses for a more rhythmic sound.

Notes

1 Story Logic

1. Edith Wharton, "Telling a Short Story," in *The Writing of Fiction* (New York: Charles Scribner's Sons, 1924; New York: Simon & Schuster, Touchstone, 1997), 39–40.
2. Quoted in Leah Garchik column, *San Francisco Chronicle*, 23 October 2007, available at http://www.sfgate.com, accessed 3 January 2010.
3. Quoted in Debra Spark, *Curious Attractions: Essays on Fiction Writing* (Ann Arbor: The University of Michigan Press, 2005), 22.
4. Flannery O'Connor, "Writing Short Stories," in *Mystery and Manners* (New York: Farrar, Straus and Giroux, 1961), 96.
5. This comment is traditionally attributed to Aristotle. See Gottfried Wilhelm Leibniz, *Discourse on Metaphysics and Other Essays* (Indianapolis, Ind.: Hackett Publishing Co., 1994), 29.
6. O'Connor, "The Nature and Aim of Fiction," in *Mystery and Manners*, 75–6.
7. Charles Baxter, "On Defamiliarization," in *Burning Down the House: Essays on Fiction*, 2d ed. (St. Paul, Minn: Graywolf Press, 2008), 28.
8. Anton Chekhov, *The Selected Letters of Anton Chekhov*, edited by Lillian Hellman (New York: Farrar, Straus and Giroux, 1984), 56–7.
9. Milan Kundera, interview with Philip Roth, in *The Book of Laughter and Forgetting*, translated by Michael Henry Heim (New York: Penguin, 1984), 237.
10. Charles Baxter, "Against Epiphanies," in *Burning Down the House: Essays on Fiction*, 54.
11. Katherine Mansfield, "The Garden Party," in *The Stories of Katherine Mansfield* (Auckland: Oxford University Press, 1984), 499.
12. Alice Munro, "Dimensions," in *Too Much Happiness* (New York: Alfred A. Knopf, 2009), 5.
13. E. M. Forster "Plot," in *Aspects of the Novel* (New York: Harcourt, Harvest, 1927), 86.
14. The story is attributed to a number of sources; see "Brevity, the Soul of Twit," available at http://www.snopes.com/college/exam/brevity.asp, accessed 20 December 2009.

15. "Flash Fiction—Television Tropes and Idioms," available at http://tvtropes.org/pmwiki/pmwiki.php/Main, accessed 25 February 2010. Ibid.
16. John Gardner, "Interest and Truth," in *The Art of Fiction: Notes on Craft for Young Writers* (New York: Random House, Vintage Books, 1983), 68.

2 The Elusiveness at the Heart of Story Structure

1. Rust Hills says that rising action should create the effect of "something that is being stretched taut until it must snap." Rust Hills, *Writing in General and the Short Story in Particular*, rev. ed. (Boston: Houghton Mifflin, 1987), 41.
2. John Barth advises that the climax "happens relatively quickly ... a comparatively sudden and consequential effect triggered by comparatively small increments." John Barth, "Incremental Perturbation: How to Know Whether You've Got a Plot or Not," in *Creating Fiction*, edited by Julie Checkoway (Cincinnati, Ohio: Story Press, 1999), 133.
3. Janet Burroway, *Writing Fiction: A Guide to Narrative Craft*, 5th ed. (New York: Longman, 2000), 31.
4. Leonard Michaels, "What's a Story?" *Ploughshares* 12, nos. 1 & 2 (1986): 202–3.
5. T. S. Eliot, "Hamlet and His Problems," in *The Sacred Wood: Essays on Poetry and Criticism*, 7th ed. (London: Methuen & Co., 1950), 100.
6. Grace Paley, "Wants," in *The Collected Stories* (New York: Farrar, Straus and Giroux, 1994), 129.
7. Ibid., 130.
8. Ibid.
9. Ibid., 131.
10. Ibid.
11. Junot Díaz, "Fiesta, 1980," in *Drown* (New York: Riverhead, 1996), 35.
12. Ibid., 26.
13. Ibid., 28.
14. Ibid., 40.
15. Ibid., 43.
16. Gabriel García Márquez, "Light is Like Water," in *Strange Pilgrims: Twelve Stories by Gabriel García Márquez*, translated by Edith Grossman (New York: Alfred A. Knopf, 1993), 158.
17. Ibid., 159–60.
18. Ibid., 161.
19. Ibid., 158.

20. Ibid., 161.
21. H. L. Hix, "An Interview with William Gass," *The Writer's Chronicle* 32, no. 4 (February 2001): 36.
22. Alice Munro, "Fathers," in *The View from Castle Rock* (New York: Alfred A. Knopf, 2006), 182.
23. Ibid., 192.
24. Ibid., 193.
25. Ibid.
26. Ibid., 194.
27. Ibid., 196.
28. Ibid.
29. Alice Munro, "Fathers," *The New Yorker* (5 August 2002): 64–71.
30. Munro, "Fathers," in *The View from Castle Rock*, 196.

3 Chapter Structure and Shapeliness in the Novel

1. Simon Schama, *Rembrandt's Eyes* (New York: Alfred A. Knopf, 1999), 262. Schama's discussion of this painting can be found on pages 262–4.
2. William Faulkner, *Intruder in the Dust* (New York: Random House, Vintage, 1972), 3.
3. Ibid., 18.
4. Ibid., 118.
5. Ibid., 206.
6. William Faulkner, *As I Lay Dying* (New York: Random House, Vintage, 1964), 77–9.
7. J. M. Coetzee, *Diary of a Bad Year* (New York: Viking, 2007), 54.
8. Ibid., 6–7.
9. Ibid., 15.
10. Ibid., 59.
11. Ibid., 59–60.
12. Ibid., 105.
13. Ibid., 111.
14. Ibid., 120–1.
15. Ibid., 145.
16. Ibid., 226.

4 Three Key Strategies of Story Logic

1. Antonya Nelson, " 'Mom's on the Roof': The Usefulness of Jokes in Shaping Short Stories," in *Bringing the Devil to His Knees: The Craft of*

Fiction and the Writing Life, edited by Charles Baxter and Peter Turchi (Ann Arbor: University of Michigan Press, 2001), 182.

2. Ibid., 181.
3. Ernest Hemingway, *Death in the Afternoon* (1932; reprint, New York: Charles Scribner's Sons, 1960), 192.
4. Victor Shklovsky, "Art as Technique," in *Russian Formalist Criticism: Four Essays*, translated by Lee T. Lemon and Marion J. Reis (Lincoln and London: University of Nebraska Press, 1965), 12.
5. Mario Vargas Llosa, "The *Catoblepas*," in *Letters to a Young Novelist*, translated by Natasha Wimmer (New York: Picador, 2002), 20.
6. Ibid., 21.
7. Anton Chekhov, "Anna on the Neck," translated by Constance Garnett, in *Anton Chekhov's Stories*, edited by Ralph Maitlaw (New York: W. W. Norton & Co., 1979), 137.
8. Naguib Mahfouz, "The Conjurer Ran Off with the Dish," in *The Time and the Place and Other Stories*, translated by Denys Johnson-Davies (New York: Doubleday, 1991), 15.
9. Ibid., 17.
10. Ibid., 18.
11. Ibid., 19.
12. Ibid., 21.
13. Ibid., 22.
14. Ernest Hemingway, "The Gambler, the Nun, and the Radio," in *The Short Stories of Ernest Hemingway* (New York: Charles Scribner's Sons, 1953), 470.
15. Ibid., 469.
16. Ibid., 471–2.
17. Ibid., 472.
18. Ibid., 473.
19. Ibid., 475.
20. Ibid., 476.
21. Ibid., 479.
22. Ibid.
23. Ibid., 480.
24. Ibid., 484.
25. Ibid., 487.
26. Ann Ryles, "Thoughts and Prayers," in "Or Something Like That," Master's of Fine Arts thesis, University of San Francisco, 2008.
27. J. Q. Stuckley is a pseudonym for a student who gave permission for me to cite this manuscript anonymously.
28. Marion Boddy-Evans, "Negative Space in a Painting," available at http://painting.about.com/od/paintingforbeginners/ss/negative space.htm, accessed 29 June 2009.

5 Captured in Motion: Dynamic Characterization

1. The quotation from Robinson appears on the jacket copy of Paul Harding, *Tinkers* (N.p.: Bellevue Literary Press, 2008).
2. Robert Alter, "Character and the Connection with Reality," in *The Pleasures of Reading in an Ideological Age* (New York: Simon and Schuster, Touchstone, 1989), 55. In this chapter Alter takes to task structuralist and post-structuralist critics who claim that a reader's identification with character is naïve, pointing out that readers are as aware as writers of the elaborate constructedness of this game.
3. Grace Paley, "The Value of Not Understanding Everything," in *Just As I Thought* (New York: Farrar, Straus and Giroux, 1998), 187.
4. Ibid., 186.
5. Gustave Flaubert, *Madame Bovary* (New York: Dover, 1996), 38.
6. James Joyce, "The Dead," in *Dubliners: Text, Criticism and Notes*, edited by Robert Scholes and A. Walton Litz (1969; reprint, New York: Penguin, Viking Critical Library, 1977), 180–1.
7. Ibid., 213.
8. Ibid., 220–1.
9. Ibid., 220.
10. Milan Kundera, *The Art of the Novel*, translated by Linda Asher (New York: Harper & Row, 1986), 42.
11. Flannery O'Connor, "Writing Short Stories," in *Mystery and Manners* (New York: Farrar, Straus and Giroux, 1961), 90.
12. Haruki Murakami, "Sleep," in *The Elephant Vanishes* (New York: Vintage International, 1993), 108.
13. Ibid., 109.
14. Alice McDermott, *Child of My Heart* (New York: Farrar, Straus and Giroux, 2002), 215.
15. Ibid., 219.
16. E. M. Forster, "People (continued)," in *Aspects of the Novel* (New York: Harcourt, Harvest, 1927), 67, 78.
17. Edith Wharton, "Character and Situation in the Novel," in *The Writing of Fiction* (New York: Charles Scribner's Sons, 1924; Simon & Schuster, Touchstone, 1997), 99–100.
18. Ernest Hemingway, "Hills Like White Elephants," in *The Short Stories of Ernest Hemingway* (New York: Charles Scribner's Sons, 1953), 273–8.
19. Raymond Carver, "Careful," in *Where I'm Calling From: New and Selected Stories* (New York: Random House, Vintage Contemporaries, 1989), 266.
20. Ibid., 267.
21. Ibid.
22. Ibid.

23. Ibid., 268.
24. Ibid.
25. Ibid.
26. Ibid., 269.
27. Ibid.
28. Ibid., 271–2.
29. Ibid., 273.
30. Ibid.
31. Ibid., 275.

6   Point-of-View Q & A

1. Wayne Booth, "Types of Narration," in *The Rhetoric of Fiction* (Chicago: University of Chicago Press, 1961), 155.
2. Ibid., 157.
3. M. M. Bakhtin, "Discourse in the Novel," in *The Dialogic Imagination: Four Essays by M. M. Bakhtin*, edited by Michael Holquist, translated by Caryl Emerson and Michael Holquist (Austin: University of Texas Press, 1981), 263.
4. Ibid., 315.
5. George Saunders, "The Red Bow," in *In Persuasion Nation* (New York: Riverhead, 2006), 78.
6. Ibid., 82.
7. Robert Alter, "Perspective," in *The Pleasures of Reading in an Ideological Age* (New York: Simon & Schuster, Touchstone, 1989), 205.
8. Roberto Bolaño, *2666*, translated by Natasha Wimmer, vol. 1 of 3 (New York: Farrar, Straus and Giroux, 2004), 16.
9. James Wood, "Narrating," in *How Fiction Works* (New York: Farrar, Straus and Giroux, 2008), 5.
10. Booth, "Types of Narration," 159–60.
11. James Joyce, "The Dead," in *Dubliners: Text, Criticism and Notes*, edited by Robert Scholes and A. Walton Litz (1969; reprint, New York: Penguin, Viking Critical Library, 1977), 176.
12. Ibid., 177.
13. Deborah Eisenberg, "Some Other, Better Otto," in *Twilight of the Superheroes* (New York: Farrar, Straus and Giroux, 2006), 46.
14. Alter, "Perspective," 191.
15. Gustave Flaubert, *Madame Bovary* (New York: Dover, 1996), 41.
16. William Trevor, "Sitting with the Dead," in *A Bit on the Side* (New York: Viking, 2004), 3.
17. Ibid., 5.
18. Ibid., 9.

19. Ibid., 10.
20. Ibid., 11.
21. Ibid., 11, 12.
22. Ibid., 13.
23. Ibid., 17, 18.
24. Junot Díaz, *The Brief Wondrous Life of Oscar Wao* (New York: Riverhead, 2007), 12–13.
25. Ibid., 12.
26. Ibid., 11.
27. Ibid., 97.
28. Ibid., 22.
29. Booth, "Types of Narration," 159.
30. Saunders, "The Red Bow," 87.
31. Alice Munro, *The Love of a Good Woman* (New York: Alfred A. Knopf, 1998). In this collection Munro structures a long story radically disrupted by shifts in point of view ("The Love of a Good Woman"); explores the effects of distance between the third-person narrator and the main character ("The Children Stay"); flummoxes the expectation that story will clearly "belong" to one perspective character ("Jakarta"); considers how retrospective narration implicitly alters the stakes of past events ("Cortes Island"); and even violates the rule that a first-person narrator can report only events she has witnessed ("My Mother's Dream").
32. Alice Munro, "My Mother's Dream," in *The Love of a Good Woman*, 296.
33. Ibid., 307, 308.
34. Ibid., 314.
35. Ibid., 301.
36. Bakhtin, "Discourse in the Novel," 278.
37. Munro, "My Mother's Dream," 313.
38. Ibid., 314.
39. Ibid., 319.
40. Ibid., 337.

7 Synecdoche and Metonymy in Setting, Staging, and Dialogue

1. Ross King, *The Judgment of Paris* (New York: Walker Publishing Co., 2006), 95.
2. Ibid., 10.
3. Ibid., 248–51, 347.
4. Henri Matisse, "Exactitude Is Not Truth," in *Matisse on Art*, edited by Jack D. Flam (Berkeley: University of California Press, 1994), 117.

5. Quoted in Peter Turchi, *Maps of the Imagination* (San Antonio, Texas: Trinity University Press, 2004), 45.
6. Edward P. J. Corbett and Robert J. Connors, *Style and Statement* (Oxford: Oxford University Press, 1999), 62. For a lucid discussion of tropes, see "Figures of Speech" in this text. See also Raymond W. Gibbs, Jr., "Speaking and Thinking with Metonymy," in *Metonymy in Language and Thought*, edited by Klause-Uwe Panther and Günter Radden (Philadelphia: John Benjamin Publishing Co., 1999), 62.
7. Toni Morrison, *Jazz* (New York: Plume, 1992), 56.
8. Ibid., 30.
9. Ibid., 31.
10. Ernest Hemingway, "A Clean, Well-Lighted Place," in *The Short Stories of Ernest Hemingway* (New York: Charles Scribner's Sons, 1953), 379.
11. Tessa Hadley, "Sunstroke," in *Sunstroke and Other Stories* (New York: Picador, 2007), 1.
12. Ibid., 2.
13. Ibid.
14. Ibid., 4–5.
15. Ibid., 7.
16. Ibid., 17.
17. Ibid., 18.
18. Ibid., 21, 23.
19. Charles Baxter, *The Art of Subtext: Beyond Plot* (St. Paul, Minn: Graywolf Press, 2007), 13–14.
20. Gina Berriault, "The Woman in the Rose-Colored Dress," in *Women in Their Beds: New and Selected Stories* (Washington, DC: Counterpoint, 1996), 109.
21. Ibid., 110.
22. Ibid., 112.
23. Morrison, *Jazz*, 79.
24. Ibid., 77.
25. Ibid., 112.
26. Ibid.
27. Ibid., 113.

8   Patterns of Imagery

1. Robert Hass, "Images," in *Twentieth Century Pleasures: Prose on Poetry* (New York: Ecco Press, 1984), 274–75.
2. William Faulkner, "Barn Burning," in *The Faulkner Reader* (New York: Random House, Modern Library, 1931), 505.

3. Stephen Dobyns, "Metaphor and the Authenticating Act of Memory," *Best Words, Best Order* (New York: St. Martin's Press, 1996), 17.
4. Helena María Viramontes, "The Moths," in *The Moths and Other Stories*, 2d ed. (Houston: Arte Público Press, 1995), 28.
5. Ibid., 30.
6. Ibid., 31.
7. Ibid., 30.
8. Ibid., 32.
9. Anton Chekhov, "Gooseberries," translated by Ivy Litvinov, in *Anton Chekhov's Short Stories*, edited by Ralph Maitlaw (New York: W. W. Norton & Co., 1979), 192.
10. Ibid., 193.
11. Ibid., 194.
12. Ibid., 187.
13. Ibid. For articulating the notion that images (and actions) can rhyme, I am indebted to Charles Baxter, "Rhyming Action," in *Burning Down the House: Essays on Fiction*, 2d ed. (St. Paul, Minn.: Graywolf Press, 2008), 107–26.
14. Chekhov, "Gooseberries," 188.
15. Ibid., 193.
16. Ibid., 194.
17. Ibid., 192. "Gooseberries" is the second in a trilogy of related stories, and the last, "About Love," begins by slyly confirming that the beautiful Pelagea does, in fact, bear her burdens in silence: she's in love with a vicious drunk who beats her.
18. Michael Cunningham, *The Hours* (New York: Farrar, Straus and Giroux, 1998), 99–100.
19. Ibid., 103.
20. Ibid., 118.
21. Ibid., 119.
22. Ibid., 120.
23. Ibid., 119.
24. Ibid., 120.
25. Ibid., 201–2.
26. Italo Calvino, "Visibility," in *Six Memos for the Next Millenium* (New York: Vintage, 1993), 89.

9 Showing and Telling

1. Ernest Hemingway, "Fathers and Sons," in *The Short Stories of Ernest Hemingway* (New York: Charles Scribner's Sons, 1953), 496.
2. Ernest Hemingway, "The Short Happy Life of Francis Macomber," in *The Short Stories of Ernest Hemingway*, 22.

3. Joseph Conrad, preface to *The Nigger of the "Narcissus"* (New York: Doubleday & Co., 1914), 11, 14.
4. Anton Chekhov, *The Selected Letters of Anton Chekhov*, edited by Lillian Hellman (New York: Farrar, Straus and Giroux, 1984), 57.
5. A. L. Kennedy, *Day* (New York: Alfred A. Knopf, 2008), 4.
6. George Eliot, *Middlemarch* (New York: Penguin Classics, 1994), 97.
7. Ibid., 101.
8. Nadine Gordimer, "Safe Houses," in *Jump and Other Stories* (New York: Farrar, Straus and Giroux, 1991), 183–4.
9. Ibid., 185.
10. Ibid., 191.
11. Ibid., 190.
12. Ibid., 193.
13. Ibid., 194.
14. Ibid., 202.
15. Ibid., 209.
16. Tobias Wolff, *Old School* (New York: Alfred A. Knopf, 2004), 3.
17. Ibid., 4.
18. Ibid., 9.
19. Ibid., 14.
20. Ibid., 12.
21. Ibid., 15.
22. Ibid., 16.
23. Ibid., 21.
24. Ibid.
25. Ibid., 23.
26. Ibid., 24.
27. For an example of Carver's changing aesthetic, compare "The Bath," first published in 1974, to its revision as "A Small, Good Thing." Raymond Carver, "The Bath," in *What We Talk about When We Talk about Love* (New York: Alfred A. Knopf, 1981), 47–56; Raymond Carver, "A Small, Good Thing," in *Cathedral* (New York: Viking, 1989), 59–90.
28. E. M. Forster, "People," in *Aspects of the Novel* (New York: Harcourt, Harvest, 1927), 63.

10   The Sentence as a Touchstone of Style

1. Gustave Flaubert, *Madame Bovary* (New York: Dover, 1996), 134.
2. Quoted in Ellen Bryant Voigt, *The Art of Syntax* (St. Paul, Minn: Graywolf Press, 2009), 43.
3. Aaron Shurin, "King of Shadows," in *King of Shadows* (San Francisco: City Lights, 2008), 48.

4. Joseph O'Neill, *Netherland* (New York: Pantheon, 2008), 62.
5. Ibid., 62–3.
6. Gertrude Stein, "Poetry and Grammar," in *Lectures in America* (New York: Random House, 1935), 210–11.
7. Isaac Babel, "Guy de Maupassant," in *The Collected Stories* (New York: New American Library, 1955), 331.
8. George Eliot, *Middlemarch* (New York: Penguin Classics, 1994), 229.
9. William Faulkner, "Barn Burning," in *The Faulkner Reader* (New York: Random House, Modern Library, 1931), 499.
10. Babel, "Guy de Maupassant," 331–2.
11. Denis Johnson, "Car Crash," in *Jesus' Son* (New York: Harper Perennial, 1993), 10.
12. Virginia Woolf, *Mrs. Dalloway* (New York: Harcourt Brace Jovanovich, Harvest, 1925), 5.
13. Grace Paley, "An Interest in Life," in *The Collected Stories* (New York: Farrar, Straus and Giroux, 1994), 50.
14. Gabriel García Márquez, "The Last Voyage of the Ghost Ship," in *Leaf Storm and Other Stories*, translated by Gregory Rabassa (New York: Harper & Row, 1972), 123.
15. Ernest Hemingway, "The Short Happy Life of Francis Macomber," in *The Short Stories of Ernest Hemingway* (New York: Charles Scribner's Sons, 1953), 15.
16. Gertrude Stein, "Poetry and Grammar," 237.
17. Adam Thirlwell, "A Masterpiece in Miniature," *The Guardian*, 8 October 2005, available at http://books.guardian.co/uk/review/story/0,12084, accessed 3 March 2008.

Exercises

1. Mario Vargas Llosa, "Style," in *Letters to a Young Novelist*, translated by Natasha Wimmer (New York: Picador, 2002), 38.

Further Reading

Alter, Robert, *The Pleasures of Reading in an Ideological Age* (New York: Simon and Schuster, Touchstone, 1989). With the aim of deepening readers' pleasure, Alter explores how fiction is made, offering insights that are practically useful to a fiction writer as well. Focusing on close reading of classic literary works, chapters are organized according to craft elements (style, perspective, character).

Baxter, Charles, *Burning Down the House: Essays on Fiction*, 2d ed. (Minneapolis, Minn.: Graywolf Press, 2008). These essays analyze sophisticated dimensions of craft, challenging accepted formulas and considering how some of our assumptions about craft are bound up with the cultural biases of our times. In "Counterpointed Characterization," Baxter considers character in repertoire; in "Against Epiphanies," he notes the commodification of insight and argues that fiction can "arrive somewhere" without serving up insight at the climax; in "Rhyming Action," he considers how recurring images and parallel action contribute to figurative meaning.

———, *The Art of Subtext: Beyond Plot* (St. Paul, Minn: Graywolf Press, 2007). Drawing on examples from contemporary writers, this short book offers an advanced course in strategies that enable the writer to evoke the unspoken and also discusses how this process can go wrong—a writer's efforts may lead to "congested subtext," or a mechanistic deployment of devices can produce effects that are anything but subtle.

Booth, Wayne, *The Rhetoric of Fiction* (Chicago: University of Chicago Press, 1961). Referencing older classics of the Western canon and writing in an academic style, Booth explores point of view as a rhetorical strategy, with great chapters on showing and telling and on manipulating narrative distance.

Chekhov, Anton, *The Selected Letters of Anton Chekhov*, edited by Lillian Hellman (New York: Farrar, Straus and Giroux, 1984). Throughout these letters Chekhov offers observations and advice about writing craft and process, distilled to the essential.

———, *The Personal Papers of Anton Chekhov: His Notebook Diary and Letters on Writing* (Honolulu: University Press of the Pacific, 2002). This book includes selected letters on writing and Chekhov's notebooks, which offer a fascinating glimpse of a great writer's attitudinal stance toward his material.

Checkoway, Julie ed., *Creating Fiction* (Cincinnati: Story Press, 1999). This anthology of craft essays by contemporary writers is organized in sections on characterization, point of view, plot, style, and revising, editing, and marketing. Contributors include Charles Johnson, Jane Smiley, John Barth, and Lan Samantha Chang.

Corbett, Edward P. J., and Robert J. Connors, *Style and Statement* (Oxford: Oxford University Press, 1999). Primarily aimed at students who are learning argumentative writing, this book offers a great introduction to classical rhetoric, with specific analysis of sentence patterns, schemes, and tropes.

Dobyns, Stephen, *Best Words, Best Order* (New York: St. Martin's Press, 1996). Focused primarily on the craft of poetry, this book includes chapters that explore in detail how metaphor works and how word choice helps a writer to generate intricate subtextual patterns.

Forster, E. M., *Aspects of the Novel* (New York: Harcourt, Harvest, 1927). Forster's advice on plot and characterization and on pattern and rhythm in the novel remains relevant, and his comments on specific writers (often his contemporaries) are illuminating.

Kundera, Milan, *The Art of the Novel*, translated by Linda Asher (New York: Harper & Row, 1986). Observations on craft from a brilliant writer whose strategies and craft principles reference both postmodern literary theory and literary tradition.

Lodge, David, *The Art of Fiction* (New York: Penguin, 1992). A pocket dictionary of key craft concepts, with each short chapter organized around a passage from a literary work. Lodge's chapter topics (intertextuality, introducing a character, repetition) often fall through the cracks of comprehensive craft handbooks.

Nelson, Antonya, " 'Mom's on the Roof': the Usefulness of Jokes in Shaping Short Stories." In *Bringing the Devil to His Knees: The Craft of Fiction and the Writing Life*, edited by Charles Baxter and Peter Turchi (Ann Arbor: University of Michigan Press, 2001). Invaluable insights into story structure and how stories make meaning from one of the best American short story writers.

O'Connor, Flannery, *Mystery and Manners* (New York: Farrar, Straus and Giroux, 1961). In this compendium of O'Connor's essays, a radical imagination goes to work on the principles that make fiction come to life.

Paley, Grace, *Just As I Thought* (New York: Farrar, Straus and Giroux, 1998). In section IV, "A Few Reflections on Teaching and Writing," Paley's essays on fiction writing and on other writers offer pithy observations on creative process and technique.

Shklovsky, Victor, "Art as Technique." In *Russian Formalist Criticism: Four Essays*, translated by Lee T. Lemon and Marion J. Reis (Lincoln and London: University of Nebraska Press, 1965). Shklovsky articulates his concept of defamiliarization and offers a fine example of how formalist approaches to fiction can be useful to the writer.

Vargas Llosa, Mario, *Letters to a Young Novelist*, translated by Natasha Wimmer (New York: Picador, 2002). Vargas Llosa connects craft questions with process, and he explores dimensions of craft in relation to principles that encompass a range of strategies.

Wharton, Edith, *The Writing of Fiction* (New York: Charles Scribner's Sons, 1924; New York: Simon & Schuster, Touchstone, 1997). This collection of Wharton's essays on writing includes invaluable advice on telling a short story, constructing a novel, and considering the relationship between character and situation in a novel.

Wood, James, *How Fiction Works* (New York: Farrar, Straus and Giroux, 2008). Wood is especially attentive to how artifice (technique and convention) creates the illusion of verisimilitude. He offers insightful observations about everything from detail and characterization to point of view and style in the work of contemporary and classic writers.

Index